Chinese Verbs &
Essentials of Grammar

Chinese Verbs & Essentials of Grammar

Julian K. Wheatley, PhD

New York Chicago San Francisco Athens London Madrid
Mexico City Milan New Delhi Singapore Sydney Toronto

1 2 3 4 5 6 7 8 9 10   QFR/QFR   1 0 9 8 7 6 5 4

ISBN   978-0-07-171304-7
MHID   0-07-171304-2

e-ISBN   978-0-07-171342-9
e-MHID   0-07-171342-5

Library of Congress Cataloging-in-Publication Data

Wheatley, Julian K.
    Chinese verbs & essentials of grammar / Julian K. Wheatley.
        p. cm.—   (. . . . . Verbs & Essentials of Grammar)
    Includes bibliographical references and index.
    ISBN 978-0-07-171304-7   (acid-free paper) — ISBN 0-07-171304-2   (acid-free paper)—
    ISBN 978-0-07-171342-9   (e-ISBN) 1. Chinese language—Verb.   2. Chinese language—
    Grammar.   I. Title. II. Title: Chinese verbs and essentials of grammar.
    PL1235.W53   2014
    495.182'421—dc23
                                                                    2014025220

McGraw-Hill Education products are available at special quantity discounts to use as premiums and sales promotions or for use in corporate training programs. To contact a representative, please visit the Contact Us pages at www.mhprofessional.com.

This book is printed on acid-free paper.

Contents

Preface   ix
Acknowledgments   xi
Conventions   xiii

1 Background

  1. The Standard Language   1
  2. Regional Mandarin   3
  3. Regional Languages   4
  4. Origins of the Standard Spoken Language   5
  5. The Written Standard   6
  6. Writing in the Regional Languages   9
  7. Languages Related to Chinese   10
  8. Chinese Names for China   10

2 Representing Pronunciation

  9. Alternative Systems of Transcription   13
  10. The Pinyin System   15
  11. Pronunciation   17

3 The Writing System

  12. The Origin of Characters   25
  13. The Function of Characters   26
  14. The Form of Characters   27
  15. Dictionaries   29
  16. Number of Characters   31
  17. The Reading Process   32
  18. Traditional and Simplified Characters   34

4 Sentences and Sentence Processes

  19. Topic-Comment   37
  20. Other Aspects of Word Order   39
  21. Questions   41

22. Question Words as Indefinites — 44
23. Yes and No — 45
24. Negation — 46
25. Commands and Requests — 46

5   Words

26. Parts of Speech (Word Classes) — 49
27. Monosyllabic and Polysyllabic Words — 51

6   Nouns

28. Compound Nouns — 53
29. Noun Suffixes — 54
30. Pronouns and Demonstratives — 58
31. Zero-Pronominalization — 59
32. Where Are the Articles ("a" and "the")? — 60
33. Modification and the Particle *de* (的) — 61
34. The *shì-de* (是-的) Construction
    and Situational *de* (的) — 63
35. Place Words — 65
36. Time When — 68
37. Measure Words — 74

7   Verbs in General

Verb Suffixes

38. The Verb Suffix *-guo* (过) — 81
39. The Verb Suffix *-le* (了) and Sentence *le* (了) — 82
40. The Verb Suffix *-zhe* (着) — 86
41. *Zài* (在) + Verb to Signal Ongoing Action — 88
42. The Absence of a Suffix — 89
43. Verb Reduplication and Tentativeness — 90

Idiosyncratic Verbs

44. *Shì* (是): Identity and Category — 92
45. Verbs Like *shì*: Classificatory Verbs — 94
46. *Yǒu* (有): Possession and Existence — 95
47. *Zài* (在): Location — 96
48. *Gěi* (给): "Give" and Its Derivatives — 97
49. Generalized Verbs — 99
50. Modal Verbs — 102
51. Ambient Verbs — 106

8 Adjectives and Adverbs

52. Adjectives and Verbs   107
53. Adjectives as Transitive Verbs   108
54. Verb + Adjective Phrase + *yìdiǎnr*   109
55. Vivid Reduplication   111
56. Adverbs   115
57. Predicate Complements   119
58. Comparison   120
59. Intensifiers   123
60. The Three *de*s   124

9 Complex Verbs

61. Resultative Verb Compounds   127
62. Directional Verb Compounds   131
63. Potential Compounds   133

10 After the Verb

64. Objects and Complex Verbs   137
65. Postverbal Particles: Goals of Motion
    and Transformation   139
66. Verb-Plus-Object Compounds   142
67. Mock Objects   146
68. Ditransitive Verbs: Verbs with Two Objects   147
69. Embedded Object Clauses   150
70. Duration Complements   151
71. Extent Phrases   156
72. Conjunctions   157

11 Verbs and Prepositions

73. Verbs in Series   161
74. Verbs and Prepositions   162
75. Prepositions   162
76. The *bǎ* (把) Construction   164
77. The Preposition *bèi* (被)   166
78. Pivot Verbs   167

12 Miscellaneous

79. Numbers   171
80. Money   174

81. Names, Titles, and Forms of Address   176
82. Proverbs and Sayings   178

Appendix: Common Verbs Organized by Semantic Area   181
Bibliography   195
Index   197

Preface

This book is about Modern Standard Chinese, commonly called Mandarin. For those who are beginning their study of Chinese, it is an overview of basic forms and structures, a compendium of examples, and a guide to some of the issues involved in the study of the language. For those at more advanced stages, it serves as a handbook of topics for selective study or review that can supplement the fine textbooks in current use.

For those who have a lively curiosity about the world's most widely spoken language but have no plans to study it, this book provides an introduction to the language and elucidates those features that make it unusual, including its character writing system, the tones that distinguish its words, the relative simplicity of its grammar, and its relationship to Chinese regional speeches (dialects), such as Cantonese.

This book is not a phrasebook for travelers, although it cites a great deal of useful language. Nor is it a complete grammar of the language, although it does cover the main grammatical features. Rather, it is a book that keeps the needs of the learner in mind, illuminating the most prominent features of the language and providing a rich array of accessible examples of spoken usage. The book covers 82 topics, grouped in 12 chapters. While the topics follow in a logical sequence that allows for continuous reading, they can also be read singly in the manner of entries in a handbook. Each topic is illustrated with representative samples of the language as it is spoken in China today, and every attempt has been made to make these examples lifelike and accessible. However, in matters of usage—especially spoken usage—there are bound to be disagreements between one speaker and another, particularly with a language that is as widely spoken as standard Chinese. It is hoped that the reader will be able to negotiate competing claims, testing them where necessary, and ultimately noting variants and making corrections.

Verbs and Essentials of Grammar

The title of this McGraw-Hill Education series highlights verbs. In many languages, verbs undergo complicated changes in form according to grammatical categories such as tense, aspect, negation, voice, and mood. These changes are traditionally set out in tables, and one of the more onerous tasks for the student of such languages is to become familiar with at least the most commonly used forms in these tables. Chinese, you will be glad to know, has none of this. In Chinese, verbs—and, indeed, nouns and other words—are invariable. Suffixes are few in number. There are no conjugations for verbs, no declensions for nouns or pronouns, no agreement for adjectives. Chinese manages without such formal shifts as "go" ~ "went," "took" ~ "take," "child" ~ "children." Instead, it makes use of specialized words, word order, and context. Nevertheless, the verb is still the heart of the sentence. In fact, it can be argued that, as the only obligatory element of sentence structure, the verb is even more prominent in Chinese than in many other languages, since it encodes functions performed by prepositions, adjectives, and even conjunctions in languages like English.

Acknowledgments

Huì shuō de bùrú huì tīng de (会说的不如会听的): 'To speak is not so valuable as to listen' goes the Chinese saying, and in writing this book, I have listened to friends, colleagues, passing acquaintances, and passers-by too numerous to list. However, a number of people deserve special mention. They are: Dr. Liwei Jiao, from the University of Pennsylvania, who provided extensive notes on the final version of the manuscript; Professor Scott McGinnis, from the Defense Language Institute in Washington, D.C., who did the same for two earlier versions; and Ms. Fangqi Guo from Harbin, a student at Tulane University, who helped me check examples and usage. In addition, thanks go to Professor Robert Bauer in Hong Kong and Ms. Yuhan 'Shelly' Yu, from the Office of Foreign Exchange at the Shenzhen Educational Bureau. I thank them all with heartfelt gratitude.

I would also like to thank the excellent team at McGraw Hill Education who nursed this project to completion, beginning with Christopher Brown, editor and publisher. He, along with Julia Anderson Bauer, the managing editor; Gigi Grajdura, the project editor; and Elleanore Waka, the production supervisor, tolerated a lot of missed deadlines, and much to their credit, agreed to include characters that added considerably to the length of the book. Dan Franklin, Terry Yokota, and the anonymous Chinese reader managed the difficult job of copyediting a manuscript that has barely a line without some special symbol. And many thanks also to Sylvia Rebert at Progressive Publishing Alternatives, who supervised the final stages of production and proofreading.

Conventions

In order to make this book accessible to readers without knowledge of Chinese, while at the same time not discouraging those who know the language or who are in the process of learning it, Chinese examples are, where feasible, cited with four layers of representation in this book: Chinese characters; the romanized transcription known as Pinyin; a word-for-word gloss; and an idiomatic translation. However, to save space, exceptions are made for examples that are brief or simple, or otherwise judged eligible for a reduced format.

As an example of the full format, here is a Chinese saying that, incidentally, shows the balanced phrasing and rhyme typical of Chinese gnomic expressions.

师父领进门，修行在个人。   CHARACTERS (MAINLAND SET)
Shīfu lǐng jìn mén, xiūxíng zài gèrén. PINYIN TRANSCRIPTION
Master lead enter door, cultivation   WORD-FOR-WORD GLOSS
   be-at individual.
'Your teacher can lead you to the door, IDIOMATIC TRANSLATION
   [but] success is up to you.'

Unless otherwise stated, characters are cited in the simplified set that is standard on the mainland (as well as in Singapore, but not in Hong Kong). Pronunciation is cited in the official Chinese transcription called Pinyin ('putting together–sounds')—hereafter written "pinyin," without capitalizing the "p." Meaning is usually given word for word and then idiomatically (that is, in terms of the sentence or utterance). The word-for-word gloss is a rough way of indicating how the idiomatic meaning is constructed in the original language. Thus, in the example above, the glosses[1] make it clear that English words like "to" and "the" have no equivalent in Chinese and that "up to you" is represented as "be-at" + "individual." Examples cited in reduced format omit characters or word-for-word glosses, or both.

---

[1]A gloss is not a definition. It is an equivalent for a word in a particular context. A definition, on the other hand, attempts to characterize the meaning of a word in all its contexts: *mén* in the example can mean 'door' or 'doorway,' but by extension, 'opening,' 'specialized subject,' and 'school of thought.'

Summary of Conventions

Most conventions are illustrated in the saying above. Spaces demarcate words, which may be of one, two, or more syllables: *Shīfu lǐng jìn mén.* Other conventions are the following.

- [ ] enclose words not explicitly represented in one of the paired languages: '[but].'
- < > indicate optional material <*yì*>*diǎnr* = *yìdiǎnr* or *diǎnr.*
- { } indicate grammatical boundaries (word, phrase, clause, etc.): {*tāmen shuō de*} *huà.*
- **X ~ Y** indicates that X and Y are both possible: *shuō ~ jiǎng.*
- **x* indicates that x is ungrammatical or otherwise unacceptable.

Meaning is indicated as follows.

- English equivalents are marked in single quotes: '. . .'; foreign-language material (other than Chinese) cited in text rather than in separate examples is enclosed in double quotes: ". . .".
- Literal meanings are placed in parentheses and separated by hyphens: *hóngbāo* ('red-packet').
- Grammatical words for which no simple English equivalent is available are simply left as pinyin in small capital letters: DE, LE, ZHE.
- Definitions are marked as follows.
  - Synonyms of a single sense are separated by commas (,).
  - Separate senses of a word are separated by semicolons (;).
  - Glosses of separate parts of speech are also separated by semicolons (;): *hóng* (红) 'red; be popular, be in vogue; a bonus, dividend.'

The following abbreviations are used.

M	measure word
SFP	sentence-final particle
vo.	verb-plus-object compound

Chinese Verbs & Essentials of Grammar

1
Background

1. The Standard Language

It is not surprising to find that China, given its size, exhibits linguistic diversity on the scale of, say, the countries of Romance-speaking Europe. To counter this diversity, one language is recognized as a national spoken standard. On the mainland, that language is called *Pǔtōnghuà*, literally, 'the common speech.' *Pǔtōnghuà* is the language used by the media, taught in the schools, and authenticated by dictionaries, language textbooks, and other reference works. This book is about *Pǔtōnghuà*.

In English, *Pǔtōnghuà* is sometimes referred to simply as "Chinese," a usage that Chinese themselves seem to prefer (consider Chinese textbook names such as *Practical Chinese for English Speakers*). However, because Chinese can also refer to Cantonese, Shanghainese, and other speeches that would not necessarily be understood by speakers of *Pǔtōnghuà*, the name "Chinese" needs to be further qualified as "Standard Chinese."

For reasons that will be given in Section 4, in English, *Pǔtōnghuà* is also—perhaps more commonly—called Mandarin. Thus, the great Chinese linguist Yuen Ren Chao called his 1948 textbook *Mandarin Primer*. The title of my own textbook, *Learning Chinese: A Foundation Course in Mandarin*, uses "Chinese" in its narrow sense, but supports it with the term "Mandarin," just to be sure. Mandarin also covers a range of dialects, however, so it too needs to be further specified as "Standard Mandarin." In this book, in the interest of simplicity, "Chinese" and "Mandarin," unless otherwise indicated, refer to the standard language.

Other Chinese Names for Standard Chinese

Standard Chinese is, more or less, recognized as a prestige norm throughout the Chinese-speaking world, even though it has different names in different places. In Taiwan, it is referred to as *Guóyǔ* 'the national language.' In

Singapore, where Chinese is one of four official languages, it is referred to as *Huáyǔ,* 'language of the Hua.'[1]

While *Pǔtōnghuà* is used as a precise term for Standard Spoken Chinese, in contrast to regional speeches such as Cantonese, when *Pǔtōnghuà* can be assumed, speakers often refer to the language as *Zhōngwén* 'the Chinese language' or *Hànyǔ* 'the spoken language of the Han.' Here is an example.

> *Nǐ Hànyǔ shuō de hěn hǎo.*[2]
> You Chinese speak DE very well.
> 'Your Chinese is very good.'

> *Nǐ huì jiǎng Zhōngwén ma?*[3]
> You able speak Chinese MA?
> 'Do you speak Chinese?'

Different Standards

Because Chinese is associated with several political entities, it can be characterized as "pluricentric"; that is, it has several different norms. Thus, just as dictionaries of English represent standards of British, American, or Australian English (at least), so too, there are differences as to what is regarded as standard Chinese. These differences are not fully formalized, but they are to some degree registered in dictionaries published on the mainland, in Taiwan, and in Singapore that purport to define standard Chinese. Acknowledged differences are relatively few, the most salient being the choice of words (for example, 'pineapple' is usually *bōluó* or *bōluómì* (less often *fènglí*) on the mainland, usually *fènglí* in Taiwan, and *huánglí* in Singapore), the pronunciation of words (for example, the word for 'refuse, garbage' is usually pronounced *lājī* in mainland Mandarin, but *lèsè* in Taiwan Mandarin), and usage (for example, *àiren* is 'spouse' on the mainland, but 'sweetheart' or 'lover' in Taiwan).

---

[1]*Huá* is another name for Chinese. It appears, in combination with *Zhōng,* in the official names of the country: *Zhōnghuá Rénmín Gònghéguó* 'The People's Republic of China' (founded in 1949) and *Zhōnghuá Mínguó* 'The Republic of China' (founded in 1912 after the overthrow of the last emperor the year before).

[2]Rather than start the book off with a long explanation of the pinyin system of representing pronunciation, I've decided to wait until Chapter 3 to introduce the transcription system. Readers are asked to note these early citations, and then check back after reading Chapter 3.

[3]Or *Nǐ huì shuō Zhōngwén ma? Jiǎng* 'speak' has been "borrowed" into Mandarin from southern speech, but it is now well integrated in *Pǔtōnghuà.*

Number of Speakers

Based on the 2000 census, the Ethnologue website indicates that 848 million people speak varieties of Mandarin as their mother tongue (presumably meaning their first language). The figure would increase if speakers of Mandarin as a second language were included, a category that would include many speakers of regional speeches, such as Cantonese. However, even without second-language speakers, the figure would encompass a vast range of differences, from middle-class urban populations at ease with the modern standard to rural poor whose local brand of Mandarin would be barely intelligible to those who spoke only the standard.

2. Regional Mandarin

Like English, spoken Mandarin comes in many regional flavors, which is why Chinese often praise foreign speakers of Mandarin not just for speaking well, but for speaking "in a standard way"—speaking with correct pronunciation, without local coloring.

你中文说得很标准。
Nǐ Zhōngwén shuō de hěn biāozhǔn.
You Chinese speak DE very standard.
'You speak Chinese correctly.'

As a national language, Mandarin has, in relatively recent times, been promoted as a lingua franca—a common language—and has spread from its natural setting in northern China into regions where the local speech was quite different from the standard. As a result, many Chinese speak two versions of Mandarin, a local version with a regional accent and distinctive vocabulary, as well as an approximation of the standard for more formal communication.

To give a concrete example from a highly educated population, a recent tutoring position in a Mandarin program at a U.S. college produced applicants from China with slight regional accents, but none so pronounced as to be outside the range of the standard. Almost all of them noted on their application, however, that they also spoke regional versions of Mandarin, which they identified by place, as follows: Nanjing (after the city on the Yangtze), Henan (a central province), Sichuan (a province in the southwest), Shanxi (a province in the north), Dongbei (the far northeastern provinces), and Beijing (the capital, in the north). Each of these are local versions of Mandarin (Nanjing Mandarin, Henan Mandarin, and the others) that would not pass as standard. Some differ from the standard mostly in details of pronunciation, including tone; others show both pronunciation and lexical differences.

At the extremes, varieties of Mandarin are probably barely mutually intelligible, even in face-to-face interaction, where speakers tend to accommodate each other. However, they are more like each other than they are like other varieties of Chinese. Among the tutoring applicants mentioned above, a significant number noted that they were also speakers of *Yuè*, *Wú*, and *Mǐn* dialects—regional speeches not part of the Mandarin grouping. *Yuè* and *Wú* are better known colloquially as Cantonese and Shanghainese, respectfully. *Mǐn* is often called Hokkien or Fujianese.

3. Regional Languages

Mandarin dialects, though they cover a large geographical range, form just one of seven dialect groupings usually distinguished by Chinese linguists. These dialect groupings are known as *fāngyán* (方言) in Chinese, short for *dìfāng de yǔyán* (地方的语言)—literally, 'regional speeches.' The Mandarin group (to which standard Mandarin is most closely related) is the most widespread and the most uniform, even though it exhibits a considerable range of variation. Mandarin dialects are spoken in a broad arc from the northeast of China to Sichuan and Yunnan in the far southwest.

Three of the Chinese designations for the other dialect groupings are based on historical kingdoms associated with their core region. The *Yuè* grouping, known as Cantonese in English, is predominant in the province of Canton (*Guǎngdōng*) and in Hong Kong. The *Wú* dialects, Shanghainese in English, are spoken in and around Shanghai, at the mouth of the Yangtze River. The *Mǐn* dialects are spoken mainly in the province of Fujian on the east coast, in Taiwan (where Southern Min, known also as Taiwanese, has become an official language), and on Hainan Island farther south. In English, the *Mǐn* grouping is often named Fujianese for the province where it is dominant (Fujian). Fujianese is also referred to as Fukienese, representing an older spelling, and Hokkien, based on the Min pronunciation of the word "Fujian."

The *Gàn* dialects, spoken in *Jiāngxī* and *Húnán* provinces, and the *Xiāng dialects,* spoken in *Húnán* province (named for important rivers in those provinces), are less well known. Finally, scattered through the Cantonese and the southern range of the *Mǐn*-speaking populations are the *Kèjiā*, meaning 'guest-families.' In English, they are known as the Hakka, which is the Cantonese pronunciation of Mandarin *Kèjiā*.

The following chart summarizes the seven regional Chinese dialect groupings (*fāngyán*).

Chinese Name	English Name(s)	Core Locations
Guānhuà	Mandarin	Northeast to southwest
Yuè	Cantonese	Canton province, Hong Kong
Mǐn	Hokkien, Fujianese, Fukienese	Fujian province, Taiwan, Hainan
Wú	Shanghai, Shanghainese	Shanghai region
Gàn	Gan	Jiangxi and Hunan provinces
Xiāng	Xiang	Hunan province
Kèjiā	Hakka	Canton province and southern Fujian

Cantonese, Hokkien, and Hakka are particularly well represented in overseas Chinese communities. Singapore's population spoke mostly Hokkien until recent years, when Mandarin was promoted over "dialects" (particularly after the start of the Speak Mandarin Movement in 1979). Until recently, over 90 percent of American Chinese traced their ancestry to coastal villages in the province of Canton, particularly the coastal strip known as Sze Yup 'the Four Counties' (now Ng Yup 'Five Counties').

Differences Among Dialect Groupings

Cantonese, Shanghainese, and the other regional speeches are similar in many ways. They are all tonal, for example, although their tonal contours differ from each other. They have many of the same grammatical categories and share a large lexicon of roots, even if they do not use them or pronounce them in the same way. However, they also exhibit differences in word order and in the form and function of grammatical words. By and large, not only are the regional languages not mutually intelligible, but subdialects within a regional language grouping (for example, the *Táishān* and *Guǎngzhōu* dialects of Cantonese) may not be judged mutually comprehensible.

4. Origins of the Standard Spoken Language

A national speech, in the sense of a spoken norm that extends throughout the country and the Chinese-speaking world, would have been inconceivable before the development of a national school system and modern media by which it could be promulgated. Traditionally, China was a checkerboard of local languages spoken by people who, for the most part, were born, grew up, and died in one locality. Certain ways of speaking, based on the language of important national centers such as Nanjing ('southern capital') and later Beijing ('northern capital'), developed among regional and national officials so that they could communicate on matters of administration, but the language that allowed the business of government and ensured a degree of unity across such a vast area was not a spoken one, but the written language known as Classical Chinese, a language that remained more or less uniform for more than 2,000 years (see Section 5).

In the decades following the Opium Wars in the mid-nineteenth century, and even more so after the fall of imperial rule and the establishment of a republic in the twentieth century, when the need for a national spoken language became a clear imperative, the most obvious candidate was the speech of the official and literary elite—the language of the Mandarins, called *Guānhuà* in Chinese, 'the language of officials.' By this time, *Guānhuà* had become clearly associated with Beijing, the capital since the fifteenth century, and by the early decades of the twentieth century, after a long period in which various hybrid proposals were considered (in part to satisfy regional interests), it was decided that the new national norm should be based on the Beijing dialect. Today, standard Mandarin—*Pŭtōnghuà*—is defined as being based on the pronunciation of contemporary Beijing speech, the lexical usage of the northern (Mandarin) dialects, and the grammatical norms of the vernacular literary language known as *báihuà* (see Section 5).

In Chinese, the name *Guānhuà* was replaced early on by terms such as *Guóyŭ* (which survives in Taiwan usage) and, ultimately, *Pŭtōnghuà* as the name for the national language. However, the foreign term "Mandarin," first used by the Portuguese as a translation of *Guānhuà*, followed the evolution of *Guānhuà* into *Pŭtōnghuà* and remains as one of the foreign names of the modern standard speech.

5. The Written Standard

By contrast to the diversity of speeches, China has, for the past two millennia at least, had only one official written language at any one time. Before the early twentieth century, that language was Classical Chinese, a highly stylized and succinct form of communication that was standardized in the early Han Dynasty (third century BCE) but reflects writing practices going back much further.

Classical Chinese

Classical Chinese differs significantly in grammar and lexicon from modern Chinese of any variety. At the time of its inception 2,000 years ago, it would have been pronounced quite differently from any of today's dialects. But because it was written in characters, Chinese practice has been to read it out with contemporary pronunciation, although in some cases, special conservative reading pronunciations have survived for certain words. As a result, Classical Chinese remains accessible to literate Chinese and has been, and remains, a source of words, sayings, and stylistic forms in both the written and spoken language, much in the way that Shakespeare and the King James Bible have left their mark on English, albeit with a much deeper time scale for Chinese.

As an example of Classical Chinese, here are the first lines of the Confucian classic known in English as *The Analects*. This is a selection of sayings—probably recorded by followers of Confucius rather than the great man himself—that reached its present form about 2,000 years ago.

學而時習之，不亦説乎? (traditional characters)
Xué ér shí xí zhī, bù yì yuè hū?
Study and timely revise it, not also pleasant SFP?
'To learn and at due times to repeat what one has learnt, is that not after all a pleasure?' (translation by Arthur Waley)

Words are more likely to be monosyllabic in Classical Chinese than in Modern Chinese. Compounds are relatively rare: 習 *xí* in the citation would be rendered 温习 *wēnxí* in modern Chinese, for example, and 説 *yuè* would be 喜悦 *xǐyuè*. Other differences involve word choice: Classical 乎 *hū* would be Modern 吗 *ma* and Classical 亦 *yì* would be Modern 也 *yě*. Characters disguise the fact that over a period of two millennia, sound change would have altered the pronunciation of words beyond recognition. From rhyme schemes, character analysis, and information from modern dialects, it is possible to deduce that the pronunciation of 學 *xué*, for example, was something like "hak" in Confucius's time; the pronunciation of 時 *shí* was like [dəʔ].

Modern Standard Written Chinese

In the early twentieth century, the formal written medium shifted away from Classical Chinese toward a style of writing based on a northern vernacular known as *báihuà*, literally 'plain-language.' "Baihua" was the name adopted in the twentieth century for the written style(s) characteristic of the Ming and Qing novels (beginning in the fourteenth century), whose prose eschewed classical affectations and incorporated vocabulary and usage from contemporary northern (or Beijing) speech. At the time, Baihua was not considered suitable for serious writing, but by the twentieth century, its affinity with the emergent standard speech, Mandarin, and the sense that it was a language of the people rather than of the ruling classes made it a logical choice for the basis of the new written norm.

For northerners, whose spoken language—Mandarin—also had northern roots, the syntax and lexicon of the new written language were reasonably familiar. But for southerners, whose spoken languages differed from the northern standard in grammatical structure, word choice, word usage, and pronunciation, learning the new vernacular style required more of a stretch. However, there was one important ameliorating factor: the character writing system. While characters may show a degree of internal consistency in the form of phonetic sets (see Section 14), they are, like the Arabic numerals (for example, 1, 2, 3), not committed to any particular pronunciation. Classical Chinese was read out in the pronunciation of whatever language grouping the speaker belonged to—Cantonese, Hokkien, Mandarin, and so on. The practice continues with the modern written medium: it is recognizably Mandarin (although admixtures of classical diction are often added to more literary styles), but it is read in one's native idiom— Cantonese, Hokkien, Mandarin, and so on. In this respect, Chinese is just a more extreme case of what is generally true of written language: Australians, Jamaicans, Americans, and Liverpudlians apply their local pronunciations but not their local usage or grammar to a text that is otherwise just written English.

Regardless of how they speak—whether it be a local version of Mandarin or Cantonese or some other regional speech that is far from intelligible to Mandarin speakers—Chinese write the same Modern Written Chinese (or Written Mandarin). This written language, when read aloud with Mandarin pronunciation, is closer to Standard Spoken Mandarin than to any other modern speech. However, it is not identical to Spoken Mandarin. For one thing, it may range in style and genre from the relatively colloquial to the more formal, or "classical." Even for speakers of Putonghua, the written language may differ considerably from the spoken form and, in its more formal registers, may be quite different. But regardless of how colloquial the style, or how close to Mandarin speech, it does not reflect regional usage. For speakers of Shanghainese, Cantonese, and regional speeches, the standard written language of China simply does not represent the patterns and usage of their spoken languages. For all children, Written Mandarin is a medium taught in school (as, indeed, is written English), but for children whose speech is regional, their task approaches that of learning a second language.

In this sense, Chinese can be characterized as "diglossic," literally 'of two tongues.' That is, children grow up with the spoken language to which they are exposed. In school, they learn to write a language that may differ both in choice of words and in the form of sentences—grammar. The distinction was far more extreme over the 2,000-plus years throughout which Classical Chinese was the written lingua franca (well into the twentieth century). Then, the distinction was comparable to that found in Europe before the rise of the vernaculars, when the educated wrote Latin but spoke local languages—the languages that ultimately gave rise to French, Italian, Spanish, and the rest of the Romance family.

6. Writing in the Regional Languages

Two major regional languages have written traditions that differ from Modern Written Chinese: Cantonese and Taiwanese.

Cantonese

In Hong Kong, the situation has been different. Until 1997, Hong Kong was a British colony, a fact that insulated it from certain linguistic trends in the rest of China. Hong Kong retained the use of traditional characters, for example. Most of the population still speaks Cantonese, and Cantonese remains the language of education and government. For formal writing, Hong Kongers, like other Chinese, still write a language that does not directly reproduce their speech; that is, they write Modern Written Chinese that is more aligned with northern, Mandarin speech. However, Hong Kong is unusual in also making extensive use of Cantonese writing, that is, writing that reproduces Cantonese speech patterns and word usage. This writing requires the use of uniquely Cantonese characters to represent those words for which there was no appropriate character in the standard written language. Such words have either been assigned historically cognate graphs or have been provided with new graphs created on phonosemantic principles (see Section 12).[4]

Chinese governments have consistently discouraged any form of dialect writing on the reasonable grounds that it would lead to disunity. However, in Hong Kong, the two types of writing complement each other rather than compete. Written Cantonese is used when there is a need to reproduce actual speech, either because the record needs to be verbatim, as in legal proceedings, or because there are emotive reasons for reproducing local speech. Written Cantonese is now common in newspapers, in comics, in certain magazines, in advertisements, on billboards, in government public service announcements, and, of course, in texting and social networking.

Taiwanese

Táiyǔ (台语) 'Taiwanese' is another regional language that has developed a written tradition separate from the Chinese standard. Until the middle of the twentieth century, Mandarin speech and Modern Written Chinese were the norm in Taiwan (and written *Táiyǔ* was not published at all), but in the last few decades, the language of approximately 85 percent of the population, a written version of *Mǐnnányǔ* 'Southern Min,' has become a viable written

---

[4]For a thorough account of Cantonese writing, see Cheung Kwan-hin and Robert Bauer, *The Representation of Cantonese with Chinese Characters* (Journal of Chinese Linguistics, Monograph Series Number 18, 2002).

medium; called Modern Written Taiwanese, it is used not only for informal written communication, but for more serious literary endeavors, as well.

7. Languages Related to Chinese

Though the evidence is not conclusive, many scholars regard the Chinese languages (Mandarin, Cantonese, and so on) as forming a branch of a family of languages that is usually labeled Sino-Tibetan, but in recent writing has also been called simply Tibeto-Burman (with the Chinese branch lying within). This family of languages includes the major literary languages of Chinese, Tibetan, and Burmese, as well as some 250 languages spoken in western China, in Nepal and adjacent regions of the Himalayas, and to the southwest of China, particularly in Burma and adjacent countries. Grouping the languages in a single family entails that they derive ultimately from a common prehistorical language, usually referred to as Proto-Sino-Tibetan. This proto-language is inferred from the apparent survival of a significant number of its roots in the daughter languages. Not generally included in the Sino-Tibetan family are Vietnamese and related languages in the Mon-Khmer family (part of a larger grouping called Austro-Asiatic) and Thai and related languages (part of the Tai or Tai-Kadai family).

Borrowed Writing Systems

The fact that Japan, as well as Korea and Vietnam at particular times in their history, have used, or now use, a character-writing system based ultimately on the Chinese has no definitive bearing on the question of the historical origins of those languages. None of the three is thought to share an origin with Chinese. Writing systems can be borrowed by languages regardless of their origin, as the widespread use of Roman alphabets, or Indic "alpha-syllabaries," attests. The fact that Chinese, Japanese, Korean, and Vietnamese use, or have used at some time in the past, a character-writing system derived from the Chinese shows the profound cultural and political influence of Chinese in the region. However, the common use of writing symbols does not reflect a common origin of linguistic features.

8. Chinese Names for China

Names for China

The English name "China" is thought to derive from a Persian word for porcelain ("china"), which, in turn, provided an English name for the country where porcelain was originally manufactured. The Chinese name for

China is *Zhōngguó*, literally 'central-kingdom,' a name that dates back to the Zhōu (Chou) dynasty, when China was still fragmented into rival states. The *Zhōngguó* was a central state ruled by an ancient dynasty to which the other states owed some allegiance—hence, "the central kingdom."

Běijīng and *Běipíng*

When the emperor Yong Le of the Ming Dynasty moved the capital from *Nánjīng* ('Southern Capital') to *Běipíng* ('Northern Peace'), he renamed the latter city *Běijīng* ('Northern Capital'). The city has retained that name and function ever since, except for the period 1928 to 1949, when the capital was removed to the south while the Japanese occupied the north, and Beijing reverted temporarily to its old name of *Běipíng*. The nationalist government in Taiwan, refusing to recognize the legitimacy of the Communist victory in 1949 and the consequent renaming of the country as the People's Republic of China, continued to call itself (and the rest of China) the Republic of China, and to use the name *Běipíng* rather than *Běijīng*.

2
Representing Pronunciation

9. Alternative Systems of Transcription

In a book about Chinese, it is obviously necessary to be able to represent the language in a way that is accessible to people who are not able to read normal Chinese writing in characters. We need a transcription system that can represent Chinese and that can, with a little priming, be read out by readers to serve the purposes of this book—which is not to learn the language as such, but to provide a useful guide and reference book.

Transcription Systems

The Wade-Giles System

A number of transcription systems for Chinese have seen considerable use over the past century and a half. One of the earliest was the Wade-Giles system, named for British diplomats and scholars Thomas Wade and Herbert Giles, who lived in the late nineteenth and early twentieth centuries. The Wade-Giles system was widely used in the twentieth century and continues to see limited use even in the present day. Its earlier popularity is reflected in standard English spellings such as "Chou" for the Chou Dynasty (*Zhōu* in pinyin) or "Hu Shih" for the Chinese philosopher and language reformer (*Hú Shì* in pinyin). Tones are omitted when citing names in English; otherwise, tones in Wade-Giles are represented by superscript numerals: Chou[1], Hu[2]Shih[4].

The Yale System

The Yale system became popular in language-learning materials developed at Yale University and elsewhere, beginning in the 1950s. It had the advantage of being easy to type, and relatively transparent (or intuitive) for English speakers. Thus, for example, "Jōu" was used for the dynasty name, and "Hú Shř" for the philosopher. Yale indicates tones with diacritics (accent signs), as shown.

The Gwoyeu Romatzyh System: Spelling the Tones

Another system, called Gwoyeu Romatzyh (GR for short), indicates tones
by varying the spelling of vowels: thus "hau, haur, hao, haw" represents four
syllables, with tones 1, 2, 3, and 4, respectively. GR requires a greater initial
effort to learn than the other systems, but in return, gives tonal distinctions
the same status as vowels and consonants, making them more memorable.

Bopomofo: A Transcription Without Roman Letters

All of the systems mentioned above make use of letters and other symbols
familiar to speakers of European languages, but less familiar to Chinese.
One popular Chinese system of transcription, invented in the early part of
the twentieth century, took its cue from the Japanese syllabary (kana) and
made use of symbols derived from ancient characters. Thus, to cite one of
the more obvious cases, ㄕ, representing an initial *sh*, is based on the character 尸, pronounced *shī*. *Zhōu* (Chou), in this system, is written ㄓㄡ, with
symbols for *zh* + *ou* and the level tone unmarked; *Hú Shì* is written ㄏㄨˊㄕˋ,
with *h* + *u* and *sh* and rising and falling tones marked with accents. Formally,
this system is called *Zhùyīn Fúhào* ('phonetic transcription'), but informally
it is named for its first four symbols (whose names incorporate the vowel
"o"), Bopomofo.

Bopomofo is the only transcription that can be written vertically without
loss of readability, and since Taiwanese still write mostly in the traditional
top-to-bottom and right-to-left fashion, it has found an ecological niche that
has ensured its survival to the present day. In Taiwan, Bopomofo is used
mainly in schools and in other educational settings where there is a need
to indicate pronunciation alongside characters. In publications, a running
transcription in Bopomofo is placed to the right of characters, where it provides a stylistically harmonious pronunciation guide that is unobtrusive, yet
immediately accessible. Bopomofo, along with pinyin, can also be used to
input Chinese characters for word processing.

English Spellings of Chinese Names

English spellings such as Peking (for *Běijīng*), Canton (for *Guǎngzhōu*), and
Amoy (for *Xiàmén*) derive from postal spellings established in the late nineteenth century and carried over to the twentieth century and, in some cases, up to
the present day. These spellings were influenced partly by Wade-Giles romaniza-
tion (for example the "p" in Peking) and partly by the pronunciation of regional
languages. The English name Hong Kong is based on the Cantonese pronunciation of the place rather than the Mandarin. Amoy (a city on the east coast) is also
based on the local (Hokkien) pronunciation rather than the Mandarin.

Peking too, like the other "-king" cities—Nanking and Chungking—is
probably also modeled on Cantonese, which has the "k" sound in those

names. The shift in English from Peking to Beijing has not only stranded names like Peking University, Peking Duck, and Peking Opera, all of which retain the old spelling, but has led to an affected pronunciation of the capital as "bay-zhing" (with the "zh" like the "s" in "pleasure") rather than "bay-djing," which is closer to the Mandarin. (Interestingly, for many European languages, the Peking version is still current: French "Pékin," German "Peking," Italian "Pechino.")

The name Canton for the city was probably based on the name of the province, *Guăngdōng*, rather than the city, *Guăngzhōu*. In any case, the city was not called *Guăngzhōu* at the time when the name Canton was first applied to it in English.

10. The Pinyin System

The system that has become the standard transcription for almost all Chinese-speaking communities in the world is not one of those mentioned in Section 9. It is the system called *Hànyŭ Pīnyīn*, literally 'Chinese spelling,' which was developed on the mainland and adopted as the official system there in the late 1950s. Eventually, the rest of the world followed. Pinyin is now used in most Chinese language–teaching materials and reference books, in library catalogs, on road signs, in URL addresses (although these may also be in Chinese characters nowadays), and in advertising and other commercial material.

Characters and Pinyin

Just as Bopomofo appears as a pronunciation crib for vertically written Chinese characters, pinyin is often added as a pronunciation crib for horizontally written character texts, where it generally appears as isolated syllables written in small print below each character. (Microsoft Word is available with special pinyin and Bopomofo annotation functions that insert pinyin horizontally below, or Bopomofo vertically to the right of, each character.)

The Character as a Linguistic Unit

For native Chinese, the character is what the linguist Yuen Ren Chao called a "sociological word," that is, it has a psychological reality that is reinforced by the importance of character meaning in literacy. Dictionaries are generally organized first by characters and then by compounds, although nowadays, character entries are often ordered alphabetically by pinyin spelling. In colloquial speech, words—compound or otherwise—are more likely to be referred to in terms of *zì* 'characters' rather than with the more specialized term *cí* 'word,' used by linguists and other wordsmiths. For this reason,

Chinese often transcribe characters with a space around each syllable rather than around each word.

Transcribing Continuous Speech

Pinyin can also be, and is, used for transcribing continuous speech or representing written texts. As such, it can be written continuously, with full punctuation, either in conjunction with a character string or without reference to characters at all, as in some of the examples in this book. For good readability, pinyin text needs to demarcate words rather than just syllables and be properly punctuated, as in the following example.

搬起石头砸自己的脚。
Bān qǐ shí tou zá zì jǐ de jiǎo. (syllables)
Bān qǐ shítou zá zìjǐ de jiǎo. (words)
Lift up stone smash self's foot.
'Hoist with your own petard.'

Distinguishing Words and Phrases

At times, it is difficult to distinguish a compound word from an idiomatic phrase in Chinese. Should *bān qǐ* be written as two words, with a space (like the English phrasal verb "lift up"), or as a single word (*bānqǐ*), without a space?

English is not immune from similar problems: "off base," as in "way off base" (meaning "badly mistaken") is two words; "off-base" (meaning "outside the perimeter") is hyphenated; and "offside" (meaning "illegally ahead of the ball/puck") is written as a single word. Ultimately, for Chinese transcription, usage has to be modeled after dictionaries and other reference works where pinyin is used.

The Limits of Pinyin

Anything that can be understood as spoken text can be transcribed and understood in pinyin, which is, after all, a record of speech. Conversely, noncolloquial material, particularly the very succinct and elaborate styles of Classical Chinese, which cannot be read out and understood, cannot be understood written out in pinyin, either. Continuous pinyin can be found in teaching materials (for example, in my own textbook, *Learning Chinese*), and some excerpts from Chinese colloquial literature have now been transcribed from characters into pinyin as an aid to language learning. Even in such cases, pinyin has not reached the level of an orthography, with a standard spelling that transcends local variation. In American or British English, spelling is standard and does not—except for special effects—change to reflect particular pronunciations: "vase" represents British "vahz" or American "veys," for example. Pinyin, which was conceived as a tool for teaching the standard language, indicates standard pronunciation, so variant pronunciations, such as *yìhuìr* and *yìhuǐr* 'for a while,' are separately indicated.

11. Pronunciation

Once learned, pinyin consistently represents pronunciation. However, it was originally intended as a tool for Chinese speakers, so it is not especially transparent for English or other foreign speakers. Some letters do have much the same value in pinyin that they have in English: *f, k, l, m, n, p, s*, and *t*, for example. Others, such as *c, q, x, z*, and *zh*, have values quite unlike those of English. Still others have two values, depending on context. Pinyin *i*, for example, is pronounced "ee" in *qi* [tɕʰi] ("tchee"), but in the syllable *zi* "tsz," it represents a buzzing sound—a very high front vowel, written [ɿ] in the IPA system (see the following subsection).

Pinyin requires some effort to learn, but given its official status and its familiarity to both Chinese who have been through the school system and to foreigners who have studied Chinese, it seems the best option for a book like this. The goal of this section is to give an overview of the sounds of Mandarin and the way those sounds are represented in pinyin, so that readers not already familiar with the system can learn to approximate actual pronunciation when they read out examples.

Approximating Mandarin Sounds

The only way to represent sound on the printed page unambiguously is to use the International Phonetic Alphabet (IPA), a system of symbols whose phonetic values have been established by convention: IPA [i] is always "ee," IPA [u] is always "oo," and so on. Unfortunately, IPA may be as unfamiliar as pinyin for many readers of this book, so in this section, we also provide pronunciation approximations in terms of typical English spelling: *u* is like "oo," *qi* is like "tchee," *te* is like "tuh," and so on. Ultimately, of course, it will be necessary to check your pronunciation with that of a speaker of standard Chinese.

The Syllable (Initial + Rhyme)

The Chinese syllable, spoken or written, is traditionally divided into an initial and a rhyme; the latter is sometimes called a "final" in linguistic literature. Initial consonants are represented by one or two letters. In Chinese, there are no consonant clusters, like English "pl" or "st." Pinyin combinations such as *ch* and *sh* represent unit sounds, as they do in English.

Rhymes

The pinyin rhyme is represented by an obligatory vowel (V) and three optional elements: tones (T), four in number; medials (M), three in number; and endings (E), five in number.

- Tones are represented by accents above the main vowel, for example, *ā*, *á*, *ǎ*, *à*.
- Medials are either *i*, *u*, or the rarer *ü*.
- Endings are *i*, *o* or *n*, *ng* (always pronounced [ŋ], as in English "sing"). It is helpful to remember "3 medials and 4 endings." There is actually a fifth ending, *u*, which appears only in the rhyme *ou*, an exception that avoids introducing a double letter—*oo*—into the pinyin system. Vowel *o* + ending *o* gives *ou* rather than *oo*: *dōu*, *zhōu*, *lòu*.

Initial   Rhyme

$$
\begin{array}{llll}
 & & \text{T} & \\
\text{C}_i & \text{M} & \text{V} & \text{E} \\
 & i, u, ü & & i, o/u, n, ng
\end{array}
$$

Rhymes in stressed syllables—those with tone—can consist of V/T (*è*, *t-ā*, *b-ǐ*), M + V/T (*j-iā*, *j-ué*, *n-üè*), V/T + E (*t-ài*, *h-ǎo*, *t-ān*, *t-āng,* and the idiosyncratic *d-ōu*), or M + V/T + E (*k-uài*, *j-iāo*, *l-iǎn*, *q-iǎn*). Notice that if there is more than one vowel letter, the tone mark always goes over the main vowel, defined as "not a medial." With *dui*, *u* is a possible medial, so *i* must be the main vowel—hence, *duì*. With *diu*, *i* is a possible medial, so *u* is the main vowel—hence, *diū*. With *hao*, *a* is not a possible medial, so it must be the main vowel (and *o* is an ending)—hence, *hǎo*.

Note how much simpler Chinese syllable structure is than that of English, which allows many more consonant clusters than Chinese (for example "str-" as in "strike" and "-xth" [ksθ] as in "sixth"). English is said to contain about 8,000 possible syllables, while Chinese has only 1,277—or, if tonal distinctions are ignored, about 400.

Initials

In the following alphabetical list, the initial consonants of Mandarin are represented in pinyin, with pronunciations represented accurately in IPA (in square brackets) and approximately in terms of English spelling in the third column. The IPA representation includes two nonstandard symbols for "buzzing vowels," in which the flat of the tongue is so high against the roof of the mouth that little more than a buzz or a hush escapes. One is [ɹ], in which the lips are spread and the tongue is flat (*ci* [tsʰɹ] "tsz"); the other is [ɻ], in which the lips are pursed and the tongue tip is raised (*chi* [tʂʰɻ] "tchr"). Consonants that are particularly problematic (at least for English speakers) are marked with an asterisk.

Initial	IPA	English Hint	Comment
b	[p]	s**p**ell	voiceless but without aspiration
c*	[tsʰ]	ma**ts**	as in Russian "tsar"
ch	[tʂʰ]	**ch**oose	with tongue tip raised
d	[t]	s**t**ill	voiceless but without aspiration
f	[f]	**f**	
g	[k]	s**k**ill	voiceless but without aspiration
h	[x]	Ba**ch**	"h" with slight friction
j	[tɕ]	**j**eep	produced at the "y" in "yield"; unvoiced
k	[kʰ]	**k**	
l	[l]	**l**	
m	[m]	**m**	
n	[n]	**n**	
p	[pʰ]	**p**	
q*	[tɕʰ]	**ch**eese	produced at the "y" in "yield"
r	[ʐ]	**r**ill	between the "r" in "rill" and the "z" in "azure"
s	[s]	**s**	
sh	[ʂ]	**sh**rill	with tongue tip raised, lips pursed
t	[tʰ]	**t**	
w	[w]	**w**	
x*	[ɕ]	**s**ying	"s" produced at the "y" of "yield"
y	[j]	**y**	sometimes with a high degree of friction
z*	[ts]	ki**ds**	
zh*	[tʂ]	**j**ewel	with tongue tip raised, lips pursed

Initials with Select Rhymes

Chinese groups the initial consonants in sets (1, 2, 3, and so on), with those articulated in the front of the mouth (at the lips) first, then proceeding by increments toward the throat. Each consonant is provided with a vowel so that it can be pronounced, but because some Mandarin initials co-occur with only certain vowels, the citation vowels vary. Becoming familiar with this table is a good first step in learning the rest of the rhymes. All syllables can be read on the level tone.

	A	B	C	D	Column B in terms of English spelling
1	*bo* [pɔ]	*po* [pʰɔ]	*mo* [mɔ]	*fo* [fɔ]	"pʷaw"
2	*de* [tɤ]	*te* [tʰɤ]	*ne* [nɤ]	*le* [lɤ]	"tuh"
3	*zi* [tsɻ]	*ci* [tsʰɻ]	*si* [sɻ]		"tsz"
4	*zhi* [tʂɭ]	*chi* [tʂʰɭ]	*shi* [ʂɭ]	*ri* [ʐɭ]	"chr"
5	*ji* [tɕi]	*qi* [tɕʰi]	*xi* [ɕi]		"chee"
6	ge [kɤ]	*ke* [kʰɤ]	*he* [hɤ]		"kuh"

Voiceless Plain Versus Voiceless Aspirate. Examination of the IPA values for columns A and B reveals that the sounds of pinyin *b* versus *p*, *d* versus *t*, and so on are not quite like those typically associated with the same pairs of letters in English. In the English pair "b/p," the distinctive feature is voicing: [b, p]. In the Chinese case, as the IPA symbols show, the pairs are both voiceless ([pɔ], [pʰɔ]), with the distinctive feature being aspiration (the delay between the release of the lips and the onset of the voiced vowel): [pɔ, pʰɔ; tɤ, tʰɤ; and so on]. So why write *b/p* in pinyin? The answer: because it is easier to type or write *b/p* than *p/p'* (the symbols used by the Wade-Giles system) or *p/pʰ*.

A simple strategy to adjust to this difference is to produce column B initials more or less as in English (*po* = "pʷaw," *te* = "tuh," and so on), but to articulate column A initials lightly, so as to minimize the voiced mode of articulation characteristic of English: *bo* = "bʷaw," with "b" articulated lightly.

The Affricates of Rows 3, 4, and 5—the Key Rows. Otherwise, the focus needs to be on rows 3, 4, and 5 of the initials chart. Row 3 represents sounds [ts, tsʰ], which, despite the fact that they are not found at the beginning of English words, are fairly easy to reproduce. Row 4, on the other hand, represents sounds described as retroflex, because they are articulated with the tip of the tongue on the back edge of the alveolar ridge (the rough ridge behind the upper teeth), a position that, for many English speakers, is approximately that for the initial consonants of words like "drill," "trill," "shrill," and "rill." (The *h* in pinyin *zh*, *ch*, and *sh*, with its long vertical stroke, can serve as a cue to elevate the tongue tip for these sounds.)

Row 5 represents sounds that are intermediate between those of rows 3 and 4. Row 5 initials would be very hard to distinguish from rows 3 and 4 were it not for the fact that the vowels that occur with row 5 initials are quite distinct from those of either row 3 or 4. Row 5 initials (*j*, *q*, *x*) can only be followed by the sounds [i] ("ee") and [ü] ("yu"), written *i* and *u*, respectively. The initials of rows 3 and 4, on the other hand, can *never* be followed by the sounds [i] ("ee") or [ü] ("yu") (the letters *i* and *u*). Those letters, *i* and *u*, are therefore never pronounced "ee" and "yu" with row 3 and 4 initials, only buzzing "i" or "oo," as in *zī, zhī* and *zū, zhū*. Mastering row 3, 4, and 5 initials with *i* and *u* written vowels is the single most important step you can take in mastering pinyin pronunciation.

Test Yourself

Here is a short exercise that, if possible, you should do with the help of a Chinese speaker. Examine the following list of syllables, and write them in two groups according to whether their *i* vowel is pronounced "ee" or as a buzz—in IPA terms, distinguish [i] and [ɿ/ʅ].

cī   jī   shī   zī   sī   xī   chī   qī   zhī

Now, do the same for *u*. Distinguish those cases of *u* that are pronounced "oo" from those that are pronounced "yu"—in IPA terms, distinguish [u] and [ü].

zū   chū   xū   zhū   qū   jū   cū   sū   shū

Now, read the following syllables aloud. (Tones are present so that they can represent real words to Chinese speakers; however, the focus of the exercise is on the vowels.) To do this efficiently, make sure you keep in mind the contrast between the initials of rows 3 and 4 on the one hand, and those of row 5 on the other.

qī   sǐ   zhī   zì   jī   qī   sì   rì   chī
xī   shì   cì   zhǐ   qí   sī   chǐ   jí   xí

Tones—Names and Representations

Tones form an additional component, present in most (but not all) syllables. Mandarin has four tones, with each tone relatively distinct compared to Chinese regional languages, such as Cantonese. Cantonese has six tones in smooth syllables (those ending in a vowel or nasal sound) in two layers of three, one relatively high, one relatively low. It also has three tones in checked syllables (those ending in -*p*, -*t*, or -*k*); it is much richer than Mandarin in consonant endings. Cantonese also has a special morphological tone that is distinct from all the others. Mandarin tones, by contrast, form a symmetrical system that nicely fills tonal space: high and low, rising and falling.

Mandarin tones can be referred to by number, or descriptively, as follows.

Symbol	Description	Number	Concept	Tone Letter
ā	high (level)	1st	"sung out"	˥
á	rising	2nd	"doubtful"	˩
ǎ	low	3rd	"low" (with rise)	˦
à	falling	4th	"conclusive"	˩

Tone Concepts

Rather than trying to mimic a drawn contour (of the sort represented by the last column in the chart above), experience has shown that for Chinese-language learners, concepts can be a more effective prompt for producing correct tonal contours. For English speakers, singing out a first-tone syllable tends to produce a level pitch; for the second tone, uncertainty or doubt tends to produce a rising pitch; for the fourth tone, certainty or conclusiveness (for example, 4 in the sequence 1, 2, 3, 4) tends to produce the desired falling pitch. For the third tone, whose citation pitch is usually described as contoured like a V, thinking of it as low rather than falling-rising serves as a safeguard against an early or unwanted rise, particularly when a low-toned syllable is followed by a syllable with high or rising pitch: *lǎoshī* (low, then high) 'teacher,' *hěn máng* (low, then rising) 'quite busy.' It is better to think of the third tone as simply low, and then to add a slight rise when there is no closely bound following syllable (as is the case for the final syllable of *Hái hǎo* '[I'm] okay').

Paired Tones and the Low-Tone Shift

The different pitches of tones are best perceived in pairs of syllables. With four tones, one expects 16 possible pairs, but one combination, low + low, regularly undergoes a shift to rising + low: *hěn* + *hǎo* → *hén hǎo*. Thus, there are actually only 15 possible combinations. These are listed below with real words or phrases, so you can ask a Chinese-speaking friend to read them out and then practice them yourself (first by imitating, then by reading them out before hearing them).

Variable + high tone	*jiāgāo*	*tígāo*	*hěn gāo*	*bù gāo*
Variable + rising tone	*bāngmáng*	*jímáng*	*hěn máng*	*bù máng*
Variable + low tone	*ānhǎo*	*hái hǎo*	(*hěn hǎo*)	*bù hǎo*
Variable + falling tone	*zhēn lèi*	*bú lèi*	*hěn lèi*	*shòulèi*

Other Tone Shifts

Other tone shifts in Mandarin only affect individual words. The negative *bu*, which has falling tone in most contexts, has rising tone before falling tone in close juncture: *bù gāo*, *bù máng*, *bù hǎo*, but *bú lèi*.

The numeral 'one,' *yi*, behaves like *bu*, except that in citation, it is level toned: *yī*, *èr*, *sān* '1, 2, 3.' Otherwise, like *bu*, it has rising tone before falling tone, and falling tone before all others: *yì zhāng*, *yì tiáo*, *yì běn,* but *yí fèn*. Some speakers pronounce *qī* '7' and *bā* '8' with rising tone before falling tone—*qí gè*, *bá gè*—but with level tone in all other cases.

Changed tones are not usually written as such in pinyin. For teaching purposes, however, the changes associated with the particular words *bu* and *yi* will be indicated in our examples. The third-tone shift, which affects all third-tone words, is not shown; to do so would obscure the original tone of too many words. Thus, we write *yìdiǎnr* and *yí gè* (rather than *yīdiǎnr and yī gè*), *bù hǎo* and *bú lèi* (rather than *bù lèi*), but *hěn hǎo* (rather than *hén hǎo*). *Qī* '7' and *bā* '8' are always written with level tone.

Rhymes

For purposes of presentation, the rhymes of Chinese are listed below, first by main vowel (written *a, e, i, o, u,* and *ü*), then by main vowel plus ending (V + *i, o/u, n, ng*), and finally, with the medials added to the mix. The examples may all be regarded as level tone. As with initials, the pronunciation of rhymes is given in IPA transcription (in square brackets) and, as much as possible, in terms of English spelling. (In the English Hint column, syllables that do not actually occur in English are cited in quotation marks, for example, "tahn.") Especially problematical items are marked with an asterisk.

		IPA	Example	English Hint	Comment
A-Rhymes					
1	*a*	[a]	*ta*	ta[rp]	never as in "tap"
2	*a-i*	[aɪ]	*tai*	tie	
3	*a-o*	[ao]	*kao*	cow	
4	*a-n*	[an]	*tan*	short "tahn"	never as in "tan"
5	*a-ng*	[ɑŋ]	*gang*	"gahng"	never as in "gang"
6	*i-a*	[ia]	*jia*	"jyah"	
7	*i-a-o*	[iɑo]	*jiao*	"jy[h]ow"	rhymes with "how"
8*	*i-a-n*	[iɛn]	*jian*	"jyen"	
9	*i-a-ng*	[iɑŋ]	*jiang*	"jyahng"	
10	*u-a*	[ua]	*hua*	"hwah"	
11	*u-a-i*	[uai]	*chuai*	"chw-eye"	rhymes with "why"
12	*u-a-n*	[uan]	*huan*	"hwahn"	like Spanish "Juan"
		[üan]	*quan*	"ch-yu-an"	
13	*u-a-ng*	[uɑŋ]	*huang*	"hwahng"	
E-Rhymes					
14	*e*	[ə]	*zhe*	"juh"	
15	*e-i*	[ei]	*zhei*	jay	
16	*e-n*	[ən]	*zhen*	"juhn"	
17	*e-ng*	[əŋ]	*leng*	lung	
18	*we-ng*	[wəŋ]	*weng*	*"w-uh-ng"*	
19	*i-e*	[iɛ]	*jie*	"jyeh"	
20*	*u-e*	[üɛ]	*jue, lüe*	"j-yu-weh," "l-yu-weh"	
I-Rhymes					
21	*i*	[i]	*li*	Lee	
22	*i-n*	[in]	*jin*	gene	
23	*i-ng*	[iŋ]	*jing*	"jeeng"	
24*	*u-i*	[uei]	*dui*	"d-way"	rhymes with "way"
25*	*i*	[ɹ]	*zi*	"dz"	
26	*i*	[ʅ]	*zhi*	"jr"	
O-Rhymes					
27*	*o*	[ʊɔ]	*bo*	"bʷaw"	
28*	*o-u*	[ou]	*zhou*	Joe	
29	*o-ng*	[uŋ]	*zhong*	"joong"	
30	*i-o-ng*	[iuŋ]	*jiong*	"jyong"	
31	*u-o*	[ʊɔ]	*duo*	"dʷaw"	

	IPA	Example	English Hint	Comment
U-Rhymes				
32 *u*	[u]	*shu*	shoe	
33* *u-n*	[un]	*shun*	"shwoon"	
34* *i-u*	[iu ~ io]	*qiu*	"chyoo"	between "you" and "yo"
35* *u*	[ü]	*xu*	"syoo"	
36 *u-n*	[ün]	*qun*	"chyoon"	

The *r*-Ending

In addition to the two final consonants *n* and *ng*, there is also a retroflex ending, -*r*, which appears in only a small number of words (or morphemes) pronounced -*er*. The most common of these are *èr* (二) 'two,' *ěr* (耳) 'ear,' and *ér* (儿) 'child.'

The -*r* Suffix

The last example above, *ér* (儿) 'child,' is also the source of an -*r* suffix frequently added to everyday nouns (rarely to verbs) in the speech of Beijing and other northern areas (see Section 26). This suffix affects the syllable in ways too complicated to fully enumerate here. Here is an example: *yìdiǎn* 'a bit, a little' is pronounced with the -*r* suffix in northern speech. The combination is pronounced without the final nasal ("*yìdiǎr*"), but pinyin convention writes *yìdiǎnr* so that *r*-less speakers can recover the underlying form and pronounce it simply *yìdiǎn*. Here are a few more examples.

- *píng* + *ér* → *píngr* 'bottle,' pronounced "pyə^{n}r"; otherwise, *píngzi* in southern Mandarin
- *xìngrén* + *ér* → *xìngrénr* 'apricot kernel; almond,' pronounced "xingrər"; otherwise, *xìngrén*
- *nǎizuǐ* + *ér* → *nǎizuǐr* 'nipple of a feeding bottle,' pronounced "naizuər"; otherwise, *nǎizuǐ* (The colloquial word *nǎizuōzi* is also used.)

3
The Writing System

With other languages, discussion of the writing system might be consigned to an appendix. But for many people—both Chinese and non-Chinese alike—characters characterize Chinese. This is partly because of the beauty and intricacy of the symbols, but it is also because, unlike the letters of alphabetic systems such as those used for English, Russian, Hebrew, and Hindi, Chinese characters for the most part combine sound with meaning, giving them a superficial identification with words and making it seem that learning the language is simply a matter of learning the meaning (and pronunciation) of a critical mass of characters (say, 4,000). In this chapter, characters are examined in terms of their origin, their function, and their form.

12. The Origin of Characters

Characters directly ancestral to modern forms appeared at least as early as the fourteenth century BCE, with the oracle inscriptions (甲骨文 *jiǎgǔwén*) of the late Shang dynasty. Traditionally, the Chinese have distinguished six types of character formation, only four of which bear on the actual form of the character. The historical details are often complicated, but the modern learner can discern the four types in the form of modern characters. Of the four original types, two apply to simplex characters and two, to compound characters (those with two components). Simplex characters can be pictorial (e.g. 門 'door' and 魚 'fish'—with fins down). They can also be indicative—a subtype of pictorial (上 'up' and 下 'down'). Compound characters—the other two types—can be synthetic, combining two simplex characters in a blended whole (好 hǎo 'good' with 女 'woman' and 子 'son'—which can be interpreted as the prototype of "goodness"). And they can be phonosemantic, combining a sound element and a semantic element: 清 qīng 'clear' and 情 qíng 'emotions' consist of a phonetic character, 青 , pronounced qīng on its own, and semantic elements 氵 'water' (a *clear* fluid) and 忄 'heart' (the source of *emotion*) (cf. §14, 15, for details). Learners often find pictorial form in characters regardless of their actual history, beginning with graphs like 哭 *kū* 'cry,' which seems to show a crying eye, and 电 *diàn* 'electricity,' which looks like an electric plug. But once a critical mass of characters is acquired, patterns of phonetic regularity found in sets of phonosemantic graphs prove more useful (see Section 14).

13. The Function of Characters

Characters represent syllables. In some cases, they represent syllables that are also words (indicated in pinyin by spaces), for example, 黄河入海流 *Huang He rù hǎi liú* ('Yellow River enter sea flow'). In many cases, however, they represent syllables that are components of words: 东西 *dōngxi* 'thing' (with characters that would otherwise be glossed 'east' and 'west'); 似乎 *sìhū* 'seem, look like' (with a character for 'seem' and another that represents a Classical Chinese particle); 蝴蝶 *húdié* 'butterfly' (with characters unique to the compound); 胡同 *hútòngr* 'alley' (with characters chosen only for their sound, but which are otherwise used for 'nonsense' and 'same').

The last example, a loanword from Manchu, illustrates the way foreign words, place names, and personal names can be represented in Chinese: 高尔夫 *gāo ěrfū* 'golf,' 符拉迪沃斯托克 *Fúlādíwòsītuōkè* 'Vladivostok,' and 格里高利·派克 *Gélǐgāolì Pàikè* 'Gregory Peck.' In such cases, the choice of characters is motivated mainly by sound. But in other cases, particularly in the names of countries, sound and meaning may complement each other. Thus, 德国 *Déguó* 'Germany,' 法国 *Fǎguó* 'France,' and 英国 *Yīngguó* 'Britain' are represented in Chinese with characters that fit the first syllable of the foreign word (*dé* for **Deu**tschland, *fǎ* for **Fra**nce, and *yīng* for **Eng**land) while also conveying a respectful meaning: 'the countries of' *dé* 'virtue,' *fǎ* 'law,' and *yīng* 'heroes.'

Characters as Morphemes (Minimal Units of Meaning)

Despite the frequency of cases in which the meaning of individual characters is irrelevant, it is true that almost all characters can, with analysis, be associated with a meaning and are therefore not only syllables, but morphemes. Character dictionaries (*zìdiǎn* 'character-records'), which list entries by character, provide a record of such meanings. For characters that do not represent words in the modern language, however, core meanings must be inferred from the compounds in which they occur or from earlier stages of the language (represented in part by Classical Chinese), when more morphemes functioned as words. In effect, literate and highly educated speakers of Chinese are more likely to know the meanings of individual characters in compounds such as 似乎 *sìhū* 'seem, look like' or even 字典 *zìdiǎn* 'dictionary,' where the second character never appears as an independent word in the modern language. The best that can be said is that for Chinese, there is always an assumption that a character is or was at some time a meaningful unit—a morpheme.

14. The Form of Characters

Characters are formed from about a dozen basic strokes, each of which is written with a conventional gesture that is defined by onset and direction. Some of the strokes are primarily horizontal or vertical in orientation, while others are hooked, curved, or bent. Most are drawn from left to right, although a few falling strokes are right to left. Characters may be composed of a single stroke (乙) or several dozen (龘). The average number of strokes for the 2,000 commonly used characters is reported to be 11.2 for the traditional set and 9 for the simplified.[1]

Character Components

The immediate constituents of characters are not strokes, but components, which are made up of clusters of strokes. Some characters are composed of only one component, but most are composed of two, organized horizontally, vertically, or concentrically, as the following examples illustrate.

好 *hǎo* 'good'	= 女 *nǚ* next to 子 *zǐ*
河 *hé* 'river'	= 氵 (a combining form of 水 *shuǐ*) next to 可 *kě*
墨 *mò* 'ink'	= 土 *tǔ* below 黑 *hēi*
因 *yīn* 'cause'	= 大 *dà* inside 囗 *wéi*
羞 *xiū* 'shy'	= 丑 *chǒu* below (a skewed) 羊 *yáng*
鸠 *jiū* 'turtle dove'	= 九 *jiǔ* before 鸟 *niǎo*

The components to the right of the equals signs are, or have at some time been, simplex characters. Such characters tend to be representational in origin, although it is often necessary to trace them back to their earliest extant forms to perceive this. Thus, 女 'female' originally represented a (kneeling) woman, 羊 'goat' depicted the head of a goat, and 鸟 (traditional 鳥) portrayed a bird.

Phonetic Sets

In modern Chinese, the majority of characters are composite, with parts that can be identified with two simplex characters. As such, they are once

---

[1]Goonetilleke, Ravindra S., W. C. Lau, and Heloisa M. Shih. "Visual search strategies and eye movements when searching Chinese character screens." *International Journal of Human-Computer Studies* (2002) 57, 448–49.

removed from any pictorial origins. In fact, most (but not all) composite characters originated as phonosemantic compounds, with one component representing sound and the other classifying the character along very general dimensions of meaning. The process that gave rise to such characters has often been obscured by historical changes in the form and pronunciation of characters. But in some cases, it has left a clear residue of "phonetic sets" like the following.

幕 *mù*	'screen'	=	莫 + 巾 'cloth'
慕 *mù*	'long for'	=	莫 + 心 'heart'
墓 *mù*	'grave'	=	莫 + 土 'ground'
募 *mù*	'summon'	=	莫 + 力 'strength'
暮 *mù*	'sunset'	=	莫 + 日 'sun'
模 *mú*	'pattern'	=	莫 + 木 'wood; tree'

The six characters in this set all consist of a constant, 莫, and a variable (巾, 心, and so on). The constant correlates with pronunciation; the variables differentiate meaning—hence, the term "phonosemantic." They can be "read" as follows: 幕, the 莫 (*mù*) associated with 巾 'cloth,' that is, 'screen'; 慕, the 莫 (*mù*) associated with 心 'heart,' that is, 'long for'; and so on. Note that in the spoken language, the ambiguity is resolved by compounding, for example, *yínmù* 'screen [for films],' *xiànmù* 'envy,' and *fénmù* 'grave.' Native speakers are very adept at reading the phonetic hints to be found in composite characters. Learners need to adopt the same strategies, observing a phonetic element such as 莫 *mù*, then trying it out as an element in a compound (for example, 羡慕 *xiànmù*), and finally settling on a meaning that fits the context ('envy').

Phonetic Loans

The process that has given rise to phonetic sets in Chinese involved two steps. In the first step, a character representing one word is used to represent a word of the same or similar pronunciation. For example, 莫, which is thought to have originally depicted the sun (日) setting over the horizon (that is, 'sunset'), is extended or borrowed to represent another meaning, a negative ('not') that is nowadays pronounced *mò*, not *mù*. The new word may have been an extension of the 'setting' meaning along the lines of 'set' → 'disappear' → 'not,' in which case the character absorbed a new sense. Or 莫 may simply have been borrowed because its original sound was very close to that of 'not.' (Originally, the two words were closer in pronunciation than modern *mù* 'sunset' and *mò* 'not.') In either case, the new arrangement solved the problem of how to create a symbol for such an abstract notion as "not," and it did so in a way that did not add to the already large repertoire of characters.

The extension of 莫 solved one problem, but it introduced a new one: ambiguity. Unmodified, 莫 would have signaled (at least) two words, 'sunset' and 'not.' Written languages can tolerate a certain degree of ambiguity; witness the ambiguity of English 'lead' and 'can': each can be a verb and a noun of entirely unrelated meanings. But if Chinese wanted to make extensive use of phonetic loans, at some point there needed to be some way of distinguishing one meaning from another. The solution was to add an additional element, a semantic hint. Plain 莫 was used for 'not,' but to signal 'sunset' (the original meaning, as it happens), 莫 was augmented by 日 'sun' to give 暮. For 'screen,' 莫 was augmented by 巾 'cloth' to give 幕, and so on. Economy of symbols is preserved, and ambiguity is resolved.

Imperfect Phonetic Sets

Unfortunately, what began as a frugal method of expanding the repertoire of symbols was, in many cases, muddied by processes of historical change that saw the sound of some members of a set diverge from others (for example, 莫 *mò* versus 暮 *mù*). As a result, lots of "phonetic sets" in the modern language look more like the following one, based on 分 *fēn*.

粉	纷	扮	颁	盆	盼
fěn	*fēn*	*bàn*	*bān*	*pén*	*pàn*

What were presumably differences in pronunciation too small to hinder the original borrowing have diverged considerably over time. Nevertheless, the sounds remain easily relatable: *f*, *b*, and *p* are all labials, and *e* and *a* are fairly similar vowels. Although the pronunciations of individual members of such sets are not as predictable as the *mù* set, the range of variation is usually narrow and the experienced learner (and certainly the native reader) will be able to "read" the hints. For 纷纷 (the reduplicative adverbial form is more common), the silk radical on the left suggests, among other things, fine, numerous, tangled, while the phonetic element 分 on the right suggests options like *fēn*, *bàn*, *pān*, and so on, enough to help you recall *fēnfēn* 'in succession; confused; numerous' (as in people 'dropping like flies' from the heat or rising 'one after the other' to speak). In this way, Chinese characters do contain phonetic information, but not in a highly systematic and reliable form. (English, of course, has its nonsystematic features, too; consider words like "to," "too," and "two.")

15. Dictionaries

Chinese characters are not, of course, amenable to alphabetical ordering. So how are words and names to be accessed efficiently in dictionaries, library catalogs, and telephone directories? The traditional solution was inspired by the predominance of composite characters. All characters were assigned a classifying element, usually called a "radical" in English (Chinese *bùshǒu*). For compound characters, the radical was usually the semantic determinative (for example, 巾 in 幕 and 土 in 墓), which is itself usually a simplex character or a combining form of a simplex character. A simplex character that was not a radical itself had one of its strokes or parts designated as radical: Thus, 天 was assigned 一, 也 was assigned 乙 (reflecting an earlier form of the character), and 美 was assigned 羊.

Looking Up Characters

Once every character is assigned a radical, radicals can be ordered by number of strokes (一 before 力, 土, 雨, and so on), and characters can be grouped under their radical and ordered by number of additional strokes. Thus, 帖 would be under 5 strokes in radical 巾 (itself placed among three-stroke radicals). The 巾 set would include the following, in the order given.

巾	the plain radical	'cloth'
帆	+ 3 strokes	'sail'
帐	+ 4 strokes	'canopy' (extended to mean 'accounts')
帖	+ 5 strokes	'card, invitation'
帛	+ 5 strokes	'silk'
带	+ 6 strokes	'belt' (extended to mean 'bring')

Meanings of Radicals

Radicals have very general meanings, such as 'person' (人), 'female' (女), 'water' (水), and 'bird' (鸟). Historical change in the meaning of a particular character has often obscured the original impetus for a particular radical. Thus, 汉 *Hàn* 'the Han people, Chinese' contains the water radical because the Han were originally associated with the Han River in central China. 别 'other; don't' contains the 'knife' radical (with the citation form 刀), probably as a metaphor for 'separation' (extended to 'other' and 'prohibition'). In the modern language, radicals function more to distinguish one character from another than to provide semantic information; in other words, 汉 is not 叹 and 别 is not 拐.

Number of Radicals

The great *Kangxi Dictionary* of 1716 catalogued all characters under 214 radicals, a number that was standard until recent times. Before the adoption of the simplified set (see Section 18), students of Chinese would learn the more common radicals by number so they could go to the appropriate section of the dictionary without checking the radical tables: the water radical

(氵) was No. 85, the silk radical (糸) was No. 120, and so on. With the formalization of simplified characters on the mainland in the 1950s, both the number of radicals and, in some cases, the assignment of radicals to particular characters underwent changes.

Alphabetization by Pinyin

Many Chinese-to-Chinese and Chinese-to-foreign dictionaries nowadays list characters in order of their pinyin pronunciation, making alphabetical lookup possible. However, they generally list compound words under the entry of the initial character; thus, the compound *qìshuǐ* (汽水) 'carbonated drink' ('gas-water') is to be found under *qì* (汽) 'air, gas,' along with other compounds like *qìchē* (汽车) 'automobile' and *qìchuán* (汽船) 'steamship,' but not *qǐchéng* (启程) 'start on a journey' or *qǐchū* (起初) 'at first, originally,' which begin with different characters. In addition, Chinese dictionaries, even if organized around characters, generally only list compounds beginning with the citation characters, not compounds in which the character is in a second or later position: thus, 汽水 *qìshuǐ* and 汽车 *qìchē* are under the entry 汽, but not 水汽 *shuǐqì* 'vapor' or 蒸汽 *zhēngqì* 'steam,' which have 汽 in the second position—these would be under the entries 水 and 蒸, respectively. A few early dictionaries, such as *Mathews' Chinese-English Dictionary*, published in 1943, list all compounds, headfirst or not, under the citation character—a good reason to make occasional use of these dictionaries still.

Only the *ABC Chinese-English Dictionary* offers alphabetical sorting by pinyin irrespective of head character. In the *ABC*'s strict alphabetical sorting, *qìchē* (汽车) and *qìchuán* (汽船) would be separated by *qǐchéng* (启程) and *qǐchū* (起初), despite the fact that the latter two begin with different characters. The *ABC* is the only dictionary that allows words that are overheard, but for which the initial character is unknown, to be looked up—provided they can be transcribed in pinyin.

For characters whose pronunciation is not already known, dictionaries with entries ordered by pronunciation still provide the means to look up words by identifying the radical, then searching ordered lists. Of course, the need for dictionaries has been reduced for all but specialized work by computer lookup functions that give pronunciation, meaning, sample sentences, and much more, on demand.

16. Number of Characters

Chinese characters number in the thousands. The *Kangxi Dictionary*, mentioned in Section 15, is said to contain more than 47,000 characters, although that enormous number includes archaic characters found in classical works dating back thousands of years, as well as variant forms in use before standardization of the written language. Modern dictionaries often have entries for 7,000 to 8,000 individual characters—and thousands more compounds. The works of Mao Zedong, intended for the masses rather than the intelligentsia, are said to make use of only 2,900 characters. The number needed for extensive reading in different genres of contemporary literature, however, is much higher, with 5,000 to 6,000 often cited as "educated." Even 3,000, a level to which the foreign student can aim, is a staggeringly large number for rote learning, which is why learners need to focus on using phonetic hints and context.

Forming New Characters

Characters are, in principle, an open set. New characters can be created, and phonosemantic principles are almost always involved in their creation. Here is an example from the periodic table of chemical elements.

Element	Full Character	Radical	Phonetic
Helium	氦 *hài*	气 *qì* 'gas'	亥 *hài*
Neon	氖 *nǎi*	气 *qì* 'gas'	乃 *nǎi*
Argon	氩 *yà*	气 *qì* 'gas'	亚 *yà*

Characters for the three gases, *hài* 'helium,' *nǎi* 'neon,' and *yà* 'argon' (for which characters have been formed in relatively recent times) are composed of the radical 气 'gas' plus phonetic elements homophonous with the composite characters: 亥 *hài*, 乃 *nǎi*, and 亚 *yà*. In the spoken language, these characters would form compounds with 气 *qì* 'gas': 氦气 'helium gas,' and so on—providing context for the 'gas' readings. For technical terms, readers can be more confident that the phonetic elements are reliable guides to pronunciation.

A less regulated form of character creation can be found in some of the onomatopoeic words found in Chinese comics (漫画 *mànhuà*). Examples are 咔哒 *kādā* 'clip-clop,' with phonetic elements 卡 *kǎ* and 达 *dá*, and 叮当 *dīngdāng* 'jingle-jangle' (noise of keys, coins, etc.), with 丁 *dīng* and 当 *dāng*.

17. The Reading Process

The Chinese writing system is often characterized as logographic, from the Greek roots meaning "word writing": characters generally represent word-like units, or, more precisely, morphemes. People do not read in morphemes, however, but in words or phrasal units. It is more accurate, therefore, to say that characters function syllabographically, representing syllables that form words. 东西, with individual characters that mean 'east' and 'west,' would have to be read as syllables (*dōng-xī*) before the context assigned the meaning 'thing' and the pronunciation *dōngxi* to the compound, with only a dubious relationship to the root meanings of 'east' and 'west.'

Reliance on Sound

For learners, who are likely to be less familiar with the range of meanings associated with individual characters in compounds, the reading process is even more likely to depend on the assignment of sound before the recognition of meaning. This is a good argument for letting written-language learning lag behind spoken-language learning, so that character learning can focus on recognition and parsing, without introducing the added complications of learning new vocabulary, grammar, and usage. After all, Chinese, when they begin to study characters, already speak and are experts on the top-down process of using context when they read.

Are Chinese Characters Ideographic?

One also hears the term "ideographic" applied to Chinese characters, with the implication that reading involves the direct perception of character meaning without reference to sound. (This is a claim that characters are like the Arabic numerals—1, 2, 3, and so on—that can be understood when they appear in foreign languages even when their pronunciation is unknown.) Proponents of this view often point to the fact that Classical Chinese—particularly classical poems—can be understood (more or less) by Japanese (whose written language makes use of graphs originally developed for Chinese) or Koreans (who continue to make use of characters in places where succinctness is valuable—in newspaper headlines, on signs, and in advertisements). However, Classical Chinese poetry is a special genre, employing concrete images and pared-down syntax. The fact that Japanese and Korean natives can make out the meaning of Classical Chinese is, in fact, no stranger than English speakers' being able to figure out the meaning of a phrase such as "horreur, labeur dur et forcé" ('horror, hard and forced labor,' from Baudelaire's poem "Chant d'automne") without knowing how to pronounce French.

Reading as Chunking

The main argument against the notion that Chinese characters are ideographs is that reading does not take place at the level of morphemes (except perhaps very occasionally when there is ambiguity to resolve). Reading requires chunking of speech into words and larger units before meaning can be inferred. Because sound is much more concrete than character meaning—sound conjures up a word, while meaning is dependent on situation (remember the *dōngxi* example above)—it is much more efficient to chunk by sound than by character meaning.

18. Traditional and Simplified Characters

In current use, many characters, but far from all, have two forms, traditional and simplified; an example is the traditional form 中國 and the simplified form 中国 for *Zhōngguó* 'China.' The traditional (or complex) set makes use of the clerical script that has been the primary medium of printed and other formal written communication for almost 2,000 years. The set is written top to bottom and right to left. Nowadays, the traditional set has official status in Taiwan, Hong Kong, and many overseas communities. Its long history, as well as its association with classical writing, gives the traditional set a prestige that accounts for its occasional use on the mainland in formal correspondence, for example, in wedding invitations, ceremonial engravings, and business cards. Long before Chinese characters were standardized, however, they were subject to simplification and change.

The Simplified Set

The simplified set of characters is official on the mainland and in Singapore. The simplified set are written left to right (like English). The reason it was so easily accepted on the mainland after official promulgation in the mid-1950s, is that, to a large degree, it made use of what had been informal simplified forms long used in calligraphic practice and other forms of handwriting. While the two scripts continue to symbolize political positions—right versus left, traditional versus modern—literate Chinese, even if they have trouble remembering how to write both precisely, can read both without much difficulty. Many students of Chinese also learn to read both, though most now probably write the simplified set, since it is standard on the mainland and is supposedly simpler.

The Costs of Simplification

It is worth noting that what makes the simplified set easier to write—fewer strokes—can make it harder to read, by making otherwise distinct characters look very similar. As an example, traditional 東 (*dōng* 'east') and 樂 (*lè* 'happiness' / *yuè* 'music') are quite distinct, but their simplified versions, 东 and 乐, are easy to confuse. On the other hand, a few characters are better differentiated in the simplified set; for example, the nearly identical 書 *shū* and 晝 *zhòu* are 书 and 昼 in the simplified set.

The simplification of characters in modern times, as well as throughout history, has also exacted a cost in ordered phonetic sets. Thus, meteorological characters that contain 雨 *yǔ* 'rain' as the radical in the traditional set show variation in the simplified set, some retaining 雨, some not: 雪 *xuě* 'snow' remains 雪 in the simplified set; 霧 *wù* 'fog' becomes 雾 (still with the 雨 radical), but 雲 *yún* 'cloud' is reduced to 云 (thereby merging with the original 云 *yún*, a formal word for 'say, speak').

Principles and Limits of Simplification

As the example of 雪 *xuě* 'snow' shows, not all characters have two forms. In fact, not only are there quite common complicated characters with only one form (for example, 籍 *jí* 'nationality'), but there are characters that retain a large number of strokes even after simplification (for example, 踴 · 踊 *yǒng*). In general, the more common the character, the larger the distinction between traditional and simplified versions tends to be; compare 個 and 个 for the common classifier *gè* and 頭 and 头 for *tóu* 'head' (which is also a suffix in common location words). Often, the simplification process involved omitting parts: 電 · 电 and 從 · 从. Sometimes, only the radicals are simplified: 話 · 话 and 錯 · 错. Chinese readers can usually switch between simplified and traditional sets with little effort. One could argue that the linguistic differences in reading the two scripts (not writing them) are more on the scale of uppercase versus lowercase letters in English (for example, A · a and G · g), or handwriting versus print.

4
Sentences and Sentence Processes

19. Topic-Comment

In English, sentences typically have a bipartite structure, with a subject, corresponding notionally to what is being discussed, and a predicate, corresponding to what is said about the subject. The subject has a high profile in English: it determines the form of the verb ("I agree" versus "She agrees"), it shifts position in questions ("He does" versus "Does he?"), and it leaves a token of its presence even when it has no reference—in words such as "it" ("It's raining") and "there" ("There's still time").

Chinese sentences also have a bipartite structure, but in the case of Chinese, the subject has a smaller grammatical profile. There is no agreement with the verb; the subject does not shift position in questions; it can be omitted altogether; and, significantly, it can be offset from the rest of the sentence with pause particles, such as 啊 *a* and 呢 *ne*.

> 叔叔呢，是牙医。
> *Shūshu ne, ‖ shì yáyī.*
> My uncle, he's a dentist.

In this respect, subjects in Chinese are a kind of disjunct, like initial time, location, and "as for" phrases in English, which are typically offset from the rest of the sentence and require reiteration with a pronoun: "Today, it's raining heavily" and "As for China, it's changing rapidly." The looser linkage in Chinese is reflected in the preference for the more discourse-oriented terms "topic" and "comment" over the grammatical terms "subject" and "predicate." (As long as one agrees on the properties, either pair of terms can be used.) Comparing the following Chinese sentences with their English counterparts illustrates the broad latitude that is acceptable between subject and predicate—or topic and comment—in Chinese.

外国烟，劲儿比较大。
Wàiguó yān || jìnr [tɕjər] bǐjiào dà.
Foreign cigarettes, strength relatively big.
'Foreign cigarettes are stronger.'

哎，中国变化真大呀。
Āi, Zhōngguó || biànhuà zhēn dà ya.
Wow, China changes really big SFP.
'Wow, China's really undergoing big changes!'

好嘞，这个保准您满意。
Hǎo lei, zhèi ge || bǎozhǔnr nín mǎnyì.
Good SFP, this M assure you be-satisfied.
'Okay, [I] guarantee you'll be happy with this.'

今天下大雨。
Jīntiān || xià dà yǔ.
Today falls big rain.
'It's raining heavily today.'

鱼已经买回来了。
Yú || yǐjing mǎi huílai le.
Fish already buy return-come LE.
'[We] already bought the fish [and brought it back].'

Another reflection of looser linkage between Chinese subject and predicate is that verbs in Chinese often allow active or passive readings. *Chēnghu* 'address,' for example, can correspond to English "to address" or "to be addressed."

请问，您怎么称呼？
Qǐngwèn, nín || zěnme chēnghu?
Please-ask, you how address.
'How are you to be addressed, please?'

大家都称呼我魏老师。
Dàjiā || dōu chēnghu wǒ Wèi lǎoshī.
People all address me Wei teacher.
'People call me "Wei laoshi."'

Here is an ambiguous example from Yuen Ren Chao's 1968 *A Grammar of Spoken Chinese.*

这鱼不能吃了。
Zhè yú || bù néng chī le.
This fish not able eat LE.
'This fish can't be eaten.' OR 'This fish can't eat.'

Test Yourself

Provide the Chinese versions of the following sentences. Hint: Where English uses "has/have," Chinese often starts with a topic phrase set off intonationally.

1. Shanghai has a lot of tall buildings. (*dàlóu* 'buildings')
2. China's population is very large. (*rénkǒu* 'population')
3. This dish has a strange flavor. (*wèidao* 'flavor,' *qíguài* 'strange')
4. One of our classmates went to elementary school in Shanghai.

Possible Answers
1. *Shànghǎi, dàlóu hěn duō.*
2. *Zhōngguó, rénkǒu hěn duō.*
3. *Zhè cài, wèidao hěn qíguài.*
4. *Wǒmen de tóngxué, yí ge zài Shànghǎi shàng de xiǎoxué.*

20. Other Aspects of Word Order

Location and Destination Phrases

Location—the locus of the action—precedes the verb (see Section 35), while destination or goal follows the verb (see Section 65). Compare the following pairs of sentences.

她在邮局工作。
Tā zài yóujú gōngzuò. (location)
She at post-office works.
'She works at the post office.'

都得带到邮局。
Dōu děi dài dào yóujú. (destination)
All must take to post-office.
'[They] all need to be taken to the post office.'

铁锅在炉子上烧热。
Tiěguō zài lúzi shang shāorè. (location)
Iron-pan at stove on heat-hot.
'The wok's heating on the stove.'

把锅放在炉子上烧热。
Bǎ guō fàng zài lúzi shang shāorè. (destination)
Take pan put at stove on heat-hot.
'Put the pan on the stove and heat it up.'

One exception involves going and coming, in which the destination can be expressed directly after the verb or indirectly with a preposition before the verb.

他去麦加朝圣。   他到麦加去朝圣。
Tā qù Màijiā cháoshèng.   *Tā dào Màijiā qù cháoshèng.*
He go Mecca face-sacred.   He to Mecca go face-sacred.
'He went on a pilgrimage to Mecca.'

Time-When, Duration, Extent, and Measure Phrases

Time-when phrases precede the verb (in sentence-initial position or after the subject) (see Section 36); duration, extent, and measure phrases follow the verb as part of the predicate, usually preceding object[1] noun phrases, if present (see Section 70 for duration phrases and Section 71 for extent and measure complements).

我们七点吃早点。
Wǒmen qī diǎn chī zǎodiǎn. (time of event)
We seven o'clock eat breakfast.
'We eat breakfast at seven o'clock.'

以后我们多多来往，加强联系。
Yǐhòu wǒmen duōduō láiwǎng, jiāqiáng liánxì. (time of event)
Later we more-more come-and-go, increase contact.
'In the future, let us have more contact and strengthen our ties.'

你们学了几年了？   只学了一年。
Nǐmen xuéle jǐ nián le?   *Zhǐ xuéle yì nián.* (duration)
You-all study-LE how-many years LE?   Only study-LE one year.
'How many years have you been   'Only one year.'
  studying [Chinese]?'

我们也学了一年（的）日语。
Wǒmen yě xuéle yì nián (de) Rìyǔ. (duration)
We also study-LE one year (DE) Japanese.
'We've also studied a year's Japanese.'

我们打了三场球，输了两场。
Wǒmen dǎle sān chǎng qiú, shūle liǎng chǎng. (measure complement)
We played-LE three fields ball, lose-LE two fields.
'We played three games and lost two.'

Adverbial Clauses Before Main Clauses

Conditional ("if"), causal ("because"), adversative ("although"), and other types of subordinate clauses generally precede main clauses in Chinese.

---

[1]In a language without case ("he" versus "him"), without a clear active-passive distinction, and with the flexible word order of topic-comment organization, the term "object" is best left loosely defined as a noun phrase that appears after the verb as the goal of verbal action.

你要是没电脑，可以去网吧发电子邮件。
Nǐ yàoshi méi diànnǎo, kěyǐ qù wǎngbā fā diànzǐ yóujiàn.
   (conditional clause)
You if not-have computer, can go Internet-café send electronic mail.
'If you don't have a computer, you can e-mail from an Internet café.'

虽然父母是中国人，但是他没去过中国。
Suīrán fùmǔ shì Zhōngguórén, dànshì tā méi qùguo Zhōngguó.
   (adversative clause)
Although parents be Chinese, but he not-have gone-ever to China.
'Although his parents are Chinese, he's never been to China.'

English, by manipulating intonation—particularly high and low pitch—allows adverbial clauses to precede or follow main clauses, so that "You can e-mail from an Internet café if you don't have a computer" is also possible. Chinese requires the use of specially marked constructions to do the same. By and large, the subordinate clause precedes the main clause.

21. Questions

Chinese has several ways to ask questions.

Yes-No Questions

Questions seeking a "yes" or "no" response are signaled by toneless sentence-final particles (SFPs), the most common of which is *ma*.

好吃吗？	很好吃。
Hǎochī ma?	*Hěn hǎochī.*
'It's tasty, huh?'	'Very.'
你去吗？	我不去。
Nǐ qù ma?	*Wǒ bú qù.*
'Are you going?'	'No, I'm not.'
一个人吗？	是的。
Yí ge rén ma?	*Shì de.*
'One person?'	'Yes.'

Verb-Not-Verb Questions

Ma-questions anticipate a confirmatory response. Entirely neutral yes-no questions are cast as alternative questions, in the verb-not-verb pattern.

你去不去？	我不去。
Nǐ qù bu qù?	*Wǒ bú qù.*
'Are you going (or not)?'	'No, I'm not.'

学中文难不难?	很难，我觉得。
Xué Zhōngwén nán bu nán?	*Hěn nán, wǒ juéde.*
'Is learning Chinese difficult (or not)?'	'Quite difficult, I feel.'

Follow-Up Questions

Follow-up questions can be asked with the SFP *ne*.

日文呢? 学日文难不难?	也很难。
Rìwén ne? Xué Rìwén nán bu nán?	*Yě hěn nán.*
'And Japanese? Is Japanese difficult to learn?'	'Yes, it's difficult, too.'

Content Questions

Content questions are formed with question words, illustrated in the following short examples.

是什么意思?
Shì shénme yìsi?
'What does that mean?'

你为什么不去?
Nǐ wèishénme bú qù?
'Why aren't you going?'

什么时候走?
Shénme shíhou zǒu?
'When are you leaving?'

是多少钱?
Shì duōshao qián?
'How much is it?'

有几本?
Yǒu jǐ běn?
'How many [books] do you have?'

谁是下一个?
Shéi shì xià yí ge?
'Who's next?'

是谁的?
Shì shéi ~ shuí de?
'Whose is it?'

<table>
<tr><td>

哪个?

Něi ge?

'Which one?'

</td><td>

那个。

Nèi ge.

'That one.'

</td></tr>
</table>

去哪儿啊? ~ 去哪里?

Qù nǎr a? ~ Qù nǎli?

'Where are you going?'

你怎么去?

Nǐ zěnme qù?

'How are you getting there?'

Note that *wèishénme* has a more formal alternative, *hébì* (何必) 'why must' ('how-necessary'); *shénme* has a colloquial alternative, *shá* (啥); and *shéi* is pronounced *shuí* by some speakers—possibly more in the north and northeast.

Question words in Chinese are not placed at the beginning of a sentence, as they generally are in English. In English, a question and its response tend not to have the same order of elements: "Where to? / To Oz!" In Chinese, a question and its response have the same basic word order: *Qù nǎr a? / Qù Běijīng.* and *Zhǎo shéi a? / Zhǎo Wèi lǎoshī.*

Alternative Questions

"Or" questions involve options. In Chinese, these are formed with *háishi* 还是, which means 'still' in other contexts. The first option may be followed by a pause: <,>.

<table>
<tr><td>

你想吃西餐<,>还是中餐?

Nǐ xiǎng chī xīcān<,> háishi zhōngcān?

'Do you want to eat Western food or Chinese food?'

</td><td>

我们在中国，还是吃中餐好。

Wǒmen zài Zhōngguó, háishi chī zhōngcān hǎo.

'We're in China; we should eat Chinese food.'

</td></tr>
</table>

If "or" does not indicate a choice (that is, if no pause is possible between the options), the conjunction *huòzhě* (或者) or *huòshi* (或是) is used, whether in a statement or in a question (see Section 72).

酒或者果汁都行。

Jiǔ huòzhě guǒzhī dōu xíng.

'Wine or juice, either one.'

<table>
<tr><td>

你想喝酒或果汁吗?

Nǐ xiǎng hē jiǔ huò guǒzhī ma?

'You want wine or juice (as opposed to nothing)?'

</td><td>

来一杯白开水，好吗?

Lái yì bēi báikāishuǐ, hǎo ma?

'Bring a glass of boiled water, okay?'

</td></tr>
</table>

22. Question Words as Indefinites

In Chinese (and in many other languages in East and Southeast Asia, as well), words like *shénme* have two aspects: (1) in the context of questions, they serve as question words, and (2) in the context of statements, they serve as indefinites.

Shénme?　　　　　　　　　　*Méi shénme.*
'What is it?'　　　　　　　　　'It's nothing.'

Qù nǎr?　　　　　　　　　　*Bú qù nǎr.*
'Where are you going?'　　　　'Nowhere.'

It is also possible to emphasize complete exclusion or inclusion by placing the indefinite phrase before the verb and adding a supporting adverb such as *dōu* or *yě*. The difference between the plain form and the exclusive/inclusive form can be confirmed by the addition of "in particular" in the English translation of the former and "at all" in the translation of the latter. The following examples illustrate this.

Nǐmen xiǎng mǎi shénme?
'What do you want to buy?'

Wǒmen bù xiǎng mǎi shénme.　　*Wǒmen shénme dōu bù xiǎng mǎi.*
'We don't want to buy anything　　'We don't want to buy anything
　[in particular].'　　　　　　　　　[at all].'

Nǐmen dào nǎr qù?
'Where are you going?'

Wǒmen bú dào nǎr qù.　　　　　*Wǒmen nǎr yě bú qù.*
'We're not going anywhere　　　　'We're not going anywhere
　[in particular].'　　　　　　　　　[at all].'

Tāmen rènshi shéi?
'Whom do they know?'

Tāmen bú rènshi shéi.　　　　　*Tāmen shéi dōu bú rènshi.*
'They don't know anyone　　　　　'They don't know anyone
　[in particular].'　　　　　　　　　[at all].'

Other correlations between the question and the indefinites are illustrated in the following examples.

Zhōngwén shū, nǐ yǒu jǐ běn?　　*Zhōngwén shū, wǒ méi jǐ běn.*
'How many Chinese books　　　　'I don't have many Chinese
　do you have?'　　　　　　　　　　books.'

Tāmen yǒu duōshao qián?　　　*Tāmen méiyou duōshao qián.*
'How much money do they have?'　'They don't have much money.'

Tā duō gāo?
'How tall is she?'

Tā bù zěnme gāo.
'She's not that tall.'

23. Yes and No

As the examples at the beginning of Section 21 show, where an English response is "yes" or "no," Chinese often has a simple reiteration of the verb, with nothing corresponding directly to "yes" or "no."

Nǐ qù bu qù?
'Are you going?'

Wǒ bú qù.
'No, I'm not.'

This is typical. Chinese repeats the verb or verb phrase, with or without a negative, to confirm or deny. There are, however, cases where Chinese appears to have a counterpart to "yes" or "no."

那是虚拟的姓名吗?
Nà shì xūnǐ de xìngmíng ma?
'Is that a made-up name?'

是的，是虚拟的。
Shì de, shì xūnǐ de.
'Yes, it's made up.'

不是，是真实的。
Bú shì, shì zhēnshí de.
'No, it's her real one.'

Shì de and *bú shì* (or simply *bù*) appear in responses where strong confirmation or denial is appropriate. However, the correspondence with English "yes" and "no" is deceptive. In the following example, the correspondences are reversed, with Chinese *shì* corresponding to English "no" and *bú shì* to English "yes."

你从没登过长城吧!
Nǐ cóng méi dēngguo Chángchéng ba!
'So you've never climbed the Great Wall, right?'

是。从没登过。
Shì, cóng méi dēngguo.
'No, I haven't.'

不是，我登过好几次了!
Bú shì, wǒ dēngguo hǎo jǐ cì le!
'Yes, I have; I've climbed it numerous times.'

Why is this? The answer is that English "yes" and "no" have different functions than Chinese *shì* and *bú shì*. "Yes" and "no" generally substitute for the answer, which is often then reiterated: "Yes, I have" / "No, I haven't." ("No, I have" can occur, but only with strong overriding intonation.) *Shì* and *bú shì* indicate the truth of the presupposition ("is the case" / "is not the case"), so it is quite possible to follow *bú shì* with a positive statement: "It is not the case that I haven't—I have."

Other options, such as *duì* (对) 'be correct' and *bú duì* (不对) 'not be correct' or *xíng* (行) 'be possible' or *bù xíng* (不行) 'not be possible' work the same way. They confirm or deny the questioner's assumptions. Thus, "yes, it's true" that Chinese does not have words for "yes" and "no," but now you know that there's a lot more to the story!

24. Negation

Negation is consistently expressed by means of a word placed in the adverbial position, directly before the verb.

The Negative *bù* (不)

In the spoken language, *bù* (or *bú*) is used.

不忙	*bù máng*	'not busy'
不抽<烟>	*bù chōu<yān>*	'doesn't smoke'
不会	*bú huì*	'not able to; not understand'

In "noun sentences" such as *Tā guànjūn* (她冠军) 'She's a champ' ('She champion'), the addition of any kind of adverbial element, including a negative, requires the presence of the verb *shì*: *Tā bú shì guànjūn*.

The Negative *méi* (没)

The common verb *yǒu* (有) 'have, exist,' which also functions as a helping verb, is exceptional in being negated with *méi*: *méiyǒu* (没有) 'not have,' often reduced to just *méi* (没).

他们还没洗澡呢。
Tāmen hái méi xǐzǎo ne.
They still not-have bathe NE.
'They haven't bathed yet.'

Formal Negatives

A number of other words serve as formal negatives, for example, *fēi* (非) 'un-,' *wú* (无) 'not have,' and *wèi* (未) 'not yet.' These are often encountered on signs and in formal writing, as well as in compounds, such as *fēicháng* (非常) 'very, extremely' (literally, 'not-usual').

25. Commands and Requests

Explicit positive commands are directed toward a second-person audience and therefore generally omit the subject. Negative commands make use of forms such as *bié* (别) 'don't' (whose verbal meaning is 'separate') and *bú yòng* (不用) 'don't, no need' ('no use'). Colloquial northern speech often

uses *béng* for the negative, a blend of the sounds *bú* and *yòng*; it is written
甭, itself a blend of the characters 不 and 用. The following examples illustrate commands.

往前走!	滚开!	快点儿! 快藏在床底下!
Wǎng qián zǒu!	*Gǔnkāi!*	*Kuài diǎnr! Kuài cáng zài chuáng dǐxià!*
Toward front walk!	Roll-open!	Fast a-bit! Fast hide at bed under!
'Walk forward!'	'Scram!'	'Quick! Hide under the bed as fast as you can!'

甭～不用客气!	你俩别吵了!	别走了，多坐一会儿呗。
Béng ～ Bú yòng kèqi!	*Nǐ liǎ bié chǎo le!*	*Bié zǒu le, duō zuò yìhuǐr bei.*
Don't be-polite!	You two don't fight LE!	Don't leave LE, more sit awhile BEI.[2]
'Feel free!'	'Don't fight, you two!'	'Don't leave; why not stay awhile?'

A command can be softened by the addition of the SFP *ba*, which conveys
a suggestive tone.

问吧!	明天再说吧!	喝一杯吧!
Wèn ba!	*Míngtiān zài shuō ba!*	*Hē yì bēi ba!*
'Go ahead and ask!'	'Let's talk tomorrow!'	'Have a cup!'

算了吧!	我帮你拿吧!	尽管抽吧!
Suàn le ba!	*Wǒ bāng nǐ ná ba!*	*Jǐnguǎn chōu ba!*
'Forget about it!'	'Let me help you!'	'Feel free to smoke!'

Paradoxically, Chinese sometimes retains a subject where English has a
subjectless imperative form. This is the case for the common phrases *nǐ kàn*
(你看) 'look' or *nǐ shuō* (你说) 'say it.'

你看，烟火[3]!
Nǐ kàn, yānhuo!
'Look, fireworks!'

In the language of signs and other formal settings, more literary words,
such as *jìnzhǐ* 'prohibit' and *wù* 'do not,' are often used. *Wù* is common in
Classical Chinese.

---

[2] 呗 *bei* is an SFP (see Section 26) that indicates that the suggestion makes perfect sense.
[3] Also, regionally, *yànhuo* (with falling-toned *yàn*), written 焰火.

禁止吸烟。	请勿吸烟。	请勿随地吐痰。
Jìnzhǐ xīyān.	*Qǐng wù xīyān.*	*Qǐng wù suídì tǔtán.*
Forbid smoke.	Request don't smoke.	Request don't casually expectorate.
'Smoking prohibited.'	'No smoking.'	'No spitting.'

The last two examples have the form of requests, initiated by the verb *qǐng* 'invite,' which occurs in conventional expressions such as *qǐngwèn* (请问) 'excuse me' ('may I ask'); *qǐng yuánliàng* (请原谅) 'please forgive me'; and the polite request to supply information, *qǐngjiào* (请教) 'can you help me' ('invite-instruction').

5
Words

26. Parts of Speech (Word Classes)

Until very recently, Chinese-to-Chinese dictionaries did not indicate parts of speech—classes of words like noun, verb, adjective, and so on. Traditionally, the only distinction was between "full words" (*shící*) and "empty words" (*xūcí*), the latter being words like *le* or *ma* that have only grammatical functions. In modern dictionaries, the label *zhùcí*, translatable as 'particle' ('help-word'), is often used in place of *xūcí*, but otherwise, designations like noun and verb tend to be found mainly in Chinese-to-foreign dictionaries—and not in all of them.

There are two reasons for this lack of attention to parts of speech. One is that there are hardly any formal criteria to apply: no singular versus plural to define nouns, for example, or present versus past to define verbs. The other reason is characters: the character, not the word, tends to be viewed as the basic unit of speech. Characters are morphemes (*císù* 词素), the building blocks of words, and as such, they cannot be given a part-of-speech label. For example, the bound morpheme *lǚ*, represented by the character 旅, appears in both nouns such as 旅馆 *lǚguǎn* 'hotel' and verbs such as 旅行 *lǚxíng* 'travel.' Since it does not function as an independent word, its part of speech cannot be determined.

For learners, classifying words into word classes (parts of speech) provides useful information about how they function. Knowing *lǚxíng* can be a verb allows the prediction that *xiàng dōng lǚxíng* (向东旅行) 'journey east,' *qù lǚxíng* (去旅行) 'go on a journey,' and *zài lǚxíng zhōng* (在旅行中) 'during the journey' are possible utterances. (In fact, *lǚxíng* can also be a noun, 'journey,' which triggers another set of predictions.) Some modern bilingual dictionaries intended for learners of Chinese do provide information about parts of speech, even if entries continue to be organized by head character. Many of the labels for these parts of speech are comparable with those used in English: nouns, verbs, adverbs, conjunctions, pronouns, and so on. To a large degree, word classes in the two languages overlap, and a learner will not be surprised to find out that *cuìniǎo* 'kingfisher' and *kuǎnshì* 'design' are nouns, *nǐ* 'you' and *zhè* 'this' are pronouns, *rúguǒ* 'if' and *nàme* 'in that case' are conjunctions, and *huānyíng* 'welcome' and *àihù* 'cherish' are verbs. However, there are also significant differences.

Adjectives

Words corresponding to adjectives in English behave like verbs in Chinese (see Section 52). As in English, they can modify nouns: *shǎ niàntou* (傻念头) 'crazy ideas.' Unlike English, they can serve, without the support of helping verbs, as predicates: *rén shǎ, qián duō* (人傻，钱多) 'people silly, money excessive' (in answer to a question about why people spend so much money on brand names). In English, adjectives cannot be used as predicates without a form of the verb "to be": 'people <u>are</u> silly, money <u>is</u> excessive,' or more naturally, 'People are silly, and they've got too much money.' In such contexts, Chinese adjectives have a built-in "be": *huáng* (黄) 'be yellow,' *qíguài* (奇怪) 'be strange,' *lèi* (累) 'be tired,' *pàng* (胖) 'be chubby.' To underscore the congruency between adjectives and verbs in Chinese, the term "stative verb" is sometimes used instead of "adjective."

Attributives

Some words in Chinese are like adjectives in modifying nouns, but unlike adjectives in that they usually do not occur as predicates. Examples include *guójì* (国际) 'international, world' (*guójì shuǐyù* 'international waters,' *Guójì Yīnbiāo* 'International Phonetic Alphabet,' *guójì gōngzhì* 'metric system') and *diànzǐ* (电子) 'electronic' (*diànzǐ shāngmào* 'e-commerce,' *diànzǐ yóujiàn* 'e-mail,' *diànzǐ yóuxì* 'electronic games').

Classifiers and Measures

In Chinese, nouns that are counted or otherwise specified require an intermediary word—a classifier. For countable nouns, the choice of classifier is limited to only a few options. Thus, the classifier for books is *běn* (本) 'a binding': *sān běn shū* (三本书) 'three books.' For knives, the classifier is *bǎ* (把) 'a handle': *zhèi bǎ dāo* (这把刀) 'this knife.' The particular classifier associated with a noun has to be learned.

For noncount nouns ("tea," "beer," "rice"), the intermediary word can be any container or quantity: *yì bēi chá* (一杯茶) 'a cup of tea,' *liǎng píng píjiǔ* (两瓶啤酒) 'two bottles of beer,' *sān jīn mǐ* (三斤米) 'three catties of raw rice.' Noncount nouns may also occur without such "measures," but in that case, they are interpreted as varieties: *Zhè chá hěn hǎo.* (这茶很好。) 'This is great tea.' For convenience, both classifiers and measures are often referred to by a single label: "measures," or "measure words."

Prepositions

Prepositions in Chinese often derive from verbs and retain some of the properties of verbs, such as being negatable. Here are several examples.

Verb	Prepositional Phrase	Verb-Preposition Correspondence
给 *gěi* 'give'	*gěi nǐ zuò* 'do it for you'	'give' ~ 'for'
用 *yòng* 'use'	*yòng kuàizi chīfàn* 'eat with chopsticks'	'use' ~ 'with'
在 *zài* 'be at'	*bú zài jiālǐ shuìjiào* 'not sleep at home'	'be at' ~ 'at'

Prepositions are sometimes labeled co-verbs to underscore their connection to verbs.

Particles and Suffixes

Chinese makes frequent use of forms with neutral tone: *de, le, guo, ne, ba, ma* (the "empty words" of traditional Chinese grammar). These are usually called particles. They appear only after toned words or other particles. Those that modify words (and, consequently, are attached without space in pinyin), such as *le, zhe,* and *guo,* are also referred to as suffixes: *zuòzhe, chīle, kànguo.* The others modify phrases or whole sentences (and in pinyin are generally separated from previous words by a space). Those that appear at the foot of the sentence are sentence-final particles (SFPs). Under favorable conditions, strings of SFPs may fuse together into single syllables (a process that has occurred throughout the history of Chinese); thus, *le + a → la* and *le + ou → lou.*

Interjections

Interjections, or exclamations, are conventionalized carriers of emotion that can stand alone, but often provide context for a following sentence. *Wèi* (喂), for example, is used to call someone (like English "hey") or when answering the telephone: *Wèi, nín něi wèi?* 'Hello, who is it?' *Pēi* (呸) conveys disapproval: *Pēi, xiūxiu liǎn!* 'Fie, for shame!' *Āiyā* (哎呀) conveys surprise or shock: *Āiyā, wǒmen wùle huǒchē le!* 'Oh no, we've missed the train!'

Interjections can also be whole phrases or even sentences, for example, *Hǎojiāhuo!* (好家伙!) 'Goodness me!' ('Good-fellow!') and *Wǒ de tiān a!* (我的天啊!) 'Good heavens!' ('My DE heaven A!')

27. Monosyllabic and Polysyllabic Words

Words of high frequency in Chinese are often monosyllabic: *yǒu* (有) 'have,' *hěn* (很) 'quite,' *rè* (热) 'be hot,' *wǒ* (我) 'I, me,' *dǎ* (打) 'hit; do.' Disyllabic words in which individual syllables cannot be assigned a meaning do exist, but are relatively rare: *húdié* (蝴蝶) 'butterfly,' *méigui* (玫瑰) 'rose,' *hǔpò* (琥珀) 'amber,' *gāngà* (尴尬) 'be awkward, affected,' *gūlu<r>* (轱辘)

'wheel,' *húlún* (囫囵) 'whole, entire.' Otherwise, most polysyllabic words in Chinese are compounds: *yóutiáo* (油条) 'dough sticks; glib person' ('oil-lengths'), *shǒujī* (手机) 'cell or mobile phone' ('hand-machine'), *wēijī* (危机) 'crisis' ('danger-crucial point'), *chàngsuǒyùyán* (畅所欲言) 'speak out freely' ('without-restraint that-which want to-say'). The last example may look like a phrase rather than a compound word (comparable to English "don't beat around the bush"), but none of the components can stand as independent words, so there is reason to regard it as a compound. (It is more like English "forthrightness," which consists of three morphemes, two of which only occur bound to others.)

Elaborate Expressions

Chàngsuǒyùyán is, in fact, an example of an "elaborate expression," a preferred type of compound that consists of four syllables (characters) and provides rich nuances of meaning for the Chinese lexicon. Other examples are *mòmíngqímiào* (莫名其妙) 'without rhyme or reason, baffling' ('not-name-its-strangeness'), *wēirúlěiluǎn* (危如累卵) 'precarious' ('danger-like-piled-eggs'), *yíjiànrúgù* (一见如故) 'hit it off right away, take to each other at once' ('once-see-like-old'), and *chúnchǐxiāngyī* (唇齿相依) 'mutually dependent' ('lips-teeth-mutual-dependent'). The pattern extends into the commercial world, with advertising copy often being cast in the four-syllable pattern typical of elaborate written style. The description of the fine fare available at a well-known fast food chain illustrates this: *měiwèi-ānquán* 'tasty and safe,' *gāozhì-kuàijié* 'top quality and speedy,' *yíngyǎng-jūnhéng* 'balanced nutrition,' *jiànkāng-shēnghuó* 'healthy living.'

The preponderance of words that are either monosyllabic or clearly compound sets the expectation that all syllables are morphemes, and in that sense Chinese is a relatively monosyllabic language. As noted in Section 13, however, assigning meanings to the components of compounds is often quite problematical. For those who do not read, who have low literacy, or who are not familiar with Classical Chinese, words like *rúguǒ* (如果) 'if' and *máfan* (麻烦) 'troublesome; to trouble; nuisance' are likely to be unanalyzable, and in that sense, are single two-syllable morphemes. (English "cupboard" is comparable; the modern pronunciation reflects the loss of morpheme status of the original constituents, "cup" and "board.")

6
Nouns

28. Compound Nouns

Compound nouns in Chinese are often formed on a single root. *Xié* (鞋) 'shoe,' for example, is at the base of dozens of compounds formed with a preceding attributive, whose meaning is given in parentheses after each example: *bīngxié* 'skates' ('ice'), *bùxié* 'cloth shoes' ('cloth'), *gāogēnxié* 'high heels' ('high-heel'), *liángxié* 'sandals' ('cool'), *píxié* 'leather shoes' ('leather'), *tuōxié* 'slippers' ('pull; drag'), *yǔxié* 'galoshes' ('rain'). A reverse Chinese-English dictionary, organized by last character rather than first, is a useful tool for browsing the range of such compounds.

Technical Terms

The predilection for compounding in Chinese makes technical terms relatively transparent. English, too, makes extensive use of compounding ("lighthouse," "pickpocket," "cheesecake"). But in English, a lot of well-established technical terms are formed from Greek and Latin roots ("telephone," "hepatitis," "carnivore"). Chinese generally uses Chinese roots for compounds, as the following examples show.

Chinese	Pinyin	English	Word-for-Word Gloss
化学	*huàxué*	"chemistry"	'change-study'
物理<学>	*wùlǐ<xué>*	"physics"	'objects-principles <-study>'
人类学	*rénlèixué*	"anthropology"	'man-kind-study'
激光	*jīguāng*	"laser"	'excited-light'
电话	*diànhuà*	"telephone"	'electric-words'
飞机	*fēijī*	"airplane"	'flying-machine'
火车	*huǒchē*	"train"	'fire-vehicle'
象牙	*xiàngyá*	"ivory"	'elephant-tusk'
行星	*xíngxīng*	"planet"	'moving-star'

Chinese	Pinyin	English	Word-for-Word Gloss
水龙头	*shuǐlóngtóu*	"faucet" ~ "tap"	'water-dragon-head' (from the shape)
吸尘机~器	*xīchénjī ~ qì*	"vacuum cleaner"	'suck-dust-machine ~ instrument'
望远镜	*wàngyuǎnjìng*	"telescope"	'view-far-mirror'
火箭	*huǒjiàn*	"rocket"	'fire-arrow'
恐龙	*kǒnglóng*	"dinosaur"	'terrible-dragon'
丑闻	*chǒuwén*	"scandal"	'shameful-news'

Loanwords

Unlike Japanese, with its propensity for adopting even nontechnical foreign words in toto, Chinese uses compounding as a far more productive way of forming new lexical material than borrowing. Loanwords of any kind are relatively rare in nonspecialized vocabulary. Here are a few loanwords from English.

沙拉	*shālā*	'salad'
卡通	*kǎtōng*	'cartoon'
拷贝	*kǎobèi*	'copy'
博客	*bókè*	'blog'
沙丁鱼	*shādīngyú*	'sardine' (combined with native *yú* 'fish')
卡其	*kǎqí*	'khaki' (from Persian through Urdu to English)
吉他	*jítā*	'guitar'
的	*dī*	'taxi' (by way of Cantonese *dik-si* (的士))
T恤衫	*T-xùshān*	'T-shirt' (by way of Cantonese *T-xut* (T-恤))

Particularly in the commercial world, even when the sound of the brand is transcribed rather than translated, the meaning of the characters is more important than the mimicry of the sound. For example, in the world of beverages, *Kěkǒu Kělè* (可口可乐) 'Coca-Cola' is a close match to the English with characters that mean 'fit-taste fit-pleasure.' The name for Sprite, *Xuěbì*, however, strays some distance from the English name to represent it with the characters for 'snow' and 'emerald green' (雪碧). Chevrolet, on the other hand, derived from a surname, uses sound and ignores meaning in its transliteration, *Xuěfúlán*, written 雪佛兰 (composed of characters for 'snow,' 'not,' and 'orchid').

29. Noun Suffixes

While the vast majority of nouns have no formal markers, a small subset of relatively common nouns appears with untoned suffixes, mainly -*r* (儿), -*zi* (子), and -*tou* (头).

The -*r* Suffix

The -*r* suffix has several sources, but in its most common manifestation, it derives from an elided form of *ér* (儿), now a bound form but originally meaning 'child' (compare *érzi* 'son'). The original diminutive meaning of the suffix evolved into the more general functions that it has today. Excluding some cases involving tonal shifts, it is the only nonsyllabic morpheme in standard Chinese. Although called a suffix, it is actually a process of *r*-coloring that affects the whole syllable: *píngr* 'bottle' is pronounced [pʰjᵊⁿr], with the subscript "n" representing nasalization; *húzuǐr* 'spout of a kettle' ('pot-mouth') is pronounced [hútswₔr]; and *dànhuángr* 'egg yolk' ('egg-yellow') is pronounced [tànhwáⁿr]. In order to avoid a complete respelling of *r*-suffixed morphemes (and consequent loss of identity), the pinyin convention is to simply add -*r* to the root spelling and let speakers apply the pronunciation rules: *jìnr* (劲儿) 'strength; enthusiasm' is pronounced [tɕejₔr]. *R*-less speakers can drop the suffix and still recover the original *jìn*.

In a very few cases, the -*r* suffix is found in verbs and adverbs, for example, *wánr* 'play, have fun' and *yíkuàir* 'together' ('one-lump'), the latter clearly derived from a noun. Otherwise, it is found only with nouns (including noun objects of verb-object compounds, and nouns already suffixed with -*zi* or -*tou*). It is a feature of northern, mostly colloquial speech.

Because most modern textbooks aim for a speech that is neither formal nor colloquial, and emphasize language that is general rather than local, the appearance of words with the -*r* suffix tends to be limited to some common forms, such as *nǎr* 'where,' *nàr* 'there,' *zhèr* 'this,' *yìdiǎnr* 'a little,' *shìr* 'business; things to do,' *wèir* 'taste,' and the occasional expression that is clearly regional (for example, *xiànrbǐng*, a pastry snack popular in Tianjin) or colloquial (*chī lǎoběnr* 'get by on one's reputation, rest on one's laurels'). However, recorded conversation of northern (especially male) speakers—by its very nature, colloquial—reveals a far greater incidence of words with the -*r* suffix.

Types of *r*-Suffixed Nouns

R-suffixed words can be divided into three main types: (1) those that occur with or without the suffix (according to how formal the situation is); (2) those that occur only with the suffix; and (3) those in which the suffixed form has a different, though relatable, meaning from the nonsuffixed.

The -*r* suffix is optional in the following words.

尖< 儿 >	*jiān<r>*	'tip, point'
撇< 儿 >	*piě<r>*	'left downward stroke' (calligraphy)
出门< 儿 >	*chūmén<r>*	'go out, be away from home'
跷脚< 儿 >	*qiāojiǎo<r>*	'sit with legs crossed'
罐< 儿 >	*guàn<r>*	'jug, container'
面包片< 儿 >	*miànbāopiàn<r>*	'slice of bread'

栅栏<儿>	*zhàlán<r>*	'railings'
馅<儿>饼	*xiàn<r>bǐng*	'pastry with meat filling'
老本<儿>	*lǎoběn<r>*	'past reputation'
虾仁<儿>	*xiārén<r>*	'shrimp meat'
胡同<儿>	*hútòng<r>*	'lane' (in Beijing and nearby regions)

The *-r* suffix is obligatory in the following words, for which the *r*-less option is a compound or is suffixed with *-zi* or *-tou*.

wèir/wèidao	味/味道	'taste'
bànr/bànlǚ	伴/伴侣	'companion'
běnr/běnzi	本/本子	'exercise book'
píngr/píngzi	瓶/瓶子	'bottle'
qiāngzǐr/zǐdàn	枪/子弹	'bullet'

In the following pairs, *r*-suffixed and *r*-less forms have distinct, but relatable, meanings:

空	*kōng*	'empty'	BUT	空儿	*kòngr*	'spare time'
肠	*cháng*	'intestine'	BUT	肠儿	*chángr*	'sausage; intestine'
活	*huó*	'live'	BUT	活儿	*huór*	'job, work'

R-less dialects may simply produce *r*-less versions (*kōng* versus *kòng*), or they may preserve the distinction with compounding (*cháng* 'intestine' versus *xiāngcháng* 'sausage').

The -*zi* Suffix

The fully toned version of the *-zi* suffix, *zǐ* (子), also means 'child.' As such, it can occur as a second element in compounds: *wángzǐ* (王子) 'prince,' *yúzǐ* (鱼子) 'fish roe,' *zhìzǐ* (质子) 'proton' ('substance-child'). As a suffix with neutral tone, it occurs with words that are encountered in everyday life around the house or in the local environment. Here are several examples, by category.

Household Items

zhuōzi 'table'	*yǐzi* 'chair'	*zhuīzi* 'awl'
chēzi 'small vehicle'	*gōuzi* 'hook'	*dànzi* 'carrying pole'
diézi 'plate, dish'	*kuàizi* 'chopsticks'	*bēizi* 'cup'
qǐzi 'bottle opener'		

Food

| *dǔzi* 'tripe' | *bāozi* 'steamed bun' | *jiǎozi* 'dumplings' |
| *júzi* 'tangerine' | *dàozi* 'rice (plant)' | |

Parts of the Body

bízi 'nose'
jiǎowànzi 'ankle'

dùzi 'stomach'
nǎozi 'brain'

liúzi 'tumor'

Relatives

sǎozi 'sister-in-law'
lǎotóuzi '(my) old man'

qīzi 'wife'
sūnzi 'grandson'

Other People

tǔbāozi 'country bumpkin'
yángguǐzi 'foreign devil'
fēngzi 'crazy person, nut case'

Clothing

màozi 'hat'
zhānzi 'felt blanket'

kùzi 'trousers'
xiézi 'shoes'

wàzi 'socks'

Animals

chóngzi 'insect'
wénzi 'mosquito'

hàozi 'mouse, rat'
tùzi 'rabbit'

hóuzi 'monkey'

Miscellaneous

lòuzi 'loophole; flaw'
gèzi 'height; build'

dǐzi 'rough draft, copy'
jùzi 'sentence'

The -*tou* Suffix

The -*tou* suffix is a noun suffix, but it is much less productive than -*r* and -*zi*. The noun version, *tóu*, means 'head.' Here are examples of words that use the suffix.

mùtou 'wood, log'
shítou 'stone'
mǎtou 'wharf'

shétou 'tongue'
mántou 'steamed bun'
niàntou<r> 'idea'

gǔtou 'bone'
zhěntou 'pillow'
língtour 'change' (money)

Many position words (see Section 35) have forms with -*tou*, for example, *qiántou* 'in front,' *hòutou* 'behind,' *shàngtou* 'on,' and *lǐtou* 'inside.' The -*tou* suffix also combines with action verbs in a construction with *yǒu* 'have' to form nouns that imply worthiness; here are some examples.

Action Verb	Example Sentence	English Translation
盼 *pàn* 'hope, long for'	*Yǒu pàntou.*	'There's hope.'
看 *kàn* 'read'	*Yǒu kàntou.*	'It's worth reading.'
奔 *bèn* 'head for'	*Méi shénme bèntour.*	'There's nothing to strive for.'

30. Pronouns and Demonstratives

Personal and demonstrative pronouns in Chinese are described in this section.

Personal Pronouns

Personal pronouns in Chinese are relatively simple and regular. They are presented in the following chart.

Singular			Plural		
我 *wǒ*		I/me	我们 *wǒmen*		we/us
			咱们 *zánmen*		we (you and I)
你 *nǐ*, 您 *nín*		you, you (polite)	你们 *nǐmen*		you (all)
他, 她, 它 *tā*		he/him, she/her, it	他们, 她们 *tāmen*		they/them

In colloquial speech, *tā* tends to refer to people. When it refers to things, however, it is more common in object position; in other words, it is more likely to occur in the Chinese equivalent of a sentence meaning "put it away" than in "it's in the drawer."

Spoken *tā* makes no distinction between male and female or between person and nonperson. In the twentieth century, the practice of using special characters, 她 and 它 (both *tā*), for female and nonpersonal referents became customary in writing but had no effect on the spoken language.

The suffix *-men*, usually without tone, is most often found in pronouns. However, it can also combine with nouns that designate people, where it functions as a collective: *lǎoshī* 'teacher,' *lǎoshīmen* 'teachers.' It does not co-occur with numbered expressions, so it cannot be regarded as a plural marker: *sān ge lǎoshī(*men)* 'three teachers.'

Mandarin speakers from Beijing and from northern regions in general, make the distinction between *wǒmen* 'we/us' that includes the addressee(s) ('all of us'), and *zán* or *zánmen* (pronounced *zámen*, as if without the first *n*) 'we/us,' but excluding the addressee(s) ('just us'). The following example is typical:

Zánmen zǒu ba!
'We're off.' (the two of us, but not you)

Demonstrative Pronouns

Demonstrative pronouns, or simply demonstratives, are words that indicate relative proximity. The citation forms are *zhè* (这) 'this' and *nà* (那) 'that.' Usage varies, but before measure words, they may also be pronounced *zhèi* and *nèi*: *zhège* ~ *zhèige* (这个), *nàge* ~ *nèige* (那个). The location pronouns ('here' and 'there') are *zhèr/nàr* (这儿/那儿) and *zhèli/nàli* (这里/那里), with the suffixes *-r* and *-li*. The first of the alternative forms is colloquial in northern Mandarin, the second, disyllabic forms are more formal or written. The disyllabic forms are also used in southern Mandarin, where the *-r* suffix is not an option. Corresponding question words are *nǎ ~ něi* 'which' and *nǎ ~ nǎli* 'where.'

	Near	**Far**	**Question**
CITATION	*zhè* 'this'	*nà* 'that'	*nǎ* 'which'
+ M	*zhè ~ zhèige* 'this one'	*nà ~ nèige* 'that one'	*nǎ ~ něi ge* 'which one'
LOCATION	*zhèr ~ zhèli* 'here'	*nàr ~ nàli* 'there'	*nǎr ~ nǎli* 'where'
MANNER	*zhème* 'this way'	*nàme* 'that way'	*zěnme* 'which way'

Chinese and English may differ in the interpretation of proximity. *Zhè*, for example, may correspond to 'that' in English, and *nà* frequently corresponds to 'the.'

你这一点儿都不知道吗?
Nǐ zhè yìdiǎnr dōu bù zhīdào ma?
You this little all not know Q?
'You didn't even know that?'

世界上最疼我的那个人去了。
Shìjiè shang zuì téng wǒ de nà ge rén qù le.
World on most care-for me DE that M person go LE.
'The person who cared for me most in all the world has departed.'

31. Zero-Pronominalization

Not only are verbs obligatory in most types of Chinese sentences, but they tend to persist as predicatives where English would use "do" or some other verb substitute. Subjects and objects, on the other hand, can be omitted rather than be simply referenced by pronouns, as they would be in English. Compare the English response with the Chinese in the following examples.

你抽不抽烟?　　　　　　抽。
Nǐ chōu bu chōuyān?　　*Chōu.*
You draw not draw-smoke?　Draw.
'Do you smoke?'　　　　　'Yes, I do.'

要看吗?　　　　　　　　要。
Yào kàn ma?　　　　　*Yào.*
Want look MA?　　　　　Want.
'Do you want to read it?'　'Yes, I do.'

你喝什么?　　　　　　　喝茶。
Nǐ hē shénme?　　　　*Hē chá.*
'What'll you have?'　　　'Tea.'

Where English substitutes "do" for the verb phrase (or, in the last case, omits the verb phrase altogether), Chinese retains the verb (*chōu, yào,* and so on) or, more generally, the verb phrase (*hē chá*). Conversely, where English uses pronouns to mark the participants in the response, Chinese often leaves them out, a feature that is sometimes called "zero-pronominalization." Thus, in Chinese, pronouns are often not expressed when the context makes the reference clear; verbs, on the other hand, tend to be reiterated.

32. Where Are the Articles ("a" and "the")?

You will have noticed that Chinese makes minimal use of words corresponding to English "a," "the," "some," and "any"—the articles. In some cases, Chinese uses a corresponding word, such as *yí ge* for 'a' or *nèi ge ~ nà ge* for 'the.' But in most cases, the function of the articles is assumed by word order. Definiteness ("the") is associated with the subject position before the verb; indefiniteness is associated with the position after the verb. Following is the classic example.

Láile yí ge kèrén.
'A guest's arrived.' ('You have a guest.')

Kèrén lái le.
'The guest's arrived.'

If the guest is unexpected ('a guest'), 'guest' follows the verb. If the guest is expected ('the guest'), 'guest' is at the head of the sentence—the topic.

Another typical case involves a question about an unknown place ('a') and a response with a known place ('the').

Zhèr yǒu méiyou cèsuǒ?	*Cèsuǒ zài lóu shàng.*
'Is there a toilet around here?'	'The toilet's upstairs.'

Here's one more example.

下雨了。
Xià yǔ le.
Falls rain LE.
'It's raining.'

雨下得很大。
Yǔ xià de hěn dà.
'The rain's really heavy.'

33. Modification and the Particle *de* (的)

Unlike English, where some modifiers precede the noun (for example, "Chinese-speaking people") and others follow the noun (for example, "people who speak Chinese"), in Chinese, a modifier consistently precedes the noun it modifies. In the following examples, the modifying phrase is enclosed in curly brackets.

{*wǒ*} *gēge*	'{my} older brother'
{*Zhōngguó*} *fēngsú-xíguàn*	'{Chinese} customs'
{*xiǎo*} *lǐwù*	'{small} gifts'
{*chuántǒng*} *sīxiǎng*	'{traditional} thinking'
{*hěn duō*} *qián*	'{a lot of} money'

{*fēicháng dà de*} *biànhuà*
'{really big} changes'
{*tāmen shuō de*} *huà*
'the things {that they said}'
{*Zhōngguó chuántǒng sīxiǎng de*} *yǐngxiǎng*
{Chinese traditional thinking DE} influence
'the influence {of traditional Chinese thinking}'

{*jǐ bèi rén zhù zai yìqǐ de*} *dàjiātíng*
{several generations people live at together DE} big-family
'a large family {in which several generations of people live together}'

中国政府在七十年代实行的计划生育政策...
{*Zhōngguó zhèngfǔ zài qīshí niándài shíxíng de*} *jìhuà-shēngyù zhèngcè*
{China government at '70s era promote DE} family-planning policy
'family planning policies {put into practice by the Chinese government in the '70s}'

These examples are divided into two sets. Only the second set requires that the function of the modifying phrase be made explicit with the particle *de* (的). For the first set, *de* is not usually present. The general rule is that the explicit particle of modification is not required with the following.

- Pronouns before kinship terms (for example, *wǒ gēge*) or other close relationships
- Country, place, or language names (for example, *Zhōngguó fēngsú-xíguàn*)
- Unmodified adjectives (for example, *xiǎo lǐwù* and *chuántǒng sīxiǎng*)

By contrast, an adjective further modified by an adverb (for example, *fēicháng dà de biànhuà*) requires *de*, with the exception of *duō* 'be many/much' and *shǎo* 'be few,' which do not require *de* despite the fact that they are always modified (for example, *hěn duō qián*).

De for All Seasons

Word-frequency dictionaries show *de* (的) to be the most frequent of all Chinese words, even more frequent than *le* (了) and *shì* (是), which follow at some distance in second and third places, respectively. Without reference to the written language, *de* would be even more ubiquitous, since particles that are pronounced differently in some central and southern regional languages are all pronounced *de* in Mandarin. Until the middle of the twentieth century, these functions were all written with the single character 的, just as verb-*le* and sentence-*le* (pronounced differently in Cantonese and other regional languages) are written 了 in Mandarin. Nowadays, however, three *de*s are distinguished in the writing system: 的, 得, and 地. The first represents the particle discussed in this section. The other two are discussed in Sections 56, 57, and 63, and all three are summarized in Section 60.

Modifying *de* (的) serves as a marker of possession (*tāde* 'his/hers') and of modification (*yìliú de cānguǎnr* (一流的餐馆儿) 'top-notch restaurant'). When the following noun or noun phrase is omitted, *de* also serves as a nominalizer (*shì hē de* 'it's for drinking'—literally, 'is drinking one'). Here are a number of typical examples.

Něi ge shì tāde?
'Which one's hers?'

Hēi de shì tāde.
'The black one's hers.'

Tā shì cóng Rìběn lái de.
She is from Japan come DE.
'She's from Japan.' ('She's one who comes from Japan.')

哪些是水洗的，哪些是干洗的？
Něi xiē shi shuǐxǐ de, něi xiē shi gānxǐ de?
Which ones be water-wash ones, which ones be dry-clean ones?
'Which ones need washing, and which ones need dry cleaning?'

他旁边儿的那个人是谁？
Tā pángbiānr de nà ge rén shi shéi?
His side DE that M person be who?
'Who's that next to him?'

戴太阳镜的那位是奥巴马吗？
Dài tàiyángjìng de nèi wèi shì Àobāmǎ ma?
Wear sun-glasses DE that M be Obama MA?
'Is the person wearing sunglasses Obama?'

Note that where context permits, nouns may be omitted after measure words and after *de*. Both cases may elicit a translation with the English pronoun "one": *něi ge* 'which one' ... *hēi de* 'the black one.' It is important to bear in mind, therefore, that measure words appear only after numbers and demonstratives, while *de* (的) as a signal of modification appears only after adjectives, verbs, and nouns.

Test Yourself

Provide the Chinese versions of the following phrases and sentences.

1. the large one
2. that one
3. this small one
4. I only have two.
5. She didn't like those two red ones.

Possible Answers

1. *dà de*
2. *nèi ge*
3. *zhèi ge xiǎo de*
4. *Wǒ zhǐ yǒu liǎng ge.*
5. *Tā bù xǐhuan nèi liǎng ge hóng de.*

34. The *shì-de* (是-的) Construction and Situational *de* (的)

The nominalizing function is at the root of the so-called *shì-de* construction, which draws attention away from the verb and to the adverbial—when, where, how—much like the English pseudocleft construction: "It was several years ago that we met" (with intonational prominence on "several years ago"). The *de* component of the construction is obligatory, but the initial *shì*, usually with neutral tone, is optional. When present, it introduces the circumstances: <*shì*> *zuótiān mǎi de* 'bought yesterday,' <*shì*> *gēn tāmen yìqǐ qù de* 'went with them.' The event in question is usually a past event. The *shì-de* construction is one of several cases in which no head noun can be placed after *de* (的). Here are some prototypical examples.

我们是几年前认识的。
Wǒmen shì jǐ nián qián rènshi de.
We are several years before meet DE.
'We met several years ago.'

他是一个人去的 。
Tā shì yí ge rén qù de.
'He went on his own.'

他是得癌症死的。
Tā shì dé áizhèng sǐ de.
He be get cancer die DE.
'He died of cancer.'

The *shì-de* construction typically underscores particular circumstances of an event that has been established earlier in the discourse or that can be taken for granted.

Nǐ shì zài nǎr shēng de, zài nǎr zhǎngdà de?
Where were you born, and where did you grow up?

In this example, being born or growing up somewhere are not in question. Rather, it is the places that are in question.

Northern Mandarin speakers can, with no change in meaning, slip the otherwise final *de* inside the object.

他们是昨天买票的 = 买的票。
Tāmen shì zuótian mǎi piào de ~ mǎi de piào.
'They bought the tickets yesterday.' ('It was yesterday that they bought the tickets.')

At one time—at least for some speakers—*de* could only intrude before nouns, not pronouns, but nowadays, that restriction no longer seems to hold. In the following example, both options are possible even with a pronominal object, as shown.

我是在香港认识她的。
Wǒ shì zài Xiāng Gǎng rènshi tā de ~ rènshi de tā.
'I met her in Hong Kong.'

Situational *de*

De (的) also appears in certain emphatic constructions, notably in the common confirmation *shì de* (是的) 'that's right' and in insistent statements. As with the *shì-de* construction, no noun can be provided to follow *de* in this context. Examples follow.

挺好的!
Tǐng hǎo de!
'That's great!'

明天会很热的。
Míngtiān huì hěn rè de.
'Tomorrow will be hot.'

Test Yourself

Provide the Chinese versions of the following sentences.

1. I graduated in 1992. (*bìyè* (vo.) 'graduate')
2. It's going to rain on Wednesday. (*xià yǔ* 'rain')
3. You walked here?—Yes, I did. (*zǒulù* (vo.) 'walk')

4. I went to university in Sydney. (*Xīní*)
5. They are coming to see me on Sunday. (*lái kàn wǒ*)

Possible Answers

1. *Wǒ shì 1992 nián bìyè de.*
2. *Xīngqīsān huì xià yǔ de.*
3. *Nǐ shì zǒulù lái de ma? Shì de.*
4. *Wǒ shì zài Xīní shàng de dàxué ~ shàng dàxué de.*
5. *Tāmen xīngqīrì lái kàn wǒ.* (not past)

35. Place Words

A number of constructions make reference to location or destination.

Zhèr fùjìn yǒu méiyou chāoshì?
'Is there a supermarket around here?'

Jīngkèlóng zài Wénxuéguǎn Lù.
'Jinkelong [Supermarket] is on Wenxueguan Road.'

Zǒu dào nàr yào jǐ fēn zhōng?
'How many minutes will it take to walk there?'

Zhèr fùjìn, *Wénxuéguǎn Lù*, and *nàr* are all places. The first is the subject of an existential sentence (with *yǒu*), the second is an object of *zài*, and the third is an object of *dào*. Other constructions requiring place words could be cited, as well. Place words are not just nouns that make reference to places. *Chéng* 'city' is a place, but *zhèr fùjìn* could not be replaced by *chéng* 'city' in the first example, nor could *nàr* be replaced by *fángzi* 'house' in the last.

The following types of nouns can constitute place words and serve as locations and destinations.

Geographic Names

Geographic names of all types can serve as locations and destinations.

Guǎngzhōu	'Canton'
Xīnjiāpō	'Singapore'
Jiànqiáo	'Cambridge'
chìdào	'equator'

Position Words

Position words are independent words that indicate position relative to some other entity. They may be pronouns: *zhèr ~ zhèli*, *nàr ~ nàli*, and *nǎr ~ nǎli*. They may be nouns that express relative position: *wàitou* 'outside,' *qiántou* 'in front,' *xiàtou* 'below.' Most of these have alternatives with *biān<r>* 'side' and *miàn<r>* 'side, face,' for example, *wàibian<r>* and *wàimian<r>*. They include words for 'left' and 'right': *zuǒbian<r>* 'left,' *yòubian<r>* 'right.' They also include compass directions: *dōngbian<r>* 'east,' *nánbian<r>* 'south,' *dōngběi<bianr>* 'northeast.'

Institutionalized Places

Certain common nouns, such as those denoting rooms within a house and places where people congregate, can act as place words without further modification: *zài chúfáng* 'in the kitchen,' *zài chēzhàn* 'at the station,' *zài yóujú* 'at the post office,' *zài jīchǎng* 'at the airport,' *zài jiā* 'at home.' These places are uniquely identifiable and therefore tend to be referred to with "the" in English: "the kitchen," "the airport."

In contrast to institutionalized places, nouns such as *fángzi* 'house,' *shān* 'mountain,' *chéng* 'city,' and *jiē* 'street' do not count as place words and need to be supported by a position word to constitute a proper location. At the very least, the position word may be a demonstrative pronoun (*nàr* in the following example).

> *Jīntiān de bào zài tā nàr.*
> Today DE newspaper at her there.
> 'Today's paper's with her.' ('She has today's paper.')

Often, however, one of the more specific words of relative location is called for. Most of these come in two forms: (1) an independent form with a suffix (for example, *qiántou* and *xiàtou*, cited previously) and (2) a dependent form without a suffix (for example, *qián* and *xià*) that can only be used in conjunction with a preceding noun. The choice of one over the other may be influenced by rhythmic considerations, with suffixed forms tending to follow disyllabic nouns: *zài fángzi hòutou* ~ *zài fáng hòu* 'behind the house,' *zài chéngshì lǐtou* ~ *zài chéng li* 'in town.'

In the full form, it is possible to insert the *de* of modification between the noun and the relative location word, *zài fángzi de hòutou*, which reveals *hòutou* as the head noun and *fángzi* as the modifier, literally, "at the house's back." In fact, the Chinese phrase may mean both "behind the house" and "the back of the house." In any case, the order of elements is the reverse of English: *zài shān shang* 'on the mountain,' *zài chuáng dǐxia* 'underneath the bed.'

Test Yourself

Provide the Chinese versions of the following phrases and sentences.

1. on the table
2. next to the supermarket (*pángbiānr* 'next to,' *chāoshì* 'supermarket')

3. behind the television (*diànshì*)
4. Take it to her. (*ná dào* 'take to')
5. She works in town.
6. She works at the post office. (*gōngzuò* 'work,' *yóujú* 'post office')
7. What's under the bed? (*dǐxia* 'underneath')

Possible Answers

1. *zhuōzi shàng(tou)*
2. *chāoshì pángbiānr*
3. *diànshì hòutou*
4. *Ná dào tā nàr.*
5. *Tā zài chéng li gōngzuò.*
6. *Tā zài yóujú gōngzuò.*
7. *Chuáng dǐxia yǒu shénme?*

Position Words

Bound Forms		**Meaning**	**+ tou**	**+ bian\<r\>**	**+ mian\<r\>**	**Other**
上	*shàng*	'on, above'	*shàngtou*	*shàngbian\<r\>*	*shàngmian\<r\>*	
下	*xià*	'under, below'	*xiàtou*	*xiàbian\<r\>*	*xiàmian\<r\>*	
前	*qián*	'in front of'	*qiántou*	*qiánbian\<r\>*	*qiánmian\<r\>*	
后	*hòu*	'behind'	*hòutou*	*hòubian\<r\>*	*hòumian\<r\>*	
里	*lǐ*	'in, inside'	*lǐtou*	*lǐbian\<r\>*	*lǐmian\<r\>*	
外	*wài*	'outside'	*wàitou*	*wàibian\<r\>*	*wàimian\<r\>*	
旁	*páng*	'next to'		*pángbiān\<r\>*		
		'underneath'				底下 *dǐxia*
		'between, among'				中间\<儿\> *zhōngjiān\<r\>*[1]
内	*nèi*	'within, in'				
		'in the vicinity'				附近 *fùjìn*
左	*zuǒ*	'left'		*zuǒbian\<r\>*	*zuǒmian\<r\>*	
右	*yòu*	'right'		*yòubian\<r\>*	*yòumian\<r\>*	
东	*dōng*	'east'		*dōngbian\<r\>*	*dōngmian\<r\>*	
南	*nán*	'south'		*nánbian\<r\>*	*nánmian\<r\>*	
西	*xī*	'west'		*xībian\<r\>*	*xīmian\<r\>*	
北	*běi*	'north'		*běibian\<r\>*	*běimian\<r\>*	

---

[1]This is pronounced *zhōngjiànr* (with falling tone on *jiànr*) by some speakers in colloquial speech.

For those words with three variants, the *miàn* option is the least common. The *biān* and *miàn* options are toned by nonnorthern speakers. The *tou* options, however, are never toned. *Biān<r>* is consistently toned in *pángbiān<r>*.

Both *lǐ* (里) and *nèi* (内) have *wài* as their opposite, but *lǐ* is more general and *nèi* more abstract: *guónèi* 'within the country, internal,' *shìnèi* 'in the city, local.' *Nèi* is also common in time expressions: *zài sān tiān nèi* 'within three days.' Unlike *lǐ,* which has *lǐtou* and variants, *nèi* comes only as a bound form.

The four quadrants are always listed from 'east': *dōng-xī-nán-běi* or *dōng-nán-xī-běi*. In the intermediate directions, the east-west axis is always primary, so that northeast is "east-north" in Chinese: *dōngběi* 'the northeast,' *xīnán* 'the southwest,' and so on.

36. Time When

Words and expressions that make reference to time when (rather than duration) can be subjects, objects, or attributives. The following example features *jīnnián* 'this year.'

今年被称为"史上最难毕业季"。
Jīnnián bèi chēng wéi "shǐ shàng zuì nán bìyè jì."
This year get called as "history in most difficult graduate season."
'This year has been called "the toughest year to graduate in history." '

More often, time expressions provide temporal context for a verbal event. In Chinese, these expressions often appear at the head of the sentence or, if a subject is present, before or directly after the subject. These positions are frequently different from that of their English counterparts, as shown in the following examples.

Wǒmen shíyuèfèn bānjiā.
We October move-house.
'We're moving (house) in October.'

Tāmen zǎoshang hē kāfēi, xiàwǔ hē chá.
'They drink coffee in the morning and tea in the afternoon.'

Shí diǎn, wǒ děi qù bàngōngshì kàn lǎoshī.
Ten o'clock I must go office see teacher.
'At ten o'clock, I have to go to the office to see my teacher.'

吃饭的时候，你平常用筷子还是用刀叉？
Chīfàn de shíhou, nǐ píngcháng yòng kuàizi háishi yòng dāochā?
Eat-food when, you usually use chopsticks or use knife-fork?
'Do you generally use chopsticks or a knife and fork when you eat?'

Multiple time expressions are ordered from largest to smallest (like dates and addresses): *jīntiān* > *xiàwǔ* > *5 diǎn zhōng*.

我已经约好今天下午五点钟去看牙医。
Wǒ yǐjing yuēhǎo jīntiān xiàwu wǔ diǎn zhōng qù kàn yáyī.
I already arrange-good today afternoon five points clock go see dentist.
'I've already made an appointment to see the dentist at five o'clock this afternoon.'

Time expressions include divisions of the day (for example, *zǎoshang* 'morning'), dates (for example, *shíyuèfènr* 'October'), clock time (for example, *shí diǎn* 'ten o'clock'), more general time expressions (*xiànzài* 'now'), and time clauses (*chīfàn de shíhou* 'when you eat').

Divisions of the Day

Morning	**Mid-Morning**	**Noon/Midday**	**Afternoon**
早上	上午	中午	下午
zǎoshang	*shàngwǔ*	*zhōngwǔ*	*xiàwǔ*

Evening	**At Night**	**Midnight, Late at Night**	**Wee Hours**
晚上	夜里	半夜	凌晨
wǎnshang	*yèli*	*bànyè*	*língchén*

There are also several expressions for early morning, including the colloquial *yìzǎo<r>* (一早<儿>) and *qīngzǎo<r>* (清早<儿>) 'early in the morning,' as well as *yídàzǎo<r>* (一大早<儿>) 'at dawn,' *dàqīngzǎo* (大清早) 'very early morning,' and *zǎochén* (早晨) 'daybreak.'

Words Based on Units of Time

	Before Last	**Last**	**This**	**Next**	**After Next**
Day	前天	昨天	今天	明天	后天
	qiántiān	*zuótiān*	*jīntiān*	*míngtiān*	*hòutiān*
Week		上<个>星期	这<个>星期	下<个>星期	
		shàng <ge> xīngqī	*zhèi <ge> xīngqī*	*xià <ge> xīngqī*	
		上<个>礼拜	这<个>礼拜	下<个>礼拜	
		shàng <ge> lǐbài	*zhèi <ge> lǐbài*	*xià <ge> lǐbài*	
Weekend		上<个>周末	这<个>周末	下<个>周末	
		shàng <ge> zhōumò	*zhèi <ge> zhōumò*	*xià <ge> zhōumò*	

		Before			**After**
		Last	**Last**	**This**	**Next**	**Next**
Month		上<个>月	这<个>月	下<个>月	
		shàng <ge>	*zhèi <ge>*	*xià <ge>*	
		yuè	*yuè*	*yuè*	
Year	前年	去年	今年	明年	后年
	qiánnián	*qùnián*	*jīnnián*	*míngnián*	*hòunián*

The week before last can be expressed as *shàng shàng <ge> xīngqī*, and the week after next as *xià xià <ge> xīngqī*. The same pattern is used for months: *shàng shàng <ge> yuè* 'the month before last.' Alternatively, time before or after can be indicated with *yǐqián* 'before' or *yǐhòu* 'afterward': *sān <ge> xīngqī yǐqián* 'three weeks before,' *sān <ge> yuè yǐhòu* 'three months later,' *sì tiān yǐqián* 'four days before.'

Independent Time Words

There are also relative time words independent of units of time. Although some of these words correspond to adverbs in English (for example, *jìnlái* 'recently'), in Chinese, they all function as a subclass of nouns.

Current

现在	*xiànzài*	'now, nowadays'
目前	*mùqián*	'at present' ('in front of the eyes')
近来	*jìnlái*	'recently, lately'
刚才	*gāngcái*	'just now'

Before

以前	*yǐqián*	'before'
从前	*cóngqián*	'formerly'
本来	*běnlái*	'originally'

Later

以后	*yǐhòu*	'after'
后来	*hòulái*	'afterward'
将来	*jiānglái*	'in the future'

刚才那个电话是谁打来的?
Gāngcái nèi ge diànhuà shì shéi dǎlái de?
Just-now that M phone-call be who make-come DE?
'Who was that who phoned just now?'

后来他们发现他是完全无辜的。
Hòulái tāmen fāxiàn tā shì wánquán wúgū de.
Afterwards they discover he be completely not-guilty DE.
'Afterwards, they discovered that he was completely innocent.'

Clock Time

Clock time is measured in *diǎn* (点) 'hours,' *fēn* (分) 'minutes,' and *miǎo* (秒) 'seconds,' optionally followed by *zhōng* (钟) 'clock,' as shown in the following chart.

Time	Chinese	Pinyin
1:00	一点<钟>	*yì diǎn <zhōng>*
1:05	一点过五分<钟>[2]	*yì diǎn guò wǔ fēn <zhōng>*
	一点零五	*yì diǎn líng wǔ*
1:15	一点十五分<钟>	*yì diǎn shíwǔ fēn <zhōng>*
	一点<过>一刻	*yì diǎn <guò> yí kè*
1:30	一点三十分<钟>	*yì diǎn sānshí fēn <zhōng>*
	一点半	*yì diǎn bàn*
1:45	一点四十五分<钟>	*yì diǎn sìshíwǔ fēn <zhōng>*
	差一刻两点<钟>	*chà yí kè liǎng diǎn <zhōng>*
1:50	差十分两点	*chà shí fēn liǎng diǎn*

The *guò* pattern, which corresponds to English "five minutes past," indicates minutes after the hour up to but not including half past the hour. The *líng* pattern, which corresponds to English "one oh five," indicates minutes after the hour up to "one oh nine" and is never followed by *zhōng*.

After half past the hour, minutes can be given after the hour or before the hour. The latter option uses *chà* 'lack, less,' with the minutes phrase usually placed before the hour: *chà wǔ fēn liǎng diǎn* 'five minutes to two.'

'Quarter past' and 'quarter to' are expressed with *kè* 'notch' (derived from the float stick of a water clock). *Sān kè* "three quarters past" is a rare alternative for *chà yí kè* 'quarter to.'

Calendar Units

Days of the week and months are labeled by number. The standard term for week is *xīngqī*. *Lǐbài*, originally 'worship week,' is also used informally. A formal (and nowadays, quite often spoken) alternative to *xīngqī* is *zhōu* 'a cycle.'

The week begins on Monday. Spoken on Sunday, *xià xīngqisì* (下星期四) is four days hence, that is, 'this Thursday.' The only unnumbered day is Sunday, which has two forms, one with *rì* 'sun' and one with *tiān* 'sky.'

Monday	Tuesday		Saturday	Sunday
xīngqīyī	*xīngqī'èr*	...	*xīngqīliù*	*xīngqīrì ~ xīngqītiān*
lǐbàiyī	*lǐbài'èr*	...	*lǐbàiliù*	*lǐbàirì ~ lǐbàitiān*
zhōuyī	*zhōu'èr*		*zhōuliù*	*zhōurì*

[2]Final *zhōng* is optional, but it is more likely on the hour (*sān diǎn zhōng*) than when minutes are expressed.

Months are also numbered: *yīyuè, èryuè, sānyuè … shí'èryuè.* (Note that measured months are durations: *yí ge yuè* 'one month,' *liǎng ge yuè* 'two months.')

Contemporary years are mostly designated by digit rather than whole number, followed by the measure *nián* 'year': *yī-jiǔ-yī-yī nián* 'the year 1911,' *èr-líng-yī-sì nián* 'the year 2014.' The year 2000 can be *èr-líng-líng-líng nián* or *liǎng qiān nián.* Years in the distant past are often read as numbers rather than digit by digit: *bābǎi sānshíyī nián* (not *bā-sān-yī*) 'the year 831.'

Republican Dates

For official or formal purposes (for example, on newspaper banners), Taiwan still makes use of an alternative dating system that began with the Republic. 1912 is year 1, 1913 is year 2, 2014 is year 103. The Chinese have also dated the calendar from the birth date of the Yellow Emperor (*Huángdì*), a date that has been fixed at 2698 BCE, so 2014 of the Gregorian calendar is—after the lunar new year—year 4712.

Seasons

Seasons (*sìjì* 'four seasons') are *chūntiān* (春天) 'spring,' *xiàtiān* (夏天) 'summer,' *qiūtiān* (秋天) 'autumn,' and *dōngtiān* (冬天) 'winter,' usually in that order. Dates, like addresses, are listed from the largest unit to the smallest: year, month, day: 1959, *bāyuè*, 23 *hào* (1959/8/23). (The day of the month is usually written as 23 日 = *rì*.)

Holidays

Holiday	Pinyin (Characters)	Date	Comment
New Year	*Yuándàn* (元旦)	January 1	Solar new year
Chinese New Year (Spring Festival)	*Chūnjié* (春节)	1st day of 1st lunar month (late January or in February)	Lunar new year
Tomb-Sweeping Day	*Qīngmíngjié* (清明节)	April 4 or 5	Near spring equinox
Labor Day	*Láodòngjié* (劳动节)	May 1	International labor day
Dragon Boat Festival	*Duānwǔjié* (端午节)	5th day of 5th lunar month (June)	Near summer solstice
Mid-Autumn Festival	*Zhōngqiūjié* (中秋节)	15th day of 8th lunar month (September or October)	Near autumnal equinox

Holiday	Pinyin (Characters)	Date	Comment
National Day	*Guóqìngjié* (国庆节)	October 1	Founding of the People's Republic of China

Lunar Months

The lunar year—actually a lunisolar year—has special terms for the first and last months and for the first ten days of each lunar month: *zhēngyuè* (正月) 'first lunar month,' *làyuè* (腊月) 'last lunar month,' *chūyī* (初一) 'beginning-one,' *chū'èr* ... *chūshí* 'second ... tenth days' (of a lunar month).

Historical Units of Time

Decades are named with *niándài* (年代) 'period, generation': *80 niándài* 'the '80s.' Centuries are *shìjì* (世纪): *shíbā shìjì* '18th century.' BC, or BCE, is *gōngyuánqián* (公元前): *gōngyuánqián wǔshíwǔ nián* '55 BCE.' AD, or CE, is *gōngyuán* (公元), literally 'official-beginning': *gōngyuán sìbǎi bāshíwǔ nián* '485 CE.'

'Dynasty' is *cháodài* (朝代), with particular dynasties based on just the first syllable: *Zhōucháo*, *Qīngcháo*. (The sequence of Chinese dynasties can be found as an index in most Chinese dictionaries, as well as online.)

Time Clauses

Time clauses are formed with conjunctions that appear at the foot of the clause: *de shíhou* (的时候) 'when, during,' *yǐqián* (以前) 'before,' *yǐhòu* (以后) 'afterwards.' The time clause itself appears before the main clause.

> *Shàngkè de shíhou bù yīnggāi shuō Yīngwén.*
> Attend-class DE time not ought speak English.
> 'You shouldn't speak English when you're in class.'

> *Shuìjiào yǐqián bù yīnggāi hē kāfēi.*
> 'You shouldn't drink coffee before bed.'

> *Chīfàn yǐhòu bù yīnggāi yóuyǒng.*
> 'You shouldn't swim after dinner.'

De shíhou (literally, 'time of') phrases have the form of a noun modified by a clause, for example, "at the time when (class is in session)." In more formal speech and in writing, *de shíhou* is often reduced to just *shí* (时). Long or complex when-clauses can also be headed by *dāng* (当) 'at a given time' or *zài* (在) 'at.'

> *<Dāng>tā huílai de shíhou wǒmen hái zài xǐzǎo.*
> 'When he got back, we were still bathing.'

Like the English expressions "before" and "after," which were originally spatial terms, *yǐqián* and *yǐhòu* are related to *qián* 'in front' and *hòu* 'behind.' (In earlier Chinese, *yǐ* (以) could be a verb meaning 'take.') *Zhīqián* (之前) and *zhīhòu* (之后) are more formal, or written, alternatives.

37. Measure Words

As noted in Section 26, nouns cannot be counted directly in Chinese. Those that are not measured out with containers, such as *bēi* (杯) 'cup of,' or units of measure, such as *shēng* (升) 'liter,' are counted with classifiers (a sub-group of measure words) that are selected, in part, by the semantic features of their noun referents. Thus vehicles are counted with *liàng* (辆): *yí liàng zìxíngchē* 'a bicycle.' Postal letters are counted with *fēng* (封), derived from the verb meaning 'seal': *yì fēng xìn* 'a letter.' The semantic principles of classifier selection are not consistent enough, however, to have predictive value, so ultimately, the classifier assigned to a particular noun has to be learned. Dictionaries should provide this information, but most do not.

The General Classifier

The classifier *gè* (个) serves as the classifier for a wide range of nouns, including people (for example, *sān ge xuésheng* 'three students') and abstract things (for example, *liǎng ge dōngxi* 'two things,' *yí ge wèntí* 'a problem,' and *sì ge xīngqī* 'four weeks'). It also serves as a default measure in those cases where the assigned measure is unknown or there are reasons that make it unnecessary, as when pointing.

"Type" or "Kind"

Zhǒng (种) and, less commonly, *yàng* (样) and *lèi* (类) function as group measures with the meaning of 'kind, type, class.'

> *Wǒmen yǒu liǎng zhǒng; nǐ yào něi zhǒng?*
> 'We have two kinds; which do you want?'

Group measures such as *yàng* (样) and *lèi* (类) permit—and are possibly more common with—a following *de*: *zhèi yàng de xīguā* 'this type of water-melon,' *zhèi lèi de dōngxi* 'things in this category.' Classifiers, illustrated earlier, do not permit *de* before the classified noun.

A selection of the more common classifiers is listed in the following chart. Some of the items, such as *bān* (班) and *chuàn* (串), fall outside the strict definition of classifiers and may be more properly considered other types of measures. For the learner, fine distinctions are less important, so the various subtypes are mixed together in the chart.

Classifier	Literal	Used with	Example(s)
把 *bǎ*	'handle'	item with a handle	*bá chū yì bǎ dāo lai* 'pull out a knife'
班 *bān*		regularly scheduled transport	*zuì hòu yì bān chē* 'the last bus'
本 *běn*	'volume'	bound item	*Zhōngwén shū nǐ yǒu jǐ běn?* 'How many Chinese books do you have?'
部 *bù*		work of art	*Nèi bù diànyǐng wǒ kànguo liǎng cì.* 'I've seen that film twice.'
场 *chǎng*	'site, clearing'	presentation of a film, play, or sports event	*Zuìhòu yì chǎng diànyǐng* 'The last picture show' (a film title)
串 *chuàn*	'string together'	keys, beads, and so on	*yí chuàn pútao* 'a bunch of grapes,' *yí chuàn yàoshi* 'a bunch of keys'
道 *dào*	'route'	item in a sequence (for example, a step or food course)	*shěngle yí dào shǒuxù* 'save a step in a process,' *yí dào cài* 'a course' (meal)
顶 *dǐng*	'top'	item with a point or top (for example, a hat)	*dàizhe yì dǐng qíguài de màozi* 'wearing a peculiar hat'
栋 *dòng*		building	*Tā zhù zai dì-èr dòng lóufáng.* 'She lives in building No. 2.'
对 *duì*		pair	*yí duì xīnhūn fūfù* 'newlywed couple'
顿 *dùn*	'session'	meal	*zhǐ chī liǎng dùn* 'only have two meals'
朵 *duǒ*		flower	*jǐ duǒ méigui* 'a few roses'

Classifier	Literal	Used with	Example(s)
份 *fèn*	'portion'	one of a set, pile	*sòng yí fèn lǐwù* 'give a present,' *yí fèn Niǔyuē Shíbào* 'a copy of the *New York Times*'
封 *fēng*	'seal'	letter	*liǎng fēng xìn* 'two letters'
幅 *fú*		picture, textile	*yì fú yóuhuà* 'an oil painting'
副 *fù*		item that comes in pairs; emotion	*yí fù yǎnjìng* 'a pair of glasses,' *yí fù xiàoliǎn* 'a smiling face'
个 *gè*		person, thing; the default measure	*Yí ge bú gòu, liǎng ge tài duō, zěnme bàn?* 'One is not enough; two is too much. What do [I] do?'
股 *gǔ*	'limb'	strandlike item (for example, a trail, smoke, or smell)	*yì gǔ yān* 'a whiff of smoke,' *yì gǔ méiqì* 'a musty smell'
家 *jiā*	'home'	company, business	*Nèi jiā fànguǎnr zěnmeyàng?* 'How about that restaurant?'
架 *jià*	'frame'	machine, airplane	*Nǐ kàn, nèi jià fēijī, nàme dī!* 'Look how low that airplane is!'
间 *jiān*	'space'	room	*liǎng jiān wòshì* 'two bedrooms'
件 *jiàn*		item of business, article of clothing, luggage	*yí jiàn xíngli* 'an item of luggage,' *bàn sān jiàn shì* 'deal with three things'
节 *jié*	'joint'	class period	*Yì jié kè yào wǔshí fēn zhōng.* 'Class lasts 50 minutes.'
句 *jù*		sentence, utterance	*shuō jǐ jù huà* 'say a few words'

Classifier	Literal	Used with	Example(s)
棵 *kē*		tree, plant	*liǎng kē shù zhījiān* 'between two trees'
颗 *kē*		small spherical object (for example, a pearl, tooth, or bean)	*yì kē liúxīng* 'a meteor,' *diàole yì kē yá* 'lose a tooth'
课 *kè*	'lesson'	lesson	*Dì-yī kè* 'Lesson 1'
口 *kǒu*	'mouth'	person in surveys, item with a mouth (for example, a bell or well)	*Jiā li yǒu jǐ kǒu rén?* 'How many in your family?'
块 *kuài*		piece, lump, dollar	*Bǎ dàngāo qiē chéng liù kuài.* 'Cut the cake into six pieces.'
辆 *liàng*		vehicle	*bǎoyǎng liǎng liàng qìchē* 'maintain two cars'
门 *mén*	'door'	course (of study)	*xiū jǐ mén kè?* 'take how many courses?'
篇 *piān*		article, essay	*yì piān wénzhāng* 'an article'
片 *piàn*		slice, expanse	*yí piàn miànbāo* 'a slice of bread'
首 *shǒu*	'head'	poem, song	*bèisòng yì shǒu shī* 'recite a poem'
双 *shuāng*		pair	*yì shuāng kuàizi* 'a pair of chopsticks'
台 *tái*	'platform'	appliance, machine (for example, a television)	*Zhè tái zìdòng-shōuhuòjī yòu huài le.* 'This vending machine's broken again.'
堂 *táng*	'hall'	school period, class	*Xiàwǔ hái yǒu yì táng kè.* 'I have another class in the afternoon.'

Classifier	Literal	Used with	Example(s)
套 *tào*		items that come in a set	*yí tào cānjù* 'a set of tableware'
条 *tiáo*	'strip'	long, sinuous item (for example, a road, river, or fish)	*yì tiáo hé* 'a river,' *yì tiáo kùzi* 'a pair of trousers'
位 *wèi*		person (polite)	*Nín něi wèi?* 'Who is it, please?'
张 *zhāng*		flat item (for example, a table, paper)	*sān zhāng zhǐ* 'three sheets of paper,' *liǎng zhāng zhuōzi* 'two tables'
阵 *zhèn*		bout, burst (for example, of wind or rain)	*yí zhèn yǔ* 'a rain shower,' *yí zhèn fēng* 'a gust of wind'
支 *zhī*		sticklike item (for example, a pen, gun, or cigarette)	*yì zhī qiāng* 'a rifle'
只 *zhī*		item of a pair (for example, certain animals or boats)	*yì zhī shǒutào* 'one glove,' *nà zhī gǒu* 'that dog'
座 *zuò*	'seat'	large structure (for example, a bridge or mountain)	*jiàn liǎng zuò qiáo* 'construct two bridges'

There may be variation in the selection of classifiers. *Gǒu* 'dogs' can be counted with *zhī* (只) or *tiáo* (条), for example. In some cases, the choice of classifier is based on meaning: *kànle yì chǎng diànyǐng* 'saw a film' (a showing) versus *jīnnián zuì hǎo de yí bù diànyǐng* 'the best film of the year' (a product).

7
Verbs in General

Introduction

Like other words in Chinese, the verb is invariable in form and is listed that way in dictionaries and in cases where a citation form is needed: *máng* (忙) 'be busy,' *chōu* (抽) 'pull,' *xíguàn* (习惯) 'be accustomed to,' *rènshi* (认识) 'recognize, know,' *xǐzǎo* (洗澡) 'bathe.'

Separability

Compound verbs differ in their degree of bonding. *Xíguàn* (习惯) 'be accustomed to,' for example, is composed of *xí*, which is not an independent verb in the modern language, and *guàn*, which is an independent verb meaning 'be used to.' Many speakers omit the second syllable in the first part of verb-not-verb questions[1]: *Xí bu xíguàn?* 'Are you accustomed to it?'

Otherwise, the compound acts as a unitary verb. The same is true of *rènshi* 'recognize, know.' *Xǐzǎo* 'bathe,' composed of the free verb *xǐ* 'wash' and the bound form *zǎo*, has a more elastic bond between its parts. Even though the components seem to form a compound, other sentence elements can intervene between the two parts: *xǐ ge zǎo* (洗个澡) 'have a bath,' *xǐle ge zǎo* (洗了个澡) 'having bathed,' *xǐle ge liángshuǐ zǎo* (洗了个凉水澡) 'have a cold bath,' *xǐhǎo zǎo le* (洗好澡了) 'had my bath.' Other examples are *shàngdàng* (上当) 'be taken in, be fooled' (*shàngle ge dà dàng* (上了个大当) 'be totally taken in') and *shuìjiào* (睡觉) 'sleep, go to bed' (*jiào yě shuìbuzháo* (觉也睡不着) 'couldn't even get to sleep,' with *zháo* 'manage to') (see Section 61).

---

[1]The truncated pattern has gained currency in Mandarin under the influence of Cantonese, where it is normal. Older northern speakers may still prefer the full pattern (*xíguàn bu xíguàn*), but nowadays, the truncated pattern is probably no longer thought of as southern.

Because the separable element in such compounds often has a nominal origin and behaves likes an object, such compounds are often labeled verb-objects (vo.) in English-language dictionaries and vocabulary lists. In Chinese, the usual term is *líhécí* (离合词) 'separate-unite-words,' and some Chinese dictionaries mark such words with the symbol =: *chī=fàn* 'eat,' *xǐ=zǎo* 'bathe.'[2]

Plain Forms Versus Combinations

Verbs can appear in plain form: *zuò* (做) 'do,' *lái* (来) 'come,' *gěi* (给) 'give,' *dài* (带) 'bring; take,' *xíguàn* (习惯) 'be accustomed to,' *zhǎngwò* (掌握) 'master.'

你周末都做一些什么？
Nǐ zhōumò dōu zuò yì xiē shénme?
'What do you do on weekends?'

来一杯白开水。
Lái yì bēi báikāishuǐ.
'Bring a glass of boiled water.'

我给你。
Wǒ gěi nǐ.
'You can have it.' ('I give you.')

我没带钥匙。
Wǒ méi dài yàoshi.
'I didn't bring my keys.'

他们不习惯。
Tāmen bù xíguàn.
'They're not used to it.'

学生很难掌握四声。
Xuésheng hěn nán zhǎngwò sìshēng.
'It's hard for students to master the four tones.'

As often as not, verbs appear in combinations, with a second, otherwise independent verb acting as a complement and conveying an additional nuance of meaning: *zuò* 'make' ~ *zuòhǎo* (做好) 'prepare' ('make-ready'), *sǐ* 'die' ~ *sǐdiào* (死掉) 'die' ('die-fall'), *tīng* 'listen' ~ *tīngbudǒng* (听不懂) 'not understand' ('listen-not-understand'), *zǒu* 'walk, go' ~ *zǒu jìnqu* (走进去) 'enter' ('walk enter-go').

---

[2]Yuen Ren Chao borrowed a term from chemistry to describe the process whereby compound verbs can be stretched to accommodate intervening elements, calling it "ionization."

饭已经做好了。
Fàn yǐjing zuòhǎo le.
'The meal's ready.'

他是中风死掉的。
Tā shì zhòngfēng sǐdiào de.
'He died of a stroke.'

我听不懂。
Wǒ tīngbudǒng.
'I don't understand.'

他们两个两个地走进去了。
Tāmen liǎng ge liǎng ge de zǒu jìnqu le.
'They walked in two by two.'

A good deal of the work required in learning to use Chinese verbs involves learning how they combine to produce nuances of meaning. The various types of compound and complex verbs will be discussed in later sections.

Verb Suffixes

Verbs can be followed by a small number of neutral-toned suffixes that convey grammatical notions that are, by and large, different from those associated with English verbs, such as tense (present and past) and voice (active and passive). Rather than being expressed grammatically, relationship to the time of speaking—tense—is conveyed by time words and context in Chinese, as the following example, about spending a summer in Nanjing, one of China's "three furnaces," makes clear.

> *Zuótiān hěn rè, jīntiān yě hěn rè, míngtiān yě huì hěn rè de.*
> Yesterday very hot, today also very hot, tomorrow also will-be hot DE.
> 'Yesterday was hot, today's also hot, and it'll be hot tomorrow, as well.'

38. The Verb Suffix -*guo* (过)

The suffix -*guo* (过), which is related to the verb *guò* 'pass, cross,' typically follows action verbs with the meaning 'has happened' at some time in the past ("ever") or over a period of time. The negative is formed with 没 *méi* placed before the verb, and the suffix -*guo* is retained.

你去过中国吗？
Nǐ qùguo Zhōngguó ma?
'Have you [ever] been to China?'

没去过，但是很想去。
Méi qùguo, dànshì hěn xiǎng qù.
'No, I haven't, but I'd really like to [go].'

你去年回过国吗？
Nǐ qùnián huíguo guó ma?
You last-year return-GUO country MA?
'Did you go back to your country
    last year?'

回了一个月。
Huíle yí ge yuè.
Return-LE 1 M month.
'I went back for a month.'

For routine activities that are part of one's daily schedule, like eating and bathing, the *-guo* suffix need not involve a long period of time. With this meaning, *-guò* tends to be toned, as shown in the following example.

你洗过澡吗？
Nǐ xǐguò zǎo ma?
'Have you bathed?'

刚洗过。
Gāng xǐguò.
'Just.'

The meaning is obviously not "Have you ever had a bath?" but rather "Have you had your bath?" Note that forms of the English verb "have" show the same range: "Have you been to China?" expresses the "ever" meaning, while "Have you eaten?" expresses the "so far today" meaning.

39. The Verb Suffix *-le* (了) and Sentence *le* (了)

It is usual to distinguish two *le*s in Mandarin, both written 了: one is suffixed to verbs (verb suffix *-le*), and the other appears at the foot of the sentence, after objects and other complements, if present (sentence *le*). Both are present in the following sentence.

她进了医院了。
Tā jìnle yīyuàn le.
She enter-LE hospital LE.
'She's in hospital.'

The two *le*s are distinct in Cantonese and other regional languages. In fact, they have different historical sources: verb suffix *-le* is a reduced form of the verb *liǎo* 'complete,' also written 了, while sentence *le* (an SFP) is a reduced form of the verb *lái* (来) 'come.'

Verb Suffix *-le*

The suffix *-le* appears directly after verbs to underscore the completion of an event. For the learner, the completion function is clearest when *le* marks the first of a sequence of events where the second event is conditional on the first.

你上了车才买票。
Nǐ shàngle chē cái mǎi piào.
You mount-LE vehicle then-and-only-then buy ticket.
'You don't buy your ticket until *after* you get on the bus.'

The first clause (*shàngle chē*) expresses the condition that must be met before the ticket can be bought (*mǎi piào*).

Test Yourself

Consider this sentence: "I'm going home after class today—I don't feel well." What are the events? "Going home" and "getting out of class." How are they ordered? "Get out of class first, then go home." Express this with the verb suffix *-le: Jīntian wǒ xiàle kè jiù huíjiā—wǒ yǒu diǎnr bù shūfu.* (Note that this example and the one about buying a ticket also illustrate the distinction between *cái*, which implies a relatively later time, and *jiù*, which implies a relatively earlier time.)

Now, provide the Chinese versions of the following sentences.

1. I'll look for you after I eat. (*zhǎo* 'look for')
2. I'm going shopping after I leave work. (*mǎi dōngxi* 'go shopping,' *xiàbān* (vo.) 'finish work')

Possible Answers
1. *Wǒ chīle fàn jiù lái zhǎo nǐ.*
2. *Wǒ xiàle bān jiù qù mǎi dōngxi.*

The completion function is harder for learners to perceive when there is no sequence of events. In the following examples, the completion of the verbal event—doing the homework, buying things—is important to the question being asked, so it is underscored with the suffix *-le*.

你做了你的功课吗?
Nǐ zuòle nǐ de gōngkè ma?
You do-LE you DE homework MA?
'Did you do your homework?'

没有,我忘了。
Méiyǒu, wǒ wàngle.
Not-have, I forget-LE.
'No, I forgot.'

买了些什么?
Mǎile xiē shénme?
Buy-LE several what?
'What did you buy?'

我们买了两件衬衫。
Wǒmen mǎile liǎng jiàn chènshān.
We buy-LE two M shirts.
'We bought a couple of shirts.'

The suffix *-le* does not usually appear in the negative. Not having done something is expressed with *méi<yǒu>*.

Jīntiān wǒ méi qù mǎi dōngxi.
'I didn't go shopping today.'

Tāmen hái méi zuòwán gōngkè.
'They haven't finished their assignments yet.'

Sentence *le*

In the example *Tā jìnle yīyuàn le* 'She's in the hospital,' sentence *le* follows the object (*yīyuàn*). In pinyin, it is written with a space before to indicate that it modifies the prior clause or sentence, not the previous word. Sentence *le* indicates a new situation, a change of state, or a connection to the time of speaking ("up to now"), but it is only used when the change has a significant role in the narrative. Recall that sentence *le* derives from the verb *lái* 'come,' suggesting a development from "come" to "come into a state of." Here are several examples.

> *Tā bìng le.*
> 'She's ill.'

> *Diǎn cài le ma?*
> Order dishes LE MA?
> 'Time to order?'

> *Xiàyǔ le.*
> Fall-rain LE.
> '[Look!] It's raining.'

> *Wǒ rènshi tā hěn jiǔ le.*
> I know her quite long LE.
> 'I've known her for ages.'

> *Wǒ xuéle sān nián Hànyǔ le.*
> 'I've been studying Chinese for three years.'

If the verb is modified by a restrictive adverb such as *zhǐ* (只) 'only,' *gāng* (刚) 'just now,' or *cái* (才) in its meaning 'only,' the sense of "up to now" is broken and sentence *le* does not appear, even though English shows no change in the form of the verb.

> *Wǒ zhǐ xuéle yì nián.*
> 'I've only been studying for a year.'

> *Wǒ gāng rènshi tā yí ge yuè.*
> 'I've only known her a month.'

Double *le*

Verb suffix *-le* and sentence *le* often co-occur, as shown in some earlier examples, to underscore a completed event that has relevance to the present. Compare the following pair of sentences.

> *Wǒmen zǒule yí ge duō xiǎoshí.*
> 'We walked for over an hour.'

> *Wǒmen zǒule yí ge duō xiǎoshí le.*
> 'We've been walking for over an hour.'

The sentence particle can also have the effect of casting a sentence with the verb suffix *-le* into the past.

Wǒ jīntian xiàle kè jiù huíjiā.
'Today, I'm going home right after class.'

Wǒ jīntian xiàle kè jiù huíjiā le.
'Today, I went home right after class.'

Other Cases of Sentence *le*

Sentence *le* is also associated with positive statements that use the adverb *tài* 'too,' the idea being that a boundary has been crossed—hence, a "new situation."

> *Tài hǎo le!*
> 'That's great!'

> *Tài bàng le!*
> 'Terrific!'

> *Yǐjing tài chí le.*
> 'It's too late already.'

A construction using the adverb *kuài* 'fast' or *kuài yào* and sentence *le* expresses imminence and provides a convenient way to express "almost" or "soon" in Chinese.

> *Shíjiān kuài dào le.*
> 'It's almost time.'

> *Tā kuài èrshí suì le.*
> 'She'll soon be 20.'

Test Yourself

Provide the Chinese versions of the following sentences.

1. Come on, the food's ready. (*lái, lái, lái*)
2. I've already eaten a lot! It's great!
3. How come you're not eating any more?
4. I'll be going then. (*zǒu* 'leave')
5. That's just too expensive!
6. They haven't decided yet. (*juédìng* 'decide')
7. I only slept three hours last night. (*shuì* 'sleep')
8. Wait here for me—I'm going to buy an umbrella.

Possible Answers

1. *Lái, lái, lái, fàn zuòhǎo le.*
2. *Wǒ yǐjing chīle hěn duō le! Hěn hǎochī!*
3. *Nǐ zěnme bù chī le ne?*
4. *Nà, wǒ zǒu le.*
5. *Nà tài guì le!*
6. *Tāmen hái méiyǒu juédìng.*

7. *Zuótiān wǎnshang wǒ zhǐ shuìle sān ge xiǎoshí.*
8. *Zài zhèr děng wǒ—wǒ qù mǎi sǎn.* (no *le*)

40. The Verb Suffix *-zhe* (着)

The verb suffix *-le* is associated primarily with narrative, underscoring the sequencing or completion of action. Verb suffix *-zhe*, by contrast, is descriptive, associated with setting the scene in which a narrative takes place: "The curtains were drawn. There was a thermos sitting on the table. There were welcome banners hanging on the wall. A woman was standing by the window, wearing a cape and holding a sword." The English "-ing" verbs in these sentences, as well as "were drawn," could all be expressed with the verb suffix *-zhe*, which changes the focus from an action to the state that results from the action, a shift that often requires a change of verb in English: "hang" ~ "hanging"; "put on" ~ "wearing"; "put" ~ "sitting" (on the shelf, for instance).

The *-zhe* suffix is written with the same character as the two verbs *zhuó* 'come into contact with; wear' and *zháo* 'touch, be touched by': 着 in the simplified set, 著 in the traditional set. (The two graphs are now quite distinct, but 着 is, in fact, historically a redrawing of the original 著.) Presumably, the suffix is related to the verbal meanings, but the course of the semantic evolution is hard to trace.

Verbs of bodily attitude or orientation, including verbs of wearing, are particularly receptive to the *-zhe* suffix. Examples include *tǎng* (躺) 'lie down,' *zhàn* (站) 'stand,' *zuò* (坐) 'sit,' *dūn* (蹲) 'sit on one's haunches, squat,' *lèng* (愣) 'space out, be in a daze, stand idly by,' *dīng* (盯) 'stare fixedly at,' *chuān* (穿) 'wear' (clothes and shoes, for example), and *dài* (戴) 'wear' (hats and accessories, for example).

她躺着呢。
Tā tǎngzhe ne.
'She's lying down.'

她在沙发上睡着呢。
Tā zài shāfā shang shuìzhe ne.
She at sofa on sleep-ZHE NE.
'She's asleep on the sofa.'

别愣着，来帮忙！
Bié lèngzhe, lái bāngmáng!
Don't idle-ZHE, quick come help!
'Don't just stand there—give us a hand!'

As the examples show, where *-zhe* would otherwise be in final position, a final *ne* is often present, which, in very general terms, indicates a certain lively interest. Negatives with V-*zhe* are not common, but are formed with *méi<yǒu>* when needed, with the *-zhe* suffix retained.

别盯着我。
Bié dīngzhe wǒ.
Don't stare-ZHE me.
'Don't stare at me.'

刚才我没盯着你!
Gāngcái wǒ méi dīngzhe nǐ!
Just-now I not stare-ZHE you!
'I wasn't staring at you just now!'

Frequently, *-zhe* appears in existential sentences, which set the stage, as a more specific version of the *yǒu* (有) 'there is/are' pattern. Such sentences begin with a location (see Section 35), which gives them a rather different word order than their English equivalents.

桌子上放着一个花瓶。
Zhuōzi shang fàngzhe yí ge huāpíng.
Table on put-ZHE one M vase.
'There's a vase sitting on the table.'

墙上挂着一幅画儿。
Qiáng shang guàzhe yì fú huàr.
Wall on hang-ZHE one M painting.
'A painting's hanging on the wall.'

桌子底下睡着一个小娃娃。
Zhuōzi dǐxia shuìzhe yí ge xiǎo wáwa.
'A baby was sleeping under the table.'

他身上穿着一件皮大衣。
Tā shēn shang chuānzhe yí jiàn pídàyī.
He body on wear-ZHE one M leather-coat.
'He had on a leather coat.'

The suffix *-zhe* may also subordinate the first verb phrase of a series, making it in effect an adverbial indicating circumstances (see Section 56).

不应该低着头走路!
Bù yīnggāi dīzhe tóu zǒulù!
Not ought bow-ing head walk-road!
'You shouldn't walk with your head down!'

说着说着, 来了一个行人。
Shuōzhe shuōzhe, láile yí ge xíngrén.
Speak-ing speak-ing come-LE one M walk-person.
'As they were talking, along came a pedestrian.'

The suffix *-zhe* is also common with imperatives.

Názhe!
'Take it!'

Jìzhe.
'Keep this in mind.'

Test Yourself

Provide the Chinese versions of the following sentences.

1. There was a policeman standing by the window.
2. She smiled at him and said "hello." (*xiào* 'smile')
3. They're waiting for you at the door. (*zài ménkǒu* 'at the door')
4. The window's closed. (*guān* 'close')
5. I'm comfortable standing. (*shūfu* 'comfortable')

Possible Answers

1. *Chuāng qián zhànzhe yí ge jǐngchá.* (Recall existential sentences with *yǒu.* Start with the location, then, instead of *yǒu,* use the specific verb "stand." Finally, mention the item of interest—the policeman (*jǐngchá*)).
2. *Tā xiàozhe gēn tā shuō "nǐ hǎo."* (The two verbs are *xiào* 'smile' and *shuō* 'say,' with *shuō* being primary.)
3. *Tāmen zài ménkǒu děngzhe nǐ.*
4. *Chuānghu guānzhe ne.*
5. *Zhànzhe shūfu.*

41. *Zài* (在) + Verb to Signal Ongoing Action

In Chinese, ongoing action can sometimes be implied by nothing more than the presence of the final particle *ne* (呢): *Chīfàn ne* 'I'm eating.' The sense of being in progress can be made more explicit by adding *zài* (在) 'be at' or *zhèng<zài>* (正<在>) 'right now' in adverbial position before the verb.

她在吃饭呢。
Tā zài chīfàn ne.
'She's eating.'

对不起，我正在吃饭呢。
Duìbuqǐ, wǒ zhèngzài chīfàn ne.
'Sorry, I'm right in the middle of my meal.'

This ongoing sense expressed with *zài* (在) and *ne* (呢) corresponds to what is known as the progressive in English: "is eating dinner," "is putting on her coat." As shown in Section 40, however, the verb suffix *-zhe* also corresponds to the English progressive (the "-ing" form) of the verb: "is wearing," "is holding." The two forms (*zài* + verb and verb suffix *-zhe*) can be compared in the following pair of sentences.

ACTION 她正在穿大衣呢。
Tā zhèngzài chuān dàyī ne.
'She's putting on her coat right now.'

STATE 她穿着大衣呢。
Tā chuānzhe dàyī ne.
'She's wearing a coat.'

Often, the difference is simply one of perspective.

ACTION *Tā zhèngzài shuìjiào ne.*
'She's just going to sleep.'

STATE *Tā shuìzhe ne.*
'She's asleep.'

For some northern speakers, however, the functions of *zhèng<zài>* and *-zhe* can reinforce each other in the same sentence.

Zhèng<zài> xiàzhe yǔ ne.
'It's raining right now!'

42. The Absence of a Suffix

The absence of a suffix can also convey certain grammatical information. Generic statements or habitual actions, for example, are expressed with a plain verb (with no suffixes).

美国人经常九点就上班。
Měiguórén jīngcháng jiǔ diǎn jiù shàngbān.
Americans generally nine o'clock then start-work.
'Americans generally start work at nine o'clock.'

喝咖啡，我放牛奶也放糖。
Hē kāfēi, wǒ fàng niúnǎi yě fàng táng.
Drink coffee, I put milk also put sugar.
'When I drink coffee, I add milk and sugar.'

Action about to happen is also expressed with a plain verb.

你出去吗?
Nǐ chūqu ma?
'Are you going out?'

出去。上课去。
Chūqu. Shàngkè qu.
'Yes, I am. I'm off to class.'

43. Verb Reduplication and Tentativeness

Action verbs may be reduplicated to suggest tentativeness or nonchalance, which often serves to reassure or persuade listeners that minimal effort is involved. With monosyllabic verbs, the repeated verb is unstressed and in neutral tone.

Shìshi kàn.
Try-try look.
'Take a look.'

Pěngpeng chǎng.
Support-support performance.
'It's just to provide support.'

Xiūxi-xiūxi ba.
Rest-rest BA.
'Why don't you take a break?'

There are a number of variations. With monosyllabic verbs such as *kàn* 'look' and *zuò* 'sit,' *yī* 'one' can be inserted between the verbs, as if to say "look a look": *Kàn yí kàn.* The fact that the verb suffix *-le* can be added to the first verb supports the view that the second verb is an object: *Tā kànle yí kàn.* In careful speech, the verb and ensuing syllables may all be toned, but in normal to fast speech, the options are *kàn yi kàn* and *kànyikan.*

Kàn yí kàn.
'Take a look.'

Tā kànle yí kàn.
'She took a look.'

Zuò yí zuò.
'Sit for a bit.'

Tā zuòle yí zuò.
'He sat for a while.'

Disyllabic verbs do not accept medial *yī.* However, both mono- and disyllabic verbs accept a third option: adding the verbal measure *yí xià<r>* 'one time, one occasion' to the verb (see Section 71). The options, then, are as follows.

Děngdeng!   'Just a minute!' 'Wait a sec!'
Děng yi děng!
Děng yi xiàr!

Xiūxi xiūxi ba.	'Take a break.'
Xiūxi yi xiàr ba!	

Wǒ gěi nǐ jièshào jièshao.	'Let me introduce you.'
Wǒ gěi nǐ jièshào yi xiàr.	

Note that verb-plus-object combinations (see Section 66) pattern with monosyllabic verbs in allowing all three options.

Shuìshui jiào ba.	'Sleep for a bit.'
Shuì yi shuìjiào ba.	
Shuì yi xiàr jiào ba.	

Here are additional common examples.

Nǐ chángchang ba.	'Have a taste!'
Nǐ cháng yi cháng ba.	
Nǐ cháng yi xiàr ba.	

Nǐ cāi yi cāi.	'Take a guess.'
Nǐ wènwen tā ba.	'Why don't you just ask her?'
Nǐ de zìdiǎn, néng kànkan ma?	'Can I take a look at your dictionary?'
Mō yi xiàr!	'Feel [this]!'

Verbs of cognition and consideration, such as *xiǎng* (想) 'think,' *kǎolù* (考虑) 'think over, consider,' *shāngliang* (商量) 'discuss, consult,' and *tán* (谈) 'talk, chat, discuss,' are especially prone to reduplication.

Xiān gēn tā tán yi tán.
'Talk to her first.'

Zánmen shāngliang shāngliang.
'Let's talk about it.'

Ràng wǒ kǎolù yi xiàr.
'Let me think it over.'

The last example serves as a conventional way of parrying a request—a way of saying 'no.' The same can be said of another common sentence: *Yǐhòu zài shuō ba?* 'Why don't we talk about it later?'

Idiosyncratic Verbs

It is worthwhile introducing some of the most common and versatile verbs of Chinese individually. The following sections discuss *shì* (是) 'be,' *yǒu* (有) 'have,' *zài* (在) 'be at,' and *gěi* (给) 'give.' Verb suffixes do not occur with *shì* and *zài*, they are rare with *yǒu*, and they occur normally with *gěi*.

44. *Shì* (是): Identity and Category

Shì as a Copula Verb

Shì has equative and categorical functions and, as such, is often unstressed, in the neutral tone.

我是黎明。
Wǒ shì Lí Míng.
'I'm Li Ming.'

满地都是水。
Mǎndì dōu shì shuǐ.
Full-place all be water.
'The whole place is covered in water.'

黎明是中文老师。
Lí Míng shì Zhōngwén lǎoshī.
'Li Ming's a Chinese teacher.'

站台不是游乐场。
Zhàntái bú shì yóulèchǎng.
'The (station) platform isn't a playground.'

Frequently, one of the elements in an equative or categorical sentence is a nominalized verb. This is particularly common in sentences involving nationality, major courses of study, professions, and so on. The nominalized form gives the attribution a more enduring sense.

Tāmen shì cóng Rìběn lái de.
'They're from Japan.' ('people who are from . . .')

Wǒ shì gǎo yǔyán de.
'I deal with languages.' ('one who deals with . . .')

Wǒ zuì xǐhuan hē de shì chá.
'The thing I like best to drink is tea.'

In casual speech, *shì* in its copula function is often omitted: *Tā dì-yī, nǐ dì-èr.* 'He's first, you're second.' The omission of *shì* is particularly common with nationality, with dates, and in physical descriptions.

Tā <shì> Yīngguórén.
'He's British.'

Jīntiān <shì> xīngqīwǔ.
'Today's Friday.'

Tā <shì> gāo bíliáng.
'He has a prominent nose.' ('nose-bridge high')

Tā <shì> hēi tóufa.
'She has black hair.'

The result is a "noun sentence," with a noun acting as the predicate—the comment. However, any sort of adverbial modification, including the negator *bu*, requires the presence of *shì* or an equivalent: *Jīntiān bú shì xīngqīwǔ.*

Shì in Location Expressions

Existence in a location is explicitly expressed with *yǒu* (see Section 46): *Fángjiān li yǒu ge guìzi.* 'There's a cupboard in the room.' It is possible, however, to express location with *shì*, with a slightly different sense. For example, in describing a room at a hotel where the furnishings are known but not their placement, what is at issue is not what is in the room (*yǒu*), but how things are arranged (*shì*).

床对面是柜子，柜子旁边是电视机。
Chuáng duìmiàn shì guìzi, guìzi pángbiānr shì diànshìjī.
'Opposite the bed is a cupboard; next to the cupboard is a television.'

Shì in Tag Questions

Shì is also a common element in confirmatory questions or tag questions.

Zhōngwén shì bu shì bǐ biéde yǔyán nán ne?
'Is [it the case that] Chinese is harder than other languages?'

Zhōngwén bǐ biéde yǔyán nán, shì ma?
'Chinese is harder than other languages, isn't it?'

In written language and sometimes in neutral speech, the second part of a *shì bu shì* question (and in fact, the negative segment of any verb-not-verb question) can be indicated with *fǒu* (否) 'or not.'

她问我是否来自中国。
Tā wèn wǒ shìfǒu lái zì Zhōngguó.
She ask me be-the-case or-not come from China.
'She asked me if I was from China.'

Shì in Emphatic Expressions

In certain contrastive, concessive, or otherwise emphatic environments, *shì* may appear with adjectives.

是很贵，可是很有用。
Shì hěn guì, kěshì hěn yǒu yòng. (versus neutral *hěn guì*)
It *is* expensive, [granted,] but it's useful.

他们的房子看起来很是不起眼儿。
Tāmen de fángzi kan qilai hen shi bu qiyanr.
Their apartment doesn't look very attractive.

For the *shì-de* construction, see Section 34.

Shì, through close association with preceding words, has become a second element in many adverbs and a few conjunctions: *zŏngshi* (总是) 'always,' *háishi* (还是) 'still,' *yàoshi* (要是) 'if' (all usually listed in dictionaries with neutral tone on *shì*); *jiùshì* (就是) 'even,' *zhĭshì* (只是) 'only,' *kĕshì* (可是) and *dànshì* (但是) 'but' (all with full tone). *Zhēnshi* (真是)—with neutral-toned *shì*—has become an interjection expressing dissatisfaction: 'Oh, really now!'

45. Verbs Like *shì*: Classificatory Verbs

A number of verbs, while not nearly as common as *shì* (是), have many features in common with it. These are often called "classificatory verbs."

Character	Pinyin and Gloss	Example
姓	*xìng* 'be surnamed'	*Tā xìng Féng.* 'His last name is Feng.'
叫	*jiào* 'be called'	*Tā de míngzi jiào shénme?* 'What's his name?'
像	*xiàng* 'resemble'	*Tā kàn shàngqu xiàng Zhōngguórén.* 'She looks Chinese.'
属	*shŭ* 'belong to'	*Wŏ <shì> shŭ lóng de.* 'I'm the year of the dragon.'
等于	*dĕngyú* 'equal'	*Yi kuài Mĕijīn dĕngyú jĭ kuài Rénmínbì?* 'How much is a dollar in RMB?'
做	*zuò* 'act as, be'	*Tā zuò xìzhŭrèn.* 'She's department head.'
当	*dāng* 'serve as, be'	*Tā dāng bānzhăng.* 'He's the class monitor.'

In *Nín guìxìng*, the polite but idiomatic expression for inquiring about a surname, *xìng* is used as a noun. As a verb, *xìng* can only take a surname as object. *Jiào,* on the other hand, requires a name of at least two syllables as object, which makes both a full name and a two-syllable *míngzi* eligible: *Wŏ xìng Wèi, jiào <Wèi> Jiŭ'ān. Jiào* can also function transitively, meaning 'call [someone].' *Xiàng* can also be an adjective: *Tāmen hĕn xiàng.* 'They look like each other.'

Rather than asking age directly, Chinese often gauge a person's age by finding out their birth sign.

46. *Yǒu* (有): Possession and Existence

Yǒu may indicate possession.

Wǒ méiyǒu Yīng-Hàn zìdiǎn.
'I don't have an English-Chinese dictionary.'

Nǐ yǒu méiyǒu xiōngdì-jiěmèi?
'Do you have any brothers or sisters?'

However, *yǒu* is more common as an existential verb, introducing noun referents into the discourse. Note that the topic of *yǒu* in this type of sentence is usually a location, and because it comes at the head of the clause, the location is not usually marked with *zài*.

Zhèr yǒu méiyǒu cèsuǒ?   *Yǒu, zài lóu shang.*
'Is there a toilet here?'   'There is; it's upstairs.'

Fùjìn yǒu liǎng jiā bǐjiào hǎo de fànguǎnr.
'There are two relatively good restaurants around here.'

Age, weight, and other measurements often appear in (verbless) noun sentences.

Wǒ sìshíwǔ suì.
'I'm 45.'

Tā qīshí gōngjīn.
'He's 70 kilos.'

However, when a verb is needed to provide a perch for adverbs, the verb is usually *yǒu*. (In this way, Chinese is like French, which uses "have" for age and weight, rather than like English, which uses "is.")

Tā zhǐ yǒu èrshísān suì.
'She's only 23.'

Wǒ méiyǒu qīshí gōngjīn, zhǐ yǒu liùshí gōngjīn.
'I'm not 70 kilos—just 60.'

Duration complements (see Section 70) can follow *yǒu*, although in such cases, *yǒu* can be omitted.

我在北京<有>六个月了。
Wǒ zài Běijīng <yǒu> liù ge yuè le.
'I've been in Beijing six months.'

Suffixed verbs are negated with *méi<yǒu>*, either with the suffixes retained in the case of *-guo* and *-zhe* or without the suffix in the case of *le*.

Tāmen huílai le.	*Tāmen méi<yǒu> huílai.*
'They've returned.'	'They haven't returned.'
Tā chīguo Běijīng kǎoyā.	*Tā méi<yǒu> chīguo Běijīng kǎoyā.*
'He's eaten Peking duck.'	'He hasn't [ever] eaten Peking duck.'
Bié dīngzhe wǒ.	*Wǒ méi<yǒu> dīngzhe nǐ.*
'Don't stare at me.'	'I'm not staring at you.'

In colloquial (rather than formal or written) Mandarin, the asymmetry between positive *le*, *-guo*, and *-zhe* on the one hand, and the negatives with *méi<yǒu>* on the other, is resolved by associating *yǒu* with the positive, as well. This is particularly true of verb-not-verb questions and their answers.

FORMAL	*Tāmen huílai le méiyǒu?*	*Huílai le.*	*Méiyǒu <huílai>.*
COLLOQUIAL	*Tāmen yǒu méiyou huílai?*	*Yǒu.*	*Méiyǒu.*
	'Have they returned?'	'Yes.'	'No.'
FORMAL	*Nǐ qùguo Táiwān méiyǒu?*	*Qùguo.*	*Méiyǒu <qùguo>.*
COLLOQUIAL	*Nǐ yǒu méiyou qùguo Táiwān?*	*Yǒu.*	*Méiyǒu.*
	'Have you [ever] been to Taiwan?'	'Yes.'	'No.'

While there is internal logic in the colloquial forms (*yǒu* in the positive, *méi<yǒu>* in the negative), Mandarin probably absorbed this pattern from southern dialects.

47. *Zài* (在): Location

In English, identity and location are expressed by a single verb, "be": "I'm an astronaut," "I'm on the far side of the moon." In Chinese (and in many other languages), identity and location are expressed with different verbs, *shì* (是) for identity and *zài* (在) for location.

我是太空人。
Wǒ shì tàikōngrén.
I be great-emptiness-person.
'I'm an astronaut.'

我在月亮的另一边儿。
Wǒ zài yuèliang de lìng yìbiānr.
I be-at moon DE other one-side.
'I'm on the far side of the moon.'

Zài as a Preposition

Zài also has a range of other functions. Subordinated to another verb, it functions like a preposition and takes a location object: *zài jiā* 'at home,' *zài wūzi li* 'in the room.'

她在饭馆儿工作，是个厨师。
Tā zài fànguǎnr gōngzuò, shì ge chúshī.
She at restaurant work, be a chef.
'She works at a restaurant; she's a chef.'

Zài in Ongoing Action

Placed directly before a verb, *zài* indicates ongoing action.

我在吃饭呢；等一会儿再打过来，好不好？
Wǒ zài chīfàn ne; děng yìhuǐr zài dǎ guòlai, hǎo bu hǎo?
I in-the-process-of eat-meal NE; wait awhile again do pass-come, good not good?
'I'm eating; call back in a little while, okay?'

Zài as a Postverbal Particle

Zài, often untoned, may also introduce the endpoint of movement, with verbs such as *fàng* 'put' and *xiě* 'write.'

自行车放在外头，好不好？
Zìxíngchē fàng zài wàitou, hǎo bu hǎo?
'Put your bike outside, okay?'

请把名字写在黑板上。
Qǐng bǎ míngzi xiě zài hēibǎn shang.
'Write your name on the blackboard, please.'

48. *Gěi* (给): "Give" and Its Derivatives

Gěi (给) is possibly the most versatile of all Chinese verbs.

Gěi as a Verb

First of all, *gěi* can be a full verb with a single object, which can be a person or a thing. If the object is a person, it is the beneficiary and the thing given is understood. In English, if the person who benefits is expressed, the thing given usually has to be supplied, as well. For that reason, the English equivalent in the first example below has to be rephrased, without "give."

Wǒ gěi nǐ.
I give [it] to you.
'Here you are.'

与其给折扣不如给减价。
Yǔqí gěi zhékòu, bùrú gěi jiǎnjià.
Rather-than give discount, better-to give reduce-price.
'Rather than give a discount, it would be better to simply reduce the price.'

Gěi may also take two objects, like its English equivalent.

我将在一两天内给你一个答复。
Wǒ jiāng zài yī-liǎng tiān nèi gěi nǐ yí ge dáfù.
'I'll give you a reply in a day or two.'

Gěi as a Verb in a Series

Gěi is often the second verb in a series (see Section 73).

拜托您捎个信儿给他。
Bàituō nín shāo ge xìnr gěi tā.
Request you bring M message give him.
'Would you mind taking a message and giving it to him?'

Gěi as a Postverbal Particle

Gěi can follow transactional verbs to introduce a beneficiary (see Section 68).

Qǐng bǎ zìdiǎn dì gěi wǒ.
'Please pass me the dictionary.'

Gěi as a Preposition

Gěi can appear before a verb in a prepositional function to indicate the beneficiary (often translated as "for" or "to").

Duìbuqǐ, gěi nín tiān máfan le.
Sorry, for you add trouble LE.
'Sorry to impose on you.'

Gěi wǒ liúxiàle hěn shēn de yìnxiàng.
For me leave-down-LE very deep DE impression.
'It left a profound impression on me.'

The prepositional function can also extend to agency ("by"), in which case *gěi* is synonymous with the preposition *bèi* (see Section 77).

她新买的雅玛哈摩托车给人偷走了。

Tā xīn mǎi de Yámǎhā mótuōchē gěi rén tōuzǒu le.

She new buy DE Yamaha motorbike by someone steal-leave LE.

'Her newly purchased Yamaha motorbike got stolen by someone.'

In such passive contexts, *gěi* can (like *bèi*) appear without an object, indicating that the event was caused by some agency and, hence, conveying a rather fatalistic or regretful tone.

因为下大雨，我们的旅游都给搞砸了。

Yīnwei xià dà yǔ, wǒmen de lǚyóu dōu gěi gǎozá le.

Because fall big rain, our DE travel all got do-fail LE.

'Because of the heavy rain, our trip was a disaster.'

你看这空气，都是车多给闹的。

Nǐ kàn zhè kōngqì, dōu shì chē duō gěi nào de.

You look this air, all be vehicles many get mucked-up DE.

'Look at the air—it's totally messed up as a result of the number of cars.'

49. Generalized Verbs

A number of Chinese verbs can combine with such a broad range of objects that they have come to function as generic verbs. Examples include dǎ (打) 'strike, hit' and the various "do, make" verbs: the homophonous (做) and (作) *zuò*, *gǎo* (搞), *nòng* (弄), and *gàn* (干).

Dǎ (打)

Dǎ is particularly versatile in forming verb-object compounds like the following.

Chinese	Pinyin	Gloss	Example
打包	*dǎbāo*	'pack (for a trip); unpack'	*bǎ shèngcài dǎbāo* 'pack up the leftovers'
打的	*dǎdī*	'take a taxi'	*dǎ ge dī qù* 'go by taxi'
打点滴	*dǎ diǎndī*	'have an intravenous drip'	*zài dǎ diǎndī* 'be on a drip'
打电话	*dǎ diànhuà*	'make a telephone call'	*gěi tā dǎ ge diànhuà* 'give her a phone call'
打官司	*dǎ guānsi*	'sue, debate'	*dǎle jǐ nián guānsī* 'been argued about for years'

Chinese	Pinyin	Gloss	Example
打猎	*dǎliè*	'hunt'	*Jìnzhǐ dǎliè.* 'No hunting.'
打喷嚏	*dǎ pēntì*	'sneeze'	*yìzhí dǎ pēntì* 'keep sneezing'
打气	*dǎqì*	'inflate'	*gěi lúntāi dǎqì* 'inflate a tire'
打水	*dǎshuǐ*	'fetch water'	*cóng jǐng li dǎshuǐ* 'draw water from a well'
打算盘	*dǎ suànpan*	'use an abacus'	*Nǐ huì dǎ suànpan ma?* 'Can you use an abacus?'
打太极拳	*dǎ tàijíquán*	'do tai chi'	*zǎoshang dǎ tàijíquán* 'do tai chi in the morning'
打折扣	*dǎ zhékòu*	'give a discount'	*Néng bu néng dǎ zhékòu?* 'Can you give me a discount?'
打针	*dǎzhēn*	'get/give an injection'	*tǎoyàn dǎzhēn* 'hate injections'
打字	*dǎzì*	'type'	*dǎzì dǎ de hěn kuài* 'types fast'

Gǎo (搞)

Gǎo has a broad range of meanings covered by English expressions such as 'happen,' 'deal with,' 'get hold of,' 'dabble in,' 'be into.'

Zěnme gǎo de?
'What's going on?'

Tā gǎo shénme èzuòjù?
'What mischief is he up to?'

Tā shì gǎo diànnǎo de.
'She's into computers.'

Zhèr gǎo de hěn rènao!
'This place is humming!'

Jīntiān de gōngkè wǒ shì gǎobudǒng de.
'I don't have a clue about today's assignment.'

Tā zǒule hòumén wèi wǒ gǎodào piào.
'He "went through the back door" to get us tickets.'

Nòng (弄)

Nòng conveys the sense of doing something with the hands—fixing, obtaining, arranging, or dealing with something. More generally, *nòng* is often used in place of a more specific verb and, as such, tends to combine with resultative or directional complements (see Sections 61 and 62): *nònghǎo* 'fix,' *nòngcuò* 'goof, damage' (with *cuò* 'err'), *nòngzāng* 'mess up' (with *zāng* 'dirty'), *nòng zhěngqí* 'make tidy' (with *zhěngqí* 'be neat'), *nòngluàn* 'mess up' (with *luàn* 'be disordered'), *nòng bu guòlai* 'cannot deal with it all.'

这书已经绝版，很难弄到手。
Zhè shū yǐjing juébǎn, hěn nán nòng dào shǒu.
This book already out-of-print, quite difficult get to hands.
'This book is out of print and quite hard to get hold of.'

Néng bu néng nòng diǎnr chī de.
'Can you rustle up something to eat?'

Gàn (干)

The meaning of *gàn* is 'do a job' or 'deal with business.' Like *gǎo* (搞), *gàn* can be used to ask about a "line of work."

你干的是哪一行？
Nǐ gàn de shì nǎ yì háng?
'What's your line of business?'

我是干电脑的。
Wǒ shì gàn diànnǎo de.
'I deal with computers.'

The question form *gàn má* (干嘛, with 嘛 often preferred over the usual 吗 because of the full tone on *má*) is a colloquial substitute for *zuò shénme* 'doing what' or *wèi shénme* 'why.'

Zánmen jīntiān gànmá ne?
'What shall we do today?'

Nǐ gànmá wèn?
'Why do you ask?'

Otherwise, *gàn* is common in set phrases, such as *gàn gémìng* 'do revolution,' *gàn huór* 'work, do a job,' and *gànshìr* 'work, do things.'

做 and 作 *zuò*

The general verb for "do, make" is *zuò* (做).

Nǐ zài zuò shénme?
'What are you doing?'

Zuòhǎole méiyǒu?
'Have you finished?'

做 also appears in verb-object combinations, such as *zuòshì* (做事) 'do things,' *zuò shēngyi* (做生意) 'do business,' and *zuòfàn* (做饭) 'cook.'

Were it not for the fact that it is represented by two characters, *zuò* might be considered a single word with a range of senses extending from a core meaning of 'do, make.' Instead, it is more usual to recognize two *zuò*s, one written 做, described in the previous paragraph, and one written 作.

作 has narrower functions than 做. In *zuòwén* (作文), it means 'write a composition'; in *zuòbì* (作弊), it means 'practice fraud'; in *zuòduì* (作对), it means 'take an opposing position.' 作 also forms noun compounds: *zuòpǐn* (作品) 'works of literature/art,' *zuòwén* (作文) 'composition,' *gōngzuò* (工作) 'work, job,' *xiězuò* (写作) 'writing,' *zuòyè* (作业) 'homework,' *zuòjiā* (作家) 'writer.' It is also the usual choice in four-character expressions, such as *zuòjiǎn-zìfù* (作茧自缚) 'get into a fix' (literally, 'spin a cocoon around oneself').

In some cases, usage is undecided: *zuòbànr* 'be a partner,' *zuòkè* 'be a guest,' *zuòmèng* 'have dreams,' and *zuòdōng* 'be the host' (literally 'be east,' the hosting direction) are listed in dictionaries with both 做 and 作.

50. Modal Verbs

A class of auxiliary verbs (often called *zhùdòngcí* 助动词 'helping verbs') is recognized for Chinese. These are verbs that, like their English counterparts, take verbs or verb phrases as their objects: *Wǒ bú yuànyi shīqù nǐ.* 'I'm not willing to lose you.' Other features of auxiliary verbs are that they cannot be modified by verbal suffixes, such as *le* (了) (see Section 39), and that they are usually negated by *bù* (as in the example), with *méi<yǒu>* limited to much rarer cases that carry a certain nuance.

In English, auxiliaries can be divided into primary auxiliaries, which play a role in the formation of verbal categories, and modal auxiliaries, which indicate the speaker's attitude to an event or situation (hence, the term "modal"). In Chinese, the only candidate for the status of a primary auxiliary is *méi<yǒu>* in its preverbal function: *méi yǒu kàndǒng* 'didn't understand,' *méi qùguo* 'haven't ever been there.' Most dictionaries, however, list *méi<yǒu>* in this function as an adverb, like the nonverbal negative *bù* (不). Thus, auxiliaries in Chinese are modal auxiliaries, or simply modal verbs. At the core of the modals are verbs that indicate ability, possibility, likelihood, and necessity, for example, *gāi* in *gāi zǒu le* 'should be going' and *gǎn* in *bù gǎn pèng tā* 'dare not touch it.'

One particularly prominent subset are the "can" modals: *néng*, *huì*, and *kěyǐ*.

Néng (能)

Néng indicates physical capability, feasibility, or possibility. The two-syllable option, *nénggòu* (能够), is synonymous.

Bù néng<gòu> zhè yàng zuò.
'It can't be done that way.'

Bù néng chī de.
'Not edible.'

Xīwàng yǒu yì tiān néng bàodá nín.
'Hope it is possible to repay you some day.'

Wǒ zài yě bù néng jiēshòu le.
'I can't take it anymore.'

在旧政权下妇女不能选举。
Zài jiù zhèngquán xia fùnǚ bù néng xuǎnjǔ.
At old political-system under women not able select-by-vote.
'Under the old political system, women couldn't vote.'

Huì (会)

Huì is used for (1) abilities that result from learning, corresponding to English 'can, be able to, know how to,' and (2) predictions, corresponding to English 'be likely, be possible, will.'

Zhōngwén, wǒ huì jiǎng yìdiǎnr, kěshì wǒ bú huì dú.
Chinese, I can speak a-bit, but I not able-to read.
'I can speak Chinese a bit, but I can't read [it].'

Zhè jiàn chènshān bú huì qǐzhòu.
'This shirt won't wrinkle.'

Zuìhòu yíqiè dōu huì hǎo de.
'Everything will be fine in the end.'

Jīntiān bú huì hěn lěng.
'It won't be too cold today.'

Kěyǐ (可以)

Kěyǐ is used for permission and possibility, corresponding to English 'may, be permitted to; be possible, can.'

Kěyǐ bu kěyǐ mǎi bàn ge?
'Can one buy a half?'

Míngtiān kěyǐ xiūxi.
'You can take tomorrow off.'

Cóng zhèr kěyǐ kàndào dàhǎi.
'You can see the sea from here.'

Of the three "can" verbs, only *kěyǐ* can be postponed to the foot of the sentence.

带孩子上班可以不可以？
Dài háizi shàngbān kěyǐ bu kěyǐ?
'Can one bring children to work?'

Common Modal Auxiliaries

The most common modal auxiliaries are presented in the following chart.

Characters	Pinyin	Gloss	Example
不必	*bú bì*	'no need to'	*Bú bì fù fángzū.* 'No need to pay rent.'
不用	*bú yòng*	'need not, no need to'	*Bú yòng xiè.* 'My pleasure.'
得	*děi*	'must, have to'	*Wǒ děi zǒu le.* 'I've got to be going.'
敢	*gǎn*	'dare, deign to'	*Bù gǎn dāng.* '[I] don't deserve it.'
会	*huì*	'can, be good at'	*hěn huì jiǎng xiàohuà* 'good at telling jokes'
肯	*kěn*	'willing to'	*bù kěn tuǒxié* 'unwilling to compromise'
可以	*kěyǐ*	'can, may'	*Nǐ kěyǐ chàngsuǒyùyán.* 'You can express yourself freely.'
乐意	*lèyì*	'glad to'	*hěn lèyì bāngzhù tā* 'glad to help her'
能	*néng*	'can, be able to'	*bù néng bù chéngrèn* 'have to admit'
想	*xiǎng*	'want to, feel like'	*Wǒ xiǎng tí ge wèntí.* 'I'd like to ask a question.'
需要	*xūyào*	'need to, have to'	*xūyào xiūlǐ* 'needs to be repaired'
要	*yào*	'want, need to'	*Wǒ yào shuìjiào le.* 'I'm trying to sleep.'
<应>该	*<yīng>gāi*	'ought to, should'	*Yīnggāi méi shénme wèntí.* 'There shouldn't be any problems.'

Characters	Pinyin	Gloss	Example
愿意	*yuànyi*	'willing to'	*yuànyi bāngmáng* 'willing to help'
准	*zhǔn*	'allow'	*Bù zhǔn chōuyān.* 'No smoking.'

The category of modal auxiliaries shades into verbs of emotional content and intention, which can also take verbs or verb phrases as objects. In a number of analyses, some of these verbs are categorized as modals.

Common Verbs of Emotional Content and Intention

Characters	Pinyin	Gloss	Example
爱	*ài*	'love to, be fond of'	*ài dǎban* 'love to dress up'
打算	*dǎsuàn*	'intend, plan'	*dǎsuàn gǎn zǎobān de huǒchē* 'intend to catch the early train'
怕	*pà*	'afraid to'	*pà qù kàn yáyī* 'afraid of going to the dentist'
忘了	*wàngle*	'forget to'	*Bié wàngle dài piào.* 'Don't forget to bring your ticket.'
喜欢	*xǐhuan*	'like to'	*xǐhuan páshān* 'like climbing mountains'

What distinguishes this group of verbs is that in addition to taking verbal objects, they can also function as transitive verbs.

Wǒ wàngle tā de míngzi.
'I've forgotten her name.'

Tā hěn xǐhuan tiánshí.
'She loves desserts.'

In fact, the same is true of a number of core modals, as well.

Wǒ bú huì Rìyǔ.
'I'm not familiar with Japanese.'

Wǒ hěn xiǎng nǐ.
'I miss you.'

需要他时，他是会来的！
Xūyào tā shí, tā shì huì lái de!
'When you need him, he'll be there!'

51. Ambient Verbs

A number of meteorological events are expressed by the Chinese verb *xià* 'fall,' with a complement that identifies the type of precipitation. The placement of the complement follows the general principle of Chinese word order: definite ("the") before the verb, indefinite ("a/some") after the verb. Note that in Chinese, there is no source of precipitation that corresponds to "it" in English.

Xiàyǔ le.
'It's raining.'

Yǔ xià de hěn dà.
'It's raining heavily.'

Míngtiān huì bu huì xiàxuě?
'Will it snow tomorrow?'

Jiùjīnshān chángcháng xiàwù.
'It's often foggy in San Francisco.'

冰雹在屋顶上哗啦哗啦地下着。
Bīngbáo zài wūdǐng shang huālā-huālā de xiàzhe.
Hail at roof on rat-a-tat-tat DE fall-ZHE.
'The hail pounded on the roof with a rat-a-tat-tat.'

Other meteorological events tend to conform to the same pattern, albeit with different verbs.

出现了好多次闪电。
Chūxiànle hǎo duō cì shǎndiàn.
Appear-LE very many times lightning ('flash-electricity').
'There was a lot of lightning.'

8
Adjectives and Adverbs

52. Adjectives and Verbs

As noted in Section 26, adjectives like *rè* (热) 'hot' and *máng* (忙) 'busy' can act as predicates without the addition of a linking verb like "be." Unless they are rhythmically balanced (for example, *dì dà wù bó* (of China) 'land large, resources rich'), adjectives as predicates usually require at least a minimum of modification, even if it's nothing more than sentence *le*, the negative *bù*, or a minimal adverb like *hěn*.

Tā pàng le. (*pàng* 'be plump')
'He's gained weight.'

Jīntiān bú rè. (*rè* 'be hot')
'It's not hot today.'

Wǒ hěn máng. (*máng* 'be busy')
'I'm busy.'

Xīnli hěn bièniu.
Heart-in quite exasperated.
'[She] feels quite exasperated.'

Nongradable adjectives, such as *jiǎ* 'false' or a color like *huáng* 'yellow,' which are notionally all or nothing—it's either yellow or it's not—have to be nominalized to act as predicates. In this case, *shì* acts as the linking verb (as if it were between two nominals).

他说的都是假的。
Tā shuō de dōu shì jiǎ de.
'Everything he says is untrue.'

她的衬衫是黄的。
Tā de chènshān shì huáng de.
'Her blouse is yellow.'

Adjectives can be conjoined by the conjunction *ér* (而) 'and.'

暖和而晴朗的天气
nuǎnhuo ér qínglǎng de tiānqì
'warm, clear weather' ('weather that's warm and clear')

They can also be conjoined by the addition of the adverb *yòu* (又) before each adjective.

坐飞机又快又舒服。
Zuò fēijī yòu kuài yòu shūfu.
'Taking the plane is fast and comfortable.'

53. Adjectives as Transitive Verbs

A number of adjectives also function idiosyncratically as transitive verbs, with a sense of 'cause to be [adjective].' Comparable cases in English usually involve at least a slight shift in the form of the word: "hot" ~ "to heat," "clear" ~ "to clarify," "tired" ~ "to tire" (though "cool" undergoes no change). In the following example, *liáng* 'cool' is used as an adjective ('be cool'), while *rè* is used as a verb ('heat up').

饭菜都凉了，我给你热一热。
Fàncài dōu liáng le, wǒ gěi nǐ rè yi rè.
'The food's cold; I'll heat it up for you.'

One cannot predict which adjectives have this property. *Liáng* has a counterpart, *liàng* (with falling tone) 'cool': *bǎ chá liàng yi xiàr* 'cool off the tea.' But while *piányi* 'be inexpensive' has a special causative meaning of 'regard as cheap,' its opposite, *guì* 'expensive,' has only an adjectival meaning.

The following chart lists additional examples of adjectives that can function as transitive verbs.

Adjective	Adjectival Meaning	Transitive Verb Meaning	Example
dī	'be low'	'lower'	*dīzhe tóu zǒulù* 'walk with your head down'
jǐn	'be tight'	'tighten'	*jǐnjin xiédài* 'tighten your shoelaces'
lèi	'be tired'	'tire, wear out'	*Bié bǎ zìjǐ lèizhe!* 'Don't wear yourself out!'
máng	'be busy'	'be occupied with'	*Nǐ máng xiē shénme ne?* 'What are you up to?'
piányi	'be cheap'	'let [someone] off lightly' ('regard as cheap')	*Zhè huí suàn piányile nǐ!* 'This time you get off lightly!'

Adjective	Adjectival Meaning	Transitive Verb Meaning	Example
píng	'be level'	'level out'	*bǎ lù píng yi píng* 'smooth out the road'
qīngchu	'clear'	'be clear about'	*Wǒ shífēn qīngchu nà jiàn shì.* 'I'm fully aware of that fact.'
rè	'be hot'	'heat up'	*rè diǎnr shuǐ xǐ yīfu* 'heat up some water to do the washing'
sōng	'be loose'	'loosen'	*tā yì sōng shǒu* 'once he loosened his grip'

A few verbs of motion, such as *lái* 'come' and *shàng* 'go up,' commonly have causative functions; examples are *lái* 'come' ~ 'cause to come' (that is, 'bring') and *shàng* 'ascend' ~ 'cause to ascend' (that is, 'serve').

Lái ge báiqiējī, yí ge wǔxiāng-niúròu.
'Bring a poached chicken and a spicy beef [dish].'

Cài qǐng shàng màn yìdiǎnr.
'Please serve the food slowly.'

More idiomatically, *qù* 'go' may also mean 'cause to go' (that is, 'remove'): *tā bǎ yútóu qù le* 'he got rid of the fish head.'

54. Verb + Adjective Phrase + *yìdiǎnr*

Adjectives plus *yìdiǎnr*, which gives a comparative reading, also participate in a productive pattern in which they follow action verbs, with the sense of 'do _____ so as to be [faster, closer].' While the resulting verbal configuration (*shuō-kuài, zhàn-jìn*) recalls the resultative compound pattern discussed in Section 61, the properties of the combination are distinct enough to merit its own section. Here are some examples.

说快一点儿。
Shuō kuài yìdiǎnr.
Speak faster a-little.
'Speak a bit faster.'

站近一点儿。
Zhàn jìn yìdiǎnr.
Stand closer a-little.
'Stand a little closer.'

写大一点儿。
Xiě dà yìdiǎnr.
Write bigger a-little.
'Write it a bit bigger.'

走慢一点儿。
Zǒu màn yìdiǎnr.
Walk slower a-little.
'Walk a bit more slowly.'

放多一点儿。
Fàng duō yìdiǎnr.
Put more a-little.
'Put a bit more in.'

请把窗户打开。	窗户开着呢。	那，把它开大一点儿。
Qǐng bǎ chuānghu dǎkāi.	*Chuānghu kāizhe ne.*	*Nà, bǎ tā kāi dà yìdiǎnr.*
'Open the window, please.'	'The window's open.'	'Then, open it a bit wider.'

开慢一点儿，好不好? 安全第一。
Kāi màn yìdiǎnr, hǎo bu hǎo? Ānquán dì-yī.
'Drive a little more slowly, OK? Safety first!'

Test Yourself

Provide the Chinese versions of the following sentences.

1. Speak a little more slowly, please.
2. Write it a little bigger, please.
3. Let's put it up higher.

Possible Answers
1. *Shuō màn yìdiǎnr, hǎo bu hǎo?*
2. *Qǐng xiě dà yìdiǎnr.*
3. *Fàng gāo yìdiǎnr ba.*

Duō/shǎo (多/少) and *zǎo/wǎn* (早/晚) Before the Verb

A small subset of adjectives can also function as adverbs; they appear before the verb in conjunction with an object that follows and expresses an amount. For example, at the end of a meal, a host may urge you to eat more, using *duō* (多) in its adverbial function, meaning 'additionally.'

Méi shénme cài; qǐng nǐ duō chī yìdiǎnr!
Not any dishes; invite you more eat a-little!
'We've nothing special, but please do have a little more.'

This configuration is particularly common with *duō* (多), but its opposite, *shǎo* (少) 'few,' and the pair *zǎo* (早) 'early' and *wǎn* (晚) 'late' also appear in the same pattern, as illustrated in the following examples.

你少给了一块。
Nǐ shǎo gěile yí kuài.
'You're a dollar short.'

我们晚到了一个小时。
Wǒmen wǎn dàole yí ge xiǎoshí.
'We were an hour late.'

Test Yourself

Provide the Chinese versions of the following sentences.

1. Please bring another set of chopsticks (*kuàizi*). (To a waiter.)
2. You should eat fewer desserts. (*tiándiǎn* 'sweet-snacks')
3. Write it a little larger, please.
4. Speak a little more slowly, please.
5. Drink up!

Possible Answers

1. *Qǐng duō ná yì shuāng kuàizi.*
2. *Nǐ zuìhǎo shǎo chī yìdiǎnr tiándiǎn.*
3. *Qǐng xiě dà yìdiǎnr.*
4. *Qǐng shuō màn yìdiǎnr.*
5. *Duō hē yìdiǎnr ba.*

55. Vivid Reduplication

As noted in Section 43, action verbs reduplicate to convey a casual or unassuming tone: *Kànkan kěyǐ ma?* 'Mind if I look?' For such verbs, the reduplication takes the form of AA or ABAB (*xiūxi xiūxi*). Adjectives also reduplicate, but for them, reduplication conveys a lively or vivid tone; the form of the reduplication is AA or AABB.

An example of the AA form is found in the admonition to study hard and advance, often written near school entrances in China. *Hǎo* 'be well/good' is reduplicated to form an adverbial. (*Tiāntiān* in the second clause is a different form of reduplication that involves measure words.)

好好学习, 天天向上。
Hǎohǎo xuéxí, tiāntiān xiàng shàng.
Study hard and make progress every day.

An example of the AABB pattern is *huānghuangzhāngzhāng* 'flustered, in a rush, helter-skelter,' based on the adjective *huāngzhāng* (慌张) 'be flustered.'

The process of vivid reduplication is not freely productive; not all simplex adjectives have corresponding reduplicated forms, and not all reduplicated forms have corresponding simplex adjectives. For this reason, reduplicated forms have to be learned as vocabulary items, and in comprehensive dictionaries, they are listed separately.

Monosyllabic Adjectives

AA reduplicated forms are found mostly with gradable adjectives—those that permit degrees. For this reason, adjectives like *duì* 'right' and *cuò* 'wrong,' which are either-or notions, are not amenable to vivid reduplication. Generally, AA forms have favorable, or at least neutral, connotations, even if the base form does not: *lǎn* 'lazy,' but *lǎnlǎn de tǎng zài chuáng shàng* (懒懒地躺在床上) 'lying supinely on his bed.'

In colloquial rather than formal contexts in northern Mandarin, the repeated syllable in the more common expressions shifts to level tone (if it is not already level): *gāogāo* 'good and tall,' *hǎohāo* 'properly, as best one can' and *mànmān* 'nice and slow' (from *màn* 'slow'). In addition, northern speakers generally add an -*r* suffix along with the tonal shift: *gāogāor, hǎohāor, mànmānr*.

谁都躲得远远儿的。
Shéi dōu duǒ de yuǎnyuānr de.
Who all hide DE far DE.
'Everyone hid some distance away.'

咱们好好儿的玩儿几天。
Zánmen hǎohāor de wánr jǐ tiān.
'We thoroughly enjoyed ourselves for a few days.'

Disyllabic Adjectives

Not all disyllabic adjectives have reduplicated forms. *Róngyi* 'easy' does not, for example, nor does *rèqíng* 'enthusiastic, passionate.' Those that do, have primary stress on the final syllable (and secondary on the first), so if the simplex form has a neutral tone in the second syllable, full tone will be restored in the reduplication: *qīngchu* (清楚) 'be clear' ~ *qīngqīngchǔchǔ* 'crystal clear,' *kèqi* (客气) 'be polite' ~ *kèkèqiqì* 'courteous and cordial.' The second syllable of such four-syllable reduplications tends to be the least stressed and, in some cases, is pronounced (and listed in dictionaries) with neutral tone: *huāngzhāng* ~ *huānghuangzhāngzhāng* (as in an earlier example), *guīju* (规矩) 'be well behaved' ~ *guīguijǔjǔ*.

The Function of Reduplicated Forms

Reduplicated forms, whether AA or AABB, may function as adjectives or as adverbials. As adjectives, they may be attributives (modifiers) or predicatives;

in either case, they are usually followed by *de* (的). Thus, in the following nursery rhyme about tadpoles, *xì* 'delicate, thin' and *dà* 'big' are reduplicated as attributives.

> *Xiǎo kēdǒu, shuǐ li yóu, xìxì de wěiba, dàdà de tóu.*
> Small tadpole, water in swim, tiny DE tail, big DE head.
> 'The little tadpole swims in the water; his tail is tiny but his head is huge.'

In the following two examples, *yuǎn* 'far' and *gāodà* 'tall, lofty' are reduplicated as predicatives.

> 他生同学的气了，离他们远远的。
> *Tā shēng tóngxué de qì le, lí tāmen yuǎnyuǎn de.*
> He bear classmates DE anger LE, from them far DE.
> 'He was angry at his classmates, so he stayed well away from them.'

> 他像他老爸，高高大大的。
> *Tā xiàng tā lǎobà, gāogāo-dàdà de.*
> 'He's like his dad, tall and impressive.'

As adverbials, reduplicated forms directly precede the verb and are often followed by the adverbial marker *de* (地) (see Section 60).

> 请多多指教。
> *Qǐng duōduō zhǐjiào.*
> Invite more advice.
> 'Comments welcome.' (a polite formula, used when asking for comments on one's work)

> 她告别了朋友们，高高兴兴地上路了。
> *Tā gàobiéle péngyoumen, gāogāoxìngxìng de shànglù le.* (*gāoxìng* 'be happy')
> She take-leave-of-LE friends, happily DE on-road LE.
> 'She said goodbye to her friends and happily set off on her way.'

Idiosyncratic Cases

As noted above, some AABB forms have no AB root at all. There is no word *guǐsuì*, for example, that corresponds to *guǐguǐsuìsuì* (鬼鬼祟祟) 'furtive.' Moreover, even when a simplex form exists, it is not always an adjective; *tōutōu* 'stealthily' derives from the verb *tōu* 'steal.' A verb *yóuyù* 'hesitate, waver' is at the base of the following example.

> 别犹犹豫豫的了！
> *Bié yóuyóu-yùyù de le!*
> Don't dawdle!

The ABAB Pattern

There are a few exceptional cases that seem to qualify as vivid adjectives even though they show the ABAB pattern: *xuěbáixuěbái* (雪白雪白) 'snowy white' (from *xuěbái* 'snowy white' (*xuě* 'snow' + *bái* 'white')). However, cases such as the following, which may appear at first glance to derive from adjectives, turn out *not* to be cases of vivid reduplication of adjectives.

我宁可在家里轻松轻松。
Wǒ nìngkě zài jiā li qīngsōng qīngsōng.
I rather at home in relax.
'I'd rather take it easy at home.'

Qīngsōng is one of a small subset of adjectives that can have stative and causative meaning, in this case, 'be relaxed' as well as 'cause to be relaxed.' The adjectival sense reduplicates with the expected AABB pattern (*qīngqīngsōngsōng*), while the causative reduplicates with the ABAB pattern of action verbs, that is, *qīngsōng qīngsōng.* A number of other adjectives, such as *gāoxìng* 'happy' and *liángkuài* 'cool,' have the same features. Often, an explicit causative verb like *ràng* (see pivot verbs in Section 78) is also present.

他讲了几个笑话让大家高兴高兴了。
Tā jiǎngle jǐ ge xiàohuà ràng dàjiā gāoxìng gāoxìng le.
He tell-LE several M jokes make everyone happy LE.
'He told several jokes to cheer everyone up.'

Partial Reduplications

Finally, it should be noted that Chinese also has a rich repertoire of partial reduplications, such as the ABB pattern, that can also function as adjectives or adverbials.

他慢腾腾，酸溜溜地微笑了一下。
Tā màntēngtēng, suānliūliū de wēixiàole yi xiàr.
He slow-tengteng, sour-liuliu DE smile-LE an occasion.
'He broke into a slow, mournful smile.'

他整个夏天都懒洋洋的，这使他的父亲很生气。
Tā zhěnggè xiàtiān dōu lǎnyángyáng de, zhè shǐ tā de fùqin hěn shēngqì.
He whole summer all indolent DE, this make his DE father quite angry.
'He spent the whole summer lazing around, which really annoyed his father.'

56. Adverbs

At its core, the adverb category consists of words specialized for adverbial positions that involve time, degree, intensification, and manner ("how"). In Chinese, adverbs vary in their proximity and attachment to the verb. Some appear only directly before the verb, others can appear before the subject as well as after it (and before the verb), and a few can appear without any verbal support at all.

Preverbal Adverbs

This group includes all monosyllabic adverbs and quite a few disyllabic ones, as well. The list that follows includes most of the adverbs that would appear in an introductory Chinese course.

也 *yě* 'also'	都 *dōu* 'all'	很 *hěn* 'quite'	挺 *tǐng* 'very'
更 *gèng* 'even more'	还 *hái* 'still, yet'	只 *zhǐ* 'only'	就 *jiù* 'then'
才 *cái* 'only; then and only then'	刚 *gāng* 'just, a short while ago'	再 *zài* 'and then, again'	常 *cháng* 'often'
老 *lǎo* 'always'	倒 *dào* 'actually, contrary to expectations'	已经 *yǐjing* 'already'	马上 *mǎshàng* 'right away'
总是 *zǒngshì* 'always'	一块儿 *yíkuàir* = 一起 *yìqǐ* 'together with'	几乎 *jīhu* 'almost'	比较 *bǐjiào* 'rather, relatively'
先 *xiān* 'first of all'	十分 *shífēn* '100%, completely'	又 yòu 'again, in addition'	太 tài 'too, very'

Movable Adverbs

Some adverbs can appear before or after the subject. Here are examples, with *yígòng* 'altogether' and *guǒrán* 'as expected, sure enough.'

我们班一共有十五个同学。	~ 一共我们班有十五个同学。
Wǒmen bān yígòng yǒu 15 ge tóngxué.	~ *Yígòng wǒmen bān yǒu 15 ge tóngxué.*
'Our class has 15 students altogether.'	~ 'Altogether, our class has 15 students.'
我果然没说服他。	~ 果然，我没说服他。
Wǒ guǒrán méi shuōfú tā.	~ *Guǒrán, wǒ méi shuōfú tā.*
I as-expected not persuade him.	
'I failed to persuade him, as expected.'	~ 'As expected, I failed to persuade him.'

Other adverbs in this category include the following.

大概 *dàgài* 'probably'   恐怕 *kǒngpà*   也许 *yěxǔ* 'maybe,
                          'be afraid that;   perhaps'
                           probably'
一定 *yídìng* 'for sure,   原来 *yuánlái*   终于 *zhōngyú* 'finally,
   certainly'   'as it turns out'   at last'
本来 *běnlái*   当然 *dāngrán*   反正 *fǎnzhèng* 'anyway'
   'originally'   'of course'

Free Adverbs

A number of movable adverbs can appear without any verbal support at all.

Yígòng duōshao?
'How many altogether?'

Bù yídìng.
'Not necessarily.'

Yěxǔ.
'Possibly, probably.'

Yǒu shíhou.
'At times.'

Other Sources of Adverbials

While words specialized for adverbial positions are of high frequency, the repertoire of adverbs is greatly enlarged by words that function both as adjectives and adverbs. Some are monosyllabic: *màn* 'slow/slowly,' *kuài* 'fast/quickly,' *duō* 'many/more,' *hǎo* 'good/very.'

Kuài zǒu, bú yào chídào le!   *Màn zǒu, màn zǒu.*
'Come on, we can't be late!'   'Take it easy!'

More often, adverbials are formed from adjectival phrases (*hěn kuài* 'very fast' ~ *hěn kuài de* 'quickly'). These tend to be marked by a following *de* (地). Here are two sentential examples.

怎么样才能很快地减肥？
Zěnmeyàng cái néng hěn kuài de jiǎnféi?
How then-and-only-then can very quickly DE lose-weight?
'How can one lose weight quickly?'

他很不舒服地坐在了凳子上。
Tā hěn bù shūfu de zuò zàile dèngzi shang.
He very not comfortable DE sit at-LE stool on.
'He sat on the stool in some discomfort.'

More common than phrasal combinations in the adverbial position are disyllabic adjectives, with or without the adverbial marker *de* (地).

Adjective	**Example**
nàixīn 'be patient'	*nàixīn de jiěshì* 'explain patiently'
yònggōng 'be hard-working'	*yònggōng xuéxí* 'study hard'
rènzhēn 'conscientious'	*rènzhēn duìdài* 'treat seriously'

毫不客气地提出了警告
háo bú kèqi de tíchūle jǐnggào (kèqi 'be polite')
in-the-least not polite DE mention-LE warning
'issued a warning in the most direct terms'

There is a large number of such disyllabic adjectives; a few are listed below.

特别 *tèbié* 'special/specially'	平常 *píngcháng* 'usual/usually'
努力 *nǔlì* 'hard-working; with effort, hard'	严厉 *yánlì* 'strict/strictly'
好奇 *hàoqí* 'curious/curiously'	热烈 *rèliè* 'enthusiastic/ enthusiastically'
懒惰 *lǎnduò* 'lazy/lazily'	慷慨 *kāngkǎi* 'generous/ generously'

Reduplicated Forms

Reduplicated forms, of two syllables (AA) or four (AABB), are particularly common as adverbials. They are often followed by the adverbial marker *de* (地).

懒懒地晒着太阳
lǎnlǎn de shàizhe tàiyang (lǎn 'be lazy')
lazily DE soak-up-ZHE sun
'relax and soak up the sun'

kāikāi-xīnxīn de guò rìzi (kāixīn 'happy')
'pass the time happily'

guīgui-jǔjǔ de zuò shēngyì (guīju 'well-behaved')
'conduct business properly'

As noted in Section 55, not all reduplicated forms have a corresponding simplex form and not all of them derive from adjectives. For example, there is no simplex form **jiàn* that corresponds to *jiànjiàn de* (渐渐地) 'gradually.' Nor is there a simplex form **bèngtiào* that corresponds to the reduplicated adverbial *bèngbeng-tiàotiào* 'bouncy and vivacious,' illustrated in the following example.

他蹦蹦跳跳地来到我面前，笑咪咪地跟我说：…
Tā bèngbeng-tiàotiào de láidào wǒ miànqián, xiàomīmī de gēn wǒ shuō: ...
He in-a-bouncy-fashion DE come-up me face-before, with-a-smile DE
  with me say: . . .
'He bounced up to me, and said to me with a smile: . . .'

In the following example, *yáoyáo-huànghuàng* is based on the verb *yáo-huang* 'sway, shake,' rather than on an adjective.

他摇摇晃晃地走回家去了。
Tā yáoyáo-huànghuàng de zǒu hui jia qu le.
'He staggered home.'

Four-Character Expressions

Another preferred category of adverbials is four-syllable (four-character) "elaborate expressions" (see Section 27). These adverbials are numerous, and like the Beijing expression in the second example below, often regional or local in usage.

我漫无目的地上了公交。
Wǒ mànwúmùdì de shàngle gōngjiāo.
I hit-or-miss DE got-on-LE bus.
'I got on a bus without knowing where it was going.'

如今它也蔫不溜秋儿地消失了。
Rújīn tā yě niānbuliūqiūr de xiāoshī le.
Nowadays also stealthily DE disappear LE.
'Without much ado, it has disappeared from view.' (of a type of food)

Onomatopoeia

Numerous onomatopoeic or otherwise sound-symbolic expressions also appear in the adverbial position. These may be reduplicative (*dīngding-dāngdāng*) or elaborate (*pīlipālā*).

雨滴丁丁当当地打着窗棂。
Yǔdī dīngding-dāngdāng de dǎzhe chuānglíng.
Raindrops ding-dang DE hit-ZHE window-frame.
'Raindrops drummed against the window frame.'

爸爸噼里啪啦地打蚊子的声音很烦人。
Bàba pīlipālā de dǎ wénzi de shēngyīn hěn fánrén.
Dad slap-splat DE hit mosquitoes DE noise very annoying.
'The noise of dad slapping mosquitoes is very annoying.'

57. Predicate Complements

In some cases, English adverbials are expressed as predicates in Chinese.

你汉语说得真好!

Nǐ Hànyǔ shuō de zhēn hǎo!

You Chinese speak DE truly good.

'You speak Chinese really well!'

The order of words in both languages turns out to be much the same. The Chinese construction is quite different from the English, however; it involves the presence of the particle *de* (得) between the verb and the adjectival phrase. The adjectival phrase in the example above, *zhēn hǎo*, has the form of an ordinary predicate: "[It]'s really good." For this reason, the construction is usually called a "predicate complement."

Another characteristic of the construction is that because the intermediary *de* is placed directly after the verb, any object has to be displaced. The object appears in a position before the verb, as in the example above, or the verb is repeated, first with the object, and then with *de* and the adjectival phrase, as in the example below, where *jiǎngkè* is a verb-plus-object glossed as 'explain-lesson.'

他讲课讲得很清楚。

Tā jiǎngkè jiǎng de hěn qīngchu.

He explain-lesson explain DE very clear.

'He lectures very well.'

The following examples show the versatility of the predicate-complement construction.

她长得高高大大的。

Tā zhǎng de gāogāo-dàdà de.

She grow DE big and tall DE.

'She's grown up so tall!'

她住得很近。

Tā zhù de hěn jìn.

She live DE quite close.

'She lives close by.'

他写汉字写得好不好?

Tā xiě Hànzì xiě de hǎo bu hǎo?

He write characters write DE good not good?

'Does he write characters well?'

Predicate Complements Versus Manner Adverbials

As noted above, predicate complements generally correspond to English adverbials: *shuō de zhēn hǎo* 'speak really well.' However, Chinese also has adverbial constructions that place adverbs—often in reduplicated form—before the verb and that also correspond to adverbs in English: *hǎohǎo xuéxí* 'study well' (see Section 56). How are the two different?

The difference is subtle. The predicate complement focuses on result: *Shuō de zhēn hǎo.* Adverbials focus on process: *Hǎohǎo xuéxi.* Typically, evaluations take the form of a predicate complement, while instructions take the form of an adverbial modifier.

EVALUATION   *Nǐ xiě de hěn hǎo.*
               'You wrote it very nicely.'
INSTRUCTION   *Qǐng hǎohāor bǎ nǐ de míngzi xiě zai hēibǎn shang.*
               'Write your name carefully on the blackboard, please.'

Test Yourself

Provide the Chinese versions of the following sentences.

1. You write characters well.
2. I like to sing, but I don't sing well (*chàng gē*).
3. She cooks very well. (*zuòfàn* 'cook,' *hǎojíle* 'extremely well')
4. Look, he's running so fast!
5. We'd better get out of here quickly! (*líkāi* 'leave')

Possible Answers
1. *Nǐ xiězì xiě de hěn hǎo.*
2. *Wǒ hěn xǐhuan chànggē, kěshì chàng de bù hǎo.*
3. *Tā zuòfàn zuò de hǎojíle.*
4. *Nǐ kàn, tā pǎo de hěn kuài!*
5. *Wǒmen zuìhǎo kuàikuài líkāi!*

58. Comparison

In the right context, comparison can be implied by the plain adjective.

Tāmen shéi gāo?   *Tā gāo.*
'Which of them is taller?' 'She's taller.'

The comparison can be made explicit by using the preposition *bǐ* (比) 'than,' which as a full verb means 'compare.' The construction is A *bǐ* B Adjective <Amount>.

Tā bǐ wǒ gāo.
'She's taller than I.'

Modification of a comparative ("a bit taller," "much taller") follows the adjective (see Section 59 for a more complete listing).

Tā bǐ wǒ gāo yìdiǎnr.
'She's a bit taller than I.'

Càishìchǎng bǐ chāoshì yuǎn yì lǐ duō lù.
'The fresh food market is a mile or so farther than the supermarket.'

Changing Perspective

The *bǐ* construction can be negated: *Tā bù bǐ wǒ gāo.* 'She's not taller than I.' It is more common, however, to change the perspective by saying "not as . . . as": A *bǐ* B Adjective is negated as B *méi<yǒu>* A *<nàme>* Adjective.

我没有她那么高。
Wǒ méi<yǒu> tā <nàme> gāo.
I not-as she so tall.
'I'm not as tall as she.'

A formal alternative for *méiyǒu* in this context is *bùrú* (不如), which, with no adjective mentioned, means 'not as good as.' *Bùrú* is common in sayings.

百闻不如一见。
Bǎi wén bùrú yí jiàn.
One hundred hear not-as-good-as one see.
'Nothing beats seeing it for yourself.'

Specific adjectives can be added, aligning the *bùrú* construction with the *méiyǒu* construction.

Běijīng bùrú Shànghǎi dà. ~ *Běijīng méiyǒu Shànghǎi <nàme> dà.*
'Beijing's not as big as Shanghai.'

Equality

The *méiyǒu* construction just illustrated expresses lack of equality ("not as"). A positive version, with *yǒu*, indicates equality attained in regard to an adjectival quality.

Jiějie yǒu nǐ nàme cōngmíng ma?	*Yǒu, qíshí tā bǐ wǒ cōngmíng.*
Your sister have you so smart MA?	Yes; actually she than I smart.
'Is your older sister as smart as you?'	'She is. Actually, she's smarter than I.'

Equality may also be expressed with the adjective *yíyàng* (一样) 'same,' often in conjunction with the verb xiàng (像) 'be like, resemble' or with the conjunction gēn (跟) 'and, with' or hé (和) 'and': A xiàng ~ gēn ~ hé B (bù) *yíyàng 'A is (not) the same as B.'*

她的口音像你的一样。

Tā de kǒuyīn xiàng nǐde yíyàng.

Her DE accent like yours same.

'Her accent is like yours.'

日本的跟韩国的价钱不一样。

Rìběn de gēn Hánguó de jiàqián bù yíyàng.

Japan DE and Korea DE price not same.

'The price of the Japanese one isn't the same as the Korean.'

Yíyàng can also be used as an adverbial with a following adjective, meaning 'equally.'

他和我一样高。

Tā hé wǒ yíyàng gāo.

He and I same tall.

'He's the same height as I.'

这药像胆汁一样苦。

Zhè yào xiàng dǎnzhī yíyàng kǔ.

This medicine like bile same bitter.

'This medicine is as bitter as bile.'

Test Yourself

Provide the Chinese versions of the following sentences.

1. It's got a bit hotter this week.
2. She's not as busy as I am.
3. Walking is faster than taking a taxi. (*zǒulù* 'walk,' *dǎ dī* 'take a taxi')
4. She's a bit taller than I am.
5. Taking the train costs the same as flying. (*zuò huǒchē* 'take a train,' *zuò fēijī* 'take a plane')
6. He and I are not equally tall.
7. Is summer as cool as spring here? (*xiàtiān* 'summer,' *chūntiān* 'spring,' *liángkuài* 'pleasantly cool')

Possible Answers

1. *Zhèi ge xīngqī rè le yìdiǎnr.*
2. *Tā méiyǒu wǒ nàme máng. ~ Tā bùrú wǒ máng.*
3. *Zǒulù bǐ dǎ dī kuài.*
4. *Tā bǐ wǒ gāo yìdiǎnr.*
5. *Zuò huǒchē gēn zuò fēijī yíyàng guì.*
6. *Tā hé wǒ bù yíyàng gāo.*
7. *Zhèr xiàtiān yǒu chūntiān nàme liángkuài ma?*

Comparison with Evaluation

Comparisons with *bǐ* occur in predicate-complement constructions (*shuō de hěn hǎo*). There are two options: (1) the predicate complement can be stated first (*shuō de {bǐ wǒ hǎo}*) or (2) the comparison can be stated first (*bǐ wǒ {shuō de hǎo}*).

他汉语说得比我好。

Tā Hànyǔ shuō de {bǐ wǒ hǎo}.
'She speaks Chinese better than I do.'

他汉语比我说得好。

Tā Hànyǔ bǐ wǒ {shuō de hǎo}.

Test Yourself

Provide the Chinese versions of the following sentences. Express each sentence in two ways.

1. He drives more wildly than I do. (*kāi* (*chē*) 'drive (a car),' *měng* 'violent, wild')
2. He writes characters more neatly than I do. (*guīju* 'well-behaved, neat')

Possible Answers

1. *Tā kāi de bǐ wǒ měng.* ~ *Tā bǐ wǒ kāi de měng.*
2. *Tā xiězì xiě de bǐ wǒ guīju.* ~ *Tā xiězì bǐ wǒ xiě de guīju.*

59. Intensifiers

Absolute Intensifiers

Adjectives can be intensified or toned down (1) by the addition of adverbials in the preverbal position or (2) by means of various postadjectival elements. Adverbial modifiers include *yǒu yìdiǎnr* (有一点儿) 'quite, a bit,' *hěn* (很) 'quite,' and *fēicháng* (非常) 'extremely, very.'

这刀子: 有<一>点儿快 / 很快 / 非常快。

Zhè dāozi: yǒu <yì>diǎnr kuài / hěn kuài / fēicháng kuài.
'This knife is a bit sharp / quite sharp / unusually sharp.'

Postadjectival intensifiers include *jíle* (极了) 'extremely' ('to the extreme'), *de hěn* (得很) 'very,' and *bùdéliǎo* (不得了) 'extremely' ('not-get-finish').

这刀子: 快得很 / 快极了 / 快得不得了。

Zhè dāozi: kuài de hěn / kuàijíle / kuài de bùdéliǎo.
'This knife is very sharp / extremely sharp / super sharp.'

Adjectives may also be intensified by full clauses linked with *de* (得).

今天冷得谁都不敢出去。
Jīntiān lěng de shéi dōu bù gǎn chūqu.
Today cold DE anyone all not dare go-out.
'It's so cold today no one dares to go out.'

他糊涂得连自己的名字也想不起来了。
Tā hútu de lián zìjǐ de míngzi yě xiǎng bu qǐlai le.
He muddled DE even own DE name also think not rise LE.
'He's so muddled, he can't even recall his own name.'

Intensification in Comparisons

Comparative intensifiers follow their adjectives. When associated with change of state or current relevance, *yìdiǎnr* may also follow sentence *le*.

她高了一点儿。
Tā gāo le yìdiǎnr.
'She's grown a bit taller.'

Intensification ranges from *yìdiǎnr* to *de duō* to *duōle*. Alternatively, an exact amount can be placed in postverbal position, as well: *yí cùn* 'one inch,' *yì lǐ lù* 'one mile (of route).'

她比我: 高一点儿 / 高得多 / 高多了 / 高两寸。
Tā bǐ wǒ: gāo yìdiǎnr / gāo de duō / gāo duōle / gāo liǎng cùn.
'She's a bit taller / much taller / a great deal taller / taller by two inches than I.'

你这样安排好得多得多了。
Nǐ zhèi yàng ānpái hǎo de duō de duō le.
This way arrange better DE much DE much LE.
'This arrangement is very much better.'

上海人口比北京的多几百万。
Shànghǎi rénkǒu bǐ Běijīng de duō jǐ bǎiwàn.
Shanghai population than Beijing DE more several million.
'Shanghai's population is greater than Beijing's by several million.'

60. The Three *de*s

Sections 33, 56, and 57 deal with three types of constructions involving particles pronounced *de*. Conveniently, the different functions associated with this syllable are distinguished by the writing system: modifying *de* is written

的, predicate complement *de* is written 得, and adverbial *de* is written 地. This section presents a synopsis of their usage and includes 得 functions that will be encountered in Section 63.

的 *de* (see Section 33)

Modifying *de* is written 的.

Possession

我的
wǒ de
'mine'

我的伞
wǒ de sǎn
'my umbrella'

Modification

人类最好的朋友
rénlèi zuì hǎo de péngyou
'man's best friend'

中国人穿的衣服
Zhōngguórén chuān de yīfu
'clothes worn by Chinese'

Nominalized Phrase

穿短裤的
chuān duǎnkù de
'people who wear shorts'

右边儿的是谁?
Yòu biānr de shì shéi?
'Who's the one on the right?'

Shì-de Construction

是今天上午才回来的。
Shì jīntiān shàngwǔ cái huílái de.
'[I] didn't get back until this morning.'

Emphasis

炒鸭掌我是吃不来的。
Chǎoyāzhǎng wǒ shì chībulái de.
Stir-fried-duck-feet I be eat-not-able DE.
'I'm just not fond of stir-fried duck feet.'

得 *de* (see Sections 57 and 63)

Predicate complement *de* is written 得, which also represents the words *děi* 'must, need to' and *dé* 'obtain, get.'

Predicate Complement

写得又快又清楚
xiě de yòu kuài yòu qīngchu
write DE both fast and clear
'writes fast and clear'

Potential Compound

听得懂
tīngdedǒng
'able to understand'

Intensification

冷得很
lěng de hěn
'very cold'

冷得不得了
lěng de bùdéliǎo
'extremely cold'

冷得谁都不敢出去
lěng de shéi dōu bù gǎn chūqu
'so cold no one dares to go out'

地 *de* (see Section 56)

Adverbial *de* is written 地, which also represents the word *dì* 'place.'

不停地来来往往
bùtíng de láilái wǎngwǎng
without-stopping DE come and go
'endlessly coming and going'

渐渐地恢复起来了
jiànjiàn de huīfù qǐlai le
gradually DE recover rise LE
'gradually recover'

9
Complex Verbs

61. Resultative Verb Compounds

In Chinese, the core functions of a verb are often elaborated by the addition of a second verb that indicates result; the combination is often called a "resultative verb compound." For example, *tīng* 'hear' combines with *dǒng* 'comprehend' to form *tīngdǒng* (听懂), literally, 'hear and understand,' that is, 'understand.' *Mǎi* 'buy' combines with *dào* 'arrive, reach' to form *mǎidào* (买到) 'buy and succeed,' that is, 'manage to buy.' Here are other examples of resultative verb compounds.

看见	*kànjiàn*	'see' ('look-perceive')
做完	*zuòwán*	'complete' ('do-finish')
打死	*dǎsǐ*	'kill' ('hit-die')
洗干净	*xǐgānjìng*	'clean' ('wash-clean')
睡着	*shuìzháo*	'get to sleep' ('sleep-succeed')
拿走	*názǒu*	'take away' ('take-leave')
卖掉	*màidiào*	'sell off' ('sell-drop')

A sense of the range of resultative verb compounds can be gained from the following four examples, which involve modifications on the verb *chī* 'eat.'

小宝贝吃惯了奶瓶，不吃母乳，怎么办？
Xiǎo bǎobèi chīguànle nǎipíng, bù chī mǔrǔ, zěnme bàn? ('eat-be accustomed')
'"Little treasure" has gotten used to feeding from a bottle and won't breast-feed; what should we do?'

谢谢，不吃了，我吃饱了。
Xièxie, bù chī le, wǒ chībǎo le. ('eat-full')
'No more, thanks; I'm full.' (on being offered more food)

我已经吃腻了美食！

Wǒ yǐjing chīnìle měishí! ('eat-cloying')

'I've had enough of rich food!'

吃好早餐事半功倍。

Chīhǎo zǎocān shìbàn-gōngbèi. ('eat-good')

Eat-proper breakfast business-half success-twice.

'Eating a good breakfast gives you twice the bang for half the buck.'

Resultative verb compounds are comparable to English phrasal verbs, which consist of a verb and particle (typically, an adverb or preposition): "hand in," "hand out," "clam up," "wind down," and so on. Like the result verbs in the Chinese compounds, the English particles are drawn from a limited set, and many of the combinations are idiosyncratic and have to be learned: "die off" (not "die up") and "mess up" (not "mess off"). In Chinese, a repertoire of resultative verb compounds has to be built up incrementally on the basis of examples in context.

A large number of verbs can appear in second position in resultative verb compounds. The following chart lists common result verbs on the left and typical first verbs with which they combine on the right. A pound sign (#) signifies that the number of possible combinations is few or limited to the ones shown. An ellipsis (. . .) signifies that the number of possible combinations is large or not listable.

Chinese	Pinyin	Gloss	Example(s)
饱	*bǎo*	'be full'	*chībǎo* 'eat one's fill,' *hēbǎo* 'drink one's fill' #
错	*cuò*	'be mistaken'	*xiěcuò* 'write incorrectly,' *rèncuò* 'wrongly recognize,' *gǎocuò* 'mistake [something] for,' *shuōcuò* 'say it wrong' . . .
倒	*dǎo*	'topple'	*shuāidǎo* 'fall down,' *guādǎo* 'be blown over' . . .
到	*dào*	'reach'	*zhǎodào* 'manage to find,' *mǎidào* 'manage to buy,' *shōudào* 'receive,' *zuòdào* 'succeed in doing' . . .
掉	*diào*	'fall off, drop' ~ 'disappear'	*sǐdiào* 'die,' *wàngdiào* 'forget,' *màidiào* 'sell' . . .
懂	*dǒng*	'understand'	*kàndǒng* 'understand (by seeing),' *tīngdǒng* 'understand (by listening),' *nòngdǒng* 'try to make sense of' #
对	*duì*	'be correct'	*xiěduì* 'write correctly,' *tīngduì* 'hear correctly' . . .

Chinese	Pinyin	Gloss	Example(s)
光	guāng	'smooth' ~ 'bare, use up'	*màiguāng* 'sell out,' *chīguāng* 'eat [it] all up' . . .
过	guò	'pass'	*zǒuguò* 'walk by,' *cuòguò* 'miss [an opportunity]' . . .
好	hǎo	'well' ~ 'do to satisfaction'	*zuòhǎo* 'finish,' *zhǔnbèihǎo* 'get ready,' *kǎohǎo* 'finish an exam,' *bànhǎo* 'finish dealing with' . . .
会	huì	'master'	*xuéhuì* 'learn' #
见	jiàn	'perceive'	*kànjiàn* 'see,' *tīngjiàn* 'hear,' *pèngjiàn* 'run into [someone]' #
开	kāi	'open up'	*dǎkāi* 'open up,' *lākāi* 'pull open,' *zǒukāi* 'clear off' . . .
腻	nì	'bored with'	*tīngnì* 'fed up with hearing,' *chīnì* 'had enough of' . . .
清楚	qīngchu	'clear'	*shuō qīngchu* 'say clearly,' *gǎo qīngchu* 'make clear' . . .
死	sǐ	'die' ~ 'to death'	*dǎsǐ* 'beat to death,' *shāsǐ* 'slay' . . .
完	wán	'finish'	*zuòwán* 'finish doing,' *xiěwán* 'finish writing' . . .
着	zháo	'hit the mark' ~ 'manage to'	*mǎizháo* 'manage to buy,' *zhǎozháo* 'find successfully,' *shuìzháo* 'get to sleep' . . .
住	zhù	'stay' ~ 'stick, fix'	*názhù* 'catch,' *wènzhù* 'stump (by questioning),' *jìzhù* 'remember,' *kǎzhù* 'jam, clog,' *tiēzhù* 'affix' ('stick-fix') . . .
走	zǒu	'leave'	*názǒu* 'take away,' *tōuzǒu* 'steal,' *bānzǒu* 'move away' . . .

Test Yourself

Provide the Chinese versions of the following sentences.

1. Have you finished your assignment? (*zuòyè* 'assignment')
2. Open the window. (*chuānghu* 'window')
3. I'm full; I can't eat any more.
4. Did you remember?
5. I didn't see her.
6. Food's ready.
7. They've sold out of today's paper. (*jīntiān de bào* 'today's paper')

8. You've written it wrong.
9. We didn't find the keys. (*yàoshi* 'key')
10. Mind you don't fall down. (*xiǎoxīn* 'be careful')

Possible Answers

1. *Zuòyè zuòwán le ma?*
2. *Bǎ chuānghu dǎkāi.*
3. *Wǒ chībǎo le, bù néng zài chī le.*
4. *Jìzhù le ma?*
5. *Wǒ méi kànjiàn tā.*
6. *Fàn zuòhǎo le.*
7. *Jīntiān de bào màiguāng le.*
8. *Nǐ xiěcuò le.*
9. *Yàoshi méi zhǎozháo.*
10. *Xiǎoxīn shuāidǎo.*

The Versatility of Resultative Verb Compounds

Only the most common resultative verbs are listed in the chart above. The pattern is very productive and allows all sorts of linguistic creativity. One writer on a Chinese blog, for example, described two students facing the pressure of examinations in the following succinct way.

一个考哭了，一个考吐了。
Yí ge kǎokūle, yí ge kǎotùle.
1 M test-cry-LE, 1 M test-vomit-LE.
'One cried on account of the test, one threw up on account of the test.'

In other cases, the addition of a result verb to an otherwise intransitive verb can introduce a relevant body part as an object. For example, *kū* 'cry' can combine with *zhǒng* 'swell' in a resultative compound that requires the addition of *yǎnjing* 'eyes.' In the case of "cry," English achieves more or less the same effect with the addition of "out," as the following example shows.

他哭肿了眼睛。
Tā kūzhǒngle yǎnjing.
'He cried his eyes out.'

Superficially, this sentence is a blend of two sentences: *Tā kū le.* 'He cried.' and *Tā yǎnjing zhǒng le.* 'His eyes swelled.' In the blended sentence, however, the body part becomes the object of the resultative compound: *kūzhǒng yǎnjing* 'cry the eyes swollen.' Other examples follow.

她哭红了眼睛。
Tā kūhóngle yǎnjing.
'She cried till her eyes were red.'

站疼了脚，怎么办？

Zhànténgle jiǎo, zěnme bàn?

Stand-hurt-LE feet, how deal-with?

'What do you do when your feet hurt from standing?'

吃饱肚子也能减肥吗？

Chībǎo dùzi yě néng jiǎnféi ma?

Eat-full stomach also can lose-weight MA?

'Can you eat your fill and still lose weight?'

62. Directional Verb Compounds

Directional verb compounds can be considered a subclass of resultative verb compounds. They may be composed of an action verb plus *lái* (来) 'come' or *qù* (去) 'go,' indicating direction toward the speaker or away from the speaker, respectively. In this function, *lái* and *qù* are usually unstressed (and untoned). Here is an example of each with the verb *ná* 'carry.'

我给你拿来吧。	我给你拿去吧.
Wǒ gěi nǐ nálai ba.	*Wǒ gěi nǐ náqu ba.*
'I'll get it for you.'	'I'll take it for you.'

Action verbs may also be complemented by one of seven verbs of directed movement.

上	*shàng*	'go up' ~ 'up; on'
下	*xià*	'go down' ~ 'down'
进	*jìn*	'enter' ~ 'in'
出	*chū*	'exit' ~ 'out'
过	*guò*	'pass' ~ 'over'
回	*huí*	'return' ~ 'back'
起	*qǐ*	'rise' ~ 'up'

As complements, these verbs create shifts in meaning, as shown in the following examples.

考上大学	*kǎoshang dàxué*	'pass an entrance exam for a university'
戴上帽子	*dàishang màozi*	'put on a hat'
坐下	*zuòxià*	'sit down'
走进教室	*zǒujìn jiàoshì*	'walk into the room'
提起一件事	*tíqǐ yí jiàn shì*	'bring up an issue'

These directional verb compounds are often expanded with the addition of the directional particles *lái* and *qù*, forming 13 possible combinations.

(*Qǐqu does not occur—presumably because it is semantically anomalous to both raise something and remove it at the same time.) The following chart shows all possible combinations of the seven verbs of movement and the two directional particles.

Movement Verb	*lái* Combination	*qù* Combination
shàng 'up'	*shànglai* 'come up'	*shàngqu* 'go up'
xià 'down'	*xiàlai* 'come down'	*xiàqu* 'go down'
jìn 'in'	*jìnlai* 'come in'	*jìnqu* 'go in'
chū 'out'	*chūlai* 'come out'	*chūqu* 'go out'
guò 'over'	*guòlai* 'come over'	*guòqu* 'go over'
huí 'back'	*huílai* 'come back'	*huíqu* 'go back'
qǐ 'rise'	*qǐlai* 'come up'	—

Meanings are mostly additive, as the following examples show.

ná shànglai 'bring it up here'   *ná xiàqu* 'take it down there'
fàng jìnlai 'put it in here'   *fàng jìnqu* 'put it in there'
zǒu guòlai 'walk over here'   *zǒu guòqu* 'walk over there'
zhàn qǐlai 'stand up'

However, just as English particles such as "on" and "up" have gained idiomatic meanings ("put on" versus "move on," "lift up" versus "shut up"), certain directional verb combinations have come to have idiomatic meanings. This is particularly true of the *qǐlai* combination, in which the literal sense of 'rise up' or 'upward' is extended to 'rise in number,' 'recall,' and 'when it comes to.'

来宾多起来了。
Láibīn duō qǐlai le.
'There have been a lot more visitors.'

说起来容易，做起来难。
Shuō qǐlai róngyi, zuò qǐlai nán.
'Talking about it is easy, [but] doing it is not.'

想了半天也没想起来。
Xiǎngle bàntiān yě méi xiǎng qǐlai.
Think-LE a-long-time also not-have think up.
'I tried for a long time, but just couldn't remember it.'

Other combinations may also have specialized meanings; examples include *shàngqu* 'appraise outwardly,' *xiàlai* 'record,' and *chūlai* 'figure out.'

那些花看上去是假的。
Nèi xiē huā kàn shàngqu shì jiǎ de.
Those several flowers look on-away be fake ones.
'Those flowers look fake.'

我把号码记下来，好不好？
Wǒ bǎ hàomǎ jì xiàlai, hǎo bu hǎo?
I BA number note down-come, OK not OK?
'Let me jot down the number, OK?'

我可以从她的口音上听出来她是新加坡人。
Wǒ kěyǐ cóng tāde kǒuyīn shang tīng chūlai tā shì Xīnjiāpō rén.
I can from her accent on hear out-come she be Singapore person.
'I can tell from her accent that she's from Singapore.'

Test Yourself

Provide the Chinese versions of the following sentences.

1. Please wait here; I'll drive the car over.
2. Sorry, I didn't catch that. (something spoken)
3. I couldn't make out who it was.
4. Please write it down for me.
5. Put it in [there].
6. Put it back over there.
7. Lift it up.
8. When you lift it, (you'll find) it's quite heavy. (*zhòng* 'heavy')

Possible Answers

1. *Qǐng zài zhèr děng, wǒ bǎ chē kāi guòlai.*
2. *Duìbuqǐ, wǒ méi tīngdǒng.*
3. *Wǒ kàn bu chūlai shì shéi.*
4. *Qǐng bǎ tā xiě xiàlai.*
5. *Bǎ tā fàng jìnqu.*
6. *Bǎ tā fàng huíqu.*
7. *Bǎ tā ná qǐlai.*
8. *Ná qǐlai hěn zhòng.*

63. Potential Compounds

Resultative verb compounds—including its subset, directional verb compounds—permit the insertion of infixes *de* and *bu* to create potential compounds: *tīngdedǒng* (听得懂) 'can understand,' *tīngbudǒng* (听不懂) 'cannot understand,' *fàng de shàngqu* (放得上去) 'can put [them] up there,' *fàng bu shàngqu* (放不上去) 'cannot put [them] up there.' The potential complement expresses the possibility or impossibility of a result.

你听得懂他们在说什么吗？
Nǐ tīngdedǒng tāmen zài shuō shénme ma?
'Do you understand what they are talking about?'

你猜得出来我是谁吗?　　　猜不出来。
Nǐ cāi de chūlai wǒ shi shéi ma?　*Cāi bu chūlai.*
You guess DE out-come I be who MA?　Guess not out-come.
'Can you guess who I am?'　　　'No, I can't.'

那个 "餐" 字我怎么写也写不对。
Nèi ge "cān" zì, wǒ zěnme xiě yě xiěbuduì.
That M *cān* word, I however write also write-not-right.
'That character for *cān*, no matter how I write it, I can't get it right.'

Potential compounds may also have idiomatic meanings. Combinations with *qǐ* 'rise,' for example, mean 'afford to' (the idea being "in reach" or "out of reach").

燕窝、鱼翅这类的东西太贵了，我吃不起。
Yànwō, yúchì zhèi lèi de dōngxi tài guì le; wǒ chībuqǐ.
'Things like bird's nest soup and shark fin are too expensive; I can't afford to eat them.'

Test Yourself
Provide the Chinese versions of the following sentences.

1. I can't see it. (literally)
2. He says he can't learn foreign languages. (*wàiyǔ* 'foreign language')
3. This window won't open.
4. I can't afford a new one.
5. We can't possibly eat so many dishes.
6. One bowl of rice won't be enough to fill you up.
7. It's quite steep. Can you walk up? (*dǒu* 'steep')
8. The car won't seat six.
9. I can't finish it today.

Possible Answers
1. *Wǒ kànbujiàn.*
2. *Tā shuō tā xuébuhuì wàiyǔ.*
3. *Zhè chuānghu dǎbukāi.*
4. *Wǒ mǎibuqǐ yíge xīn de.*
5. *Zhème duō cài wǒmen chībuliǎo.*
6. *Yì wǎn fàn chībubǎo.*
7. *Lù hěn dǒu. Nǐ zǒu de shàngqu ma?*
8. *Chē zuòbuxià liù ge rén.*
9. *Wǒ jīntiān zuòbuwán.*

Generic Potential Compounds

There are also generic potential compounds, whose function is little more than to make a potential form available to a particular verb. The most productive of these is *liǎo,* from a verb meaning 'complete' (which is also thought to be the source of the verb suffix *-le*): *zuòbuliǎo* 'cannot do [it],' *nádeliǎo* 'can manage to carry [them].' Potential compounds with *liǎo* often suggest possibility despite, or impossibility because of, an amount, size, weight, difficulty, or other obstacle. The other generic second verb is *lái* 'come,' which is not so productive: *chīdelái* 'suit one's taste,' *kàndelái* 'be able to perceive (meaning, for example),' *tándelái* 'able to get along.'

车太多了，我们五点到不了。
Chē tài duō le, wǒmen wǔ diǎn dàobuliǎo.
'Too many cars—we won't be able to make it by five o'clock.'

这么多菜，我一个人怎么吃得了呢？
Zhème duō cài, wǒ yí ge rén zěnme chīdeliǎo ne?
'Such a lot of dishes—how can I eat them all myself?'

她做不来，我也做不来。
Tā zuòbulái, wǒ yě zuòbulái (= zuòbuliǎo).
'She can't do it, nor can I.'

我当不来那种唯唯诺诺的儿子。
Wǒ dàngbulái (= dàngbuliǎo) nà zhǒng wéiwéi-nuònuò de érzi.
I take role-not-capable that kind obsequious DE son.
'I can't be one of those goody-goody sons.'

我和他很谈得来。
Wǒ hé tā hěn tándelái.
'I get along very well with him.'

Test Yourself

Provide the Chinese versions of the following sentences.

1. I can't manage this on my own! (*bàn* 'manage,' *zhè jiàn shì* 'this [business],' *yí ge rén* 'on my own')
2. Could he have written such nice characters? (*piàoliang* 'nice' = 'pretty')
3. You can't carry all those things—let me help you. (*ná* 'carry,' *bāng* 'help')
4. I can't eat all this sandwich—why don't you have half? (*sānmíngzhì* 'sandwich,' *yíbàn* 'half')
5. I'll never forget them.

Possible Answers

1. *Wǒ yí ge rén bànbuliǎo zhèi jiàn shì.*
2. *Tā xiědeliǎo nàme piàoliang de Hànzì ma?*
3. *Nǐ nábuliǎo nàme duō dōngxi; wǒ bāng nǐ ná ba.*
4. *Zhèi ge sānmíngzhì wǒ chībuliǎo, nǐ lái chī yíbàn ba.*
5. *Wǒ wàngbuliǎo tāmen.*

10
After the Verb

64. Objects and Complex Verbs

There are a number of options for the placement of objects with complex verbs. Where feasible, erstwhile objects (at least from an English perspective) can be placed at the head of the clause, using one of several strategies, such as stating the object first or making use of the preposition *bǎ*.

鱼已经买回来了。
Yú yǐjing mǎi huílai le.
'[We] already bought the fish [and brought it back].'

他把箱子拿进去了。
Tā bǎ xiāngzi ná jìnqu le.
'He took the trunk inside.'

In some cases, objects can appear after the verb complex.

和尚打死蚊子算杀生吗？
Héshang dǎsǐ wénzi suàn shāshēng ma?
Monk hit-dead mosquito regard kill-life MA?
'Does a monk killing a mosquito count as destroying life?'

她戴上表，关上门，就出去了。
She wear-on watch, close-on door, then exit-go LE.
Tā dàishang biǎo, guānshang mén, jiù chūqu le.
'She put on her watch, closed the door, and went out.'

打倒帝国主义。
Dǎdǎo dìguózhǔyì!
Hit-topple imperial-ism!
'Down with imperialism!'

Under certain conditions, objects may also appear after directional compound verbs. In such cases, if the object is a single word, northern speakers, at least, usually delay the final *lái* or *qù* until after the object. This is not so strange if you recall that *lái* and *qù* in directional complements act more like directional particles than fully functioning verbs. They are neutral in tone and serve to indicate direction toward or away from the speaker.

站住，不要动！举起手来！
Zhànzhù, bú yào dòng! Jǔ qǐ shǒu lai!
Stand-still, not need move! Raise up hands here!
'Stay still, don't move! Hands up!'

When the object is longer, however, it can often be expressed after *lái* or *qù*, as well.

我想不出好办法来。
Wǒ xiǎng bu chū hǎo bànfǎ lai. ~ Wǒ xiǎng bu chūlai hǎo bànfǎ.
I think not out good method come.
'I can't think of a good solution.'

If the object is a destination, the split pattern is the only option for both northern and southern speakers.

然后把葱姜放进鸭肚子里去。
Ránhòu bǎ cōng jiāng fàng jìn yā dùzi li qu. (*... fàng jìnqu yā dùzi li.)
'Afterwards, put the scallions and ginger in the duck's stomach.'

现在把鸭子放进烤箱里去。
Xiànzài bǎ yāzi fàng jìn kǎoxiāng li qu. (*... fàng jìnqu kǎoxiāng li.)
'Now, put the duck in the oven.'

In some Chinese dictionaries, complex verbs with separable components are indicated with a double slash between the verbs (//, as opposed to = for verb-object compounds). This applies to resultative verb compounds and directional verb compounds: *tīng//jiàn* and *kǎo//shang*. In the case of *ná//qǐ// lai*, the first // signals the possibility of splitting *ná* and *qǐ* (for example, *ná de qǐlai* 'can pick it up'), and the second // signals the possibility of splitting *qǐ* and *lai* (for example, *ná qǐ bǐ lai* 'pick up a pen').

Test Yourself

Provide the Chinese versions of the following phrases.

1. walk into town
2. take out a book
3. lift up the lamp
4. send over a gift
5. cannot say a word
6. walk to the station (*huǒchēzhàn* 'station')

Typical Answers

1. *zǒu jìn chéng li qu*
2. *ná chūlai yì běn shū ~ ná chū yì běn shū lai*
3. *bǎ táidēng ná qǐlai*
4. *sòng guòqu lǐwù ~ sòng lǐwù guòqu*
5. *shuō bu chū huà lai ~ shuō bu chūlai huà*
6. *zǒu dào huǒchēzhàn <qu>*

65. Postverbal Particles: Goals of Motion and Transformation

Destination or goal can be expressed directly after some verbs with no intervening words (like "go home" in English): *qù Běijīng* 'go to Beijing,' *lái wǒ jiā* 'come to my house,' *jìn yīyuàn* 'check into the hospital,' *shàngchē* 'get in the vehicle.' But for most verbs, the destination—or more generally, the goal of motion—requires the mediation of one of the four directional particles that serve as postverbal particles (often without tone): *dào* 'to,' *zài* 'at,' *gěi* 'for,' and *chéng* 'into.' The following chart shows examples of verb phrases, first with a simple object and then with postverbal particles. "Transform" refers to the thing that something becomes.

OBJECT	寄个包裹	*jì ge bāoguǒ*	'mail a parcel'
DESTINATION	寄到香港	*jì dào Xiānggǎng*	'mail it to Hong Kong'
PLACE	放在抽屉里	*fàng zài chōuti li*	'put it in the drawer'
BENEFICIARY	寄给哥哥	*jì gěi gēge*	'send it to my older brother'
TRANSFORM	看成事实	*kàn chéng shìshí*	'regard it as fact'

Unlike a result verb, a postverbal particle forms a constituent with the following object rather than the prior verb. Pinyin indicates this with a space. However, *dào* and *chéng* also function as result verbs in resultative verb compounds, where they are always fully toned and without objects: *shōudào* 'receive' ('receive-reach'), *zuòchéng* 'succeed in finishing' ('make-succeed').

Verb + *dào* (到)

Verbs that involve the transfer of something from one place to another generally introduce the destination with *dào* (after the verb).

她把钱包送到警察局，但是还没有人去认领。
Tā bǎ qiánbāo sòng dào jǐngchájú, dànshì hái méiyǒu rén qù rènlǐng.
She BA wallet take to police-station, but still not-have person go claim.
'She took the wallet to the police station, but no one's come to claim it yet.'

他们已经搬出去了，搬到冠城园去了。

Tāmen yǐjing bān chūqu le, bān dào Guānchéngyuán qu le.

'They've already moved out—they moved to Guanchengyuan.'

Even though there is no combination *bān dàoqu (since *dào* is not one of the seven verbs of directed movement), *qù* can appear (in neutral tone) after the destination to underscore movement away.

Verb + *zài* (在)

Verbs that emphasize placement rather than trajectory generally introduce the place where the object ends up with *zài*.

请把名字写在答题纸上。

Qǐng bǎ míngzi xiě zài dátízhǐ shang.

Please BA name write at answer-sheet on.

'Please write your name on the answer sheet.'

哎呀，我把钥匙忘在家里了。

Āiya, wǒ bǎ yàoshi wàng zài jiā li le.

Oh no!, I BA keys forget at home in LE.

'Oh no!, I left my keys at home.'

你把剪刀放在哪儿了？

Nǐ bǎ jiǎndāo fàng zài nǎr le?

You BA scissors put at where LE?

'Where did you put the scissors?'

The choice between *dào* and *zài* is not just a matter of which verb is used. A response with *fàng dào* is quite possible and would suggest a longer trajectory involved in taking the scissors back to the drawer: *Wǒ bǎ tā fàng dào chōuti li le.* 'I put them back in the drawer.'

Verb + *gěi* (给)

Many transactional verbs that involve the transfer of an object to a person or institution introduce the beneficiary with *gěi* after the verb.

他寄给我一本样书。

Tā jì gěi wǒ yì běn yàngshū.

She send to me one M sample.

'She sent me a sample book.'

他们把收入捐给我们学校了。

Tāmen bǎ shōurù juān gěi wǒmen xuéxiào le.

They BA income donate to our school LE.

'They donated the proceeds to our school.'

Verb + *chéng* (成)

Finally, verbs that involve transformation of one thing into another, introduce the final state—the transform—with *chéng* after the verb.

她把希尔顿这个名字听成喜来登了。
Tā bǎ Xī'ěrdùn zhèi ge míngzi tīng chéng Xǐláidēng le.
'She heard the name Hilton as Sheraton.'

你能把这句话翻译成英语吗？
Nǐ néng bǎ zhèi jù huà fānyì chéng Yīngyǔ ma?
You able BA this M speech translate into English MA?
'Can you translate this sentence into English?'

Preverbal Versus Postverbal Phrases

As noted in Section 20, a location phrase that indicates the locus of action usually appears before the verb, while a destination phrase generally follows it. For most verbs, the distinction is clear. With *fàng* (放) 'put,' the location is usually the place where the object ends up, so the phrase follows the verb: *fàng zài wàitou* 'put it outside.' With *gōngzuò* (工作) 'work,' the location is usually the place where the work takes place, so the phrase precedes the verb: *zài gōngchǎng gōngzuò* 'work in a factory.' With *xiě* (写) 'write,' both options are possible, depending on the nature of the phrase: *zài túshūguǎn xiěxìn* 'write letters in the library,' *xiě zài hēibǎn shang* 'write on the blackboard.'

For a few common verbs, however, the distinction between preverbal and postverbal placement is less consequential. *Shēng* (生) 'be born,' *shēnghuó* (生活) 'live,' *zhù* (住) 'live,' and *zhǎng* (长) 'grow up' allow the location to appear before the verb in some cases and after the verb in others. The following sentence is quite natural, even with the shift from postverbal at the beginning and preverbal at the end.

喜欢生活在上海的人不一定也喜欢在北京生活。
Xǐhuan shēnghuó zài Shànghǎi de rén bù yídìng yě xǐhuan zài Běijīng shēnghuó.
Like live in Shanghai DE people not necessarily also like in Beijing live.
'People who live in Shanghai wouldn't necessarily enjoy living in Beijing.'

In saying a few words about your background, you are describing a forward-moving trajectory, so presenting the locations as destinations—after the verb—is probably more natural.

Wǒ shēng zài Lìwùpǔ, zhǎng zài Lúndūn, xiànzài zhù zài Xīnjiāpō.
'I was born in Liverpool, grew up in London, and now I live in Singapore.'

66. Verb-Plus-Object Compounds

As noted at the beginning of Chapter 7, disyllabic verbs differ in their degree of separability. Verbs like *zhīdào* 'know,' *dǎban* 'dress up, pose as,' and *bāngzhù* 'help' act basically as units, although for some speakers, they can be truncated in verb-not-verb questions: *zhī<dào> bu zhīdào*.

Other disyllabic verbs are separable, but the degree of separability varies. *Chīfàn* (吃饭) 'eat' and *shuìjiào* (睡觉) 'sleep' allow their erstwhile objects to appear even before the verb.

> *Zhè jǐ tiān fàn yě chībuxià, jiào yě shuìbuzháo.*
> These several days food also eat-not-down, sleep also sleep-not-manage.
> 'These last few days, I haven't been able to eat or sleep.'

Other verbs allow only a lesser degree of separation. *Dānxīn* (担心) 'worry,' for example, allows *dānle bù shǎo xīn* 'is quite anxious,' but it does not allow *xīn* to be placed before *dān*. As noted in Section 64, in dictionaries and vocabulary lists, separable compounds are often labeled in English as verb-plus-object (vo.) compounds because of their resemblance to verbs with objects. The Chinese term *líhécí* (离合词) 'separate-unite-words' is more apt, but harder to translate into English. Chinese-English dictionaries mark verb-plus-object compounds with an equals sign: *xǐ=zǎo* 'bathe,' *dān=xīn* 'be anxious about.'

What is special about verb-plus-object compounds, and requires them to be identified in a dictionary, is that one or both of the components may be a bound form, which cannot usefully be listed alone. This is true of *shuìjiào* and *xǐzǎo,* for which neither "object" can be provided with a meaning. Even when the parts can be assigned meanings, however, the meaning of the whole may be idiomatic: *chīfàn* is literally 'eat-rice,' but the actual meaning is 'eat a meal' or just 'eat.' Many verb-plus-object compounds, in fact, correspond to simplex verbs in English, for example, *shuìjiào* 'sleep.' Their objects are generic objects, so the focus remains on the action rather than the goal of the action. If attention shifts to a particular object, the generic object is replaced by a specific object: *chī cài* 'eat dishes (of food),' *xǐ yīfu* 'wash clothes,' *shēng háizi* 'give birth to a child,' *bāng fùmǔ* 'help one's parents.'

Objects of Verb + Object Compounds

Some verb-plus-object compounds are focused on the verbal event: *shuìjiào* 'sleep,' *zǒulù* 'walk,' *shàngbān* 'start work,' *chīkǔ* 'bear hardship.' Many, however, can be construed to have an effect on people or things. For example, *chīcù* 'be jealous' (literally, 'eat-vinegar') can involve a person toward whom the emotion is directed ("jealous of someone"). If *cù* 'vinegar' occupies the object slot, how is the object of jealousy to be expressed? One possibility is to insert a possessive pronoun between the verb and its erstwhile object: *Tā zài chī wǒde cù ma?* 'Is he jealous of me?' The possessive construction is paradoxical in that, even though grammatically, the possessive phrase modifies the following noun, semantically, it serves as an object of interest ("jealous of me"). In other words, it may be *my* vinegar, but it is *he* who is eating it—that is, *he* who is jealous. Other examples follow.

bāngmáng 'help'	BUT *bāng tāde máng* 'help her'
shēngqì 'be angry'	BUT *shēng tā de qì* 'be angry at him'
	(NOT *make him angry)
shàngdàng 'be fooled'	BUT *shàng tāde dàng* 'take advantage
	of him'

Here is a list (alphabetical by pinyin) of representative verb-plus-object compounds, with example phrases or sentences.

Verb-plus-Object	Gloss	Literal
毕业 *bìyè*	'graduate'	'conclude-undertaking'

EXAMPLE *bìle yè yǐhòu* 'after graduating'

吃醋 *chīcù*	'be jealous'	'eat-vinegar'

EXAMPLE *Tā zài chī wǒde cù ma?* 'Is he jealous of me?'

吃饭 *chīfàn*	'eat (a meal)'	'eat-rice'

EXAMPLE *měitiān chī sān dùn fàn* 'eat three meals a day'

吃惊 *chījīng*	'be amazed'	'eat-surprise'

EXAMPLE *lìng tā dà chī yì jīng* 'surprised her' (literally, 'make her big eat one surprise)'

吃苦 *chīkǔ*	'bear hardship'	'eat-bitter'

EXAMPLE *yìqǐ chīguo kǔ de rén* 'people who've suffered together'

抽烟 *chōuyān*	'smoke'	'pull-smoke'

EXAMPLE *cóng méi chōuguo yān* 'never to have smoked'

打包 *dǎbāo*	'pack up'	'make-bundle'

EXAMPLE *dǎhǎo bāo* 'having wrapped up the parcel'

打岔儿 *dǎchàr*	'interrupt'	'make-branch'

EXAMPLE *Bú zài huì yǒu rén dǎchàr.* 'There won't be any more people interrupting again.'

打赌 *dǎdǔ*	'bet'	'make-bet'

EXAMPLE *Zánmen dǎ ge dǔ ba!* 'Let's make a bet.'

打盹儿 *dǎdǔnr*	'doze'	'do-doze'

EXAMPLE *dǎ yìhuǐr dǔnr* 'snooze for a while'

Verb-plus-Object	Gloss	Literal
担心 *dānxīn*	'worry, feel anxious'	'carry on shoulder-heart'

EXAMPLE   *wèi háizi dānle bù shǎo xīn* 'was very anxious about the children'

打球 *dǎqiú*	'play ball'	'hit-ball'

EXAMPLE   *Gāi dǎ yìhuǐr qiú!* 'We should play some ball.'

打气 *dǎqì*	'inflate, pump up'	'hit-air'

EXAMPLE   *Gěi tā dǎdǎqì.* 'Pump him up a bit.'

打字 *dǎzì*	'type'	'hit-word'

EXAMPLE   *dǎle bàntiān zì* 'type for quite a long time'

烦人 *fánrén*	'be annoying'	'annoy-person'

EXAMPLE   *cónglái méi zhème fánguo rén* 'has never been so annoying'

加工 *jiāgōng*	'process, polish'	'add-work'

EXAMPLE   *xūyào zài jiāgōng yíxiàr* 'needs a bit of polishing'

教书 *jiāoshū*	'teach'	'teach-book'

EXAMPLE   *Nǐ jiāoguo shū méiyou?* 'Have you ever taught?'

结婚 *jiéhūn*	'marry'	'contract for-marriage'

EXAMPLE   *Tā jiéhūn yǒu sān nián le.* 'She's been married for three years.'

结业 *jiéyè*	'graduate'	'complete-enterprise'

EXAMPLE   *Shì něinián jiéyè de?* 'Which year did [you] graduate in?'

录音 *lùyīn*	'record'	'record-sound'

EXAMPLE   *Shì lùyīn de bú shì xiànchǎng zhíbō.* 'It's recorded; it's not a live broadcast.'

排队 *páiduì*	'line up'	'order-ranks'

EXAMPLE   *Páipai duì!* 'Line up!'

上班 *shàngbān*	'start work, go to work'	'start-shift'

EXAMPLE   *jiǔ diǎn shàngbān* 'start work at nine o'clock'

上当 *shàngdàng*	'be fooled'	'start-assume'

EXAMPLE   *Bié shàng tā de dàng.* 'Don't be taken in by him.'

Verb-plus-Object	Gloss	Literal
上课 *shàngkè*	'start class, go to class'	'start-class'

EXAMPLE *Shàngwán kè jiù huíjiā le.* 'I went home right after class.'

上路 *shànglù*	'set out on a journey'	'start-road'

EXAMPLE *Wǒ zhè jiù shànglù.* 'I'm off.'

上学 *shàngxué*	'attend school, be at school'	'start-school'

EXAMPLE *qí zìxíngchē shàngxué* 'ride to school on a bike'

生气 *shēngqì*	'get angry, take offense'	'give rise-anger'

EXAMPLE *Nǐ shēng shéi de qì?* 'Whom are you angry at?'

睡觉 *shuìjiào*	'sleep'	'sleep-perceive'

EXAMPLE *shuìbuzháo jiào* 'not able to get to sleep'

说话 *shuōhuà*	'speak'	'say-speech'

EXAMPLE *Xiān shuō jǐ jù huà.* 'First, I'll say a few words.'

谈天儿 *tántiānr*	'chat, discuss'	'chat-sky'

EXAMPLE *tánle yì wǎnshang de tiānr* 'chatted the whole evening'

跳舞 *tiàowǔ*	'dance'	'jump-dance'

EXAMPLE *tiàole sān ge xiǎoshí de wǔ* 'danced for three hours'

退休 *tuìxiū*	'retire'	'retreat-rest'

EXAMPLE *tuìxiū tuì de hěn zǎo* 'retired early'

下班 *xiàbān*	'finish work, get out of work'	'finish-shift'

EXAMPLE *wǎn yìdiǎnr cái xiàbān* 'late getting out of work'

下课 *xiàkè*	'get out of class, end class'	'finish-class'

EXAMPLE *Kuài yào xiàkè le.* 'Class is almost finished.'

下台 *xiàtái*	'step down; get out of a predicament'	'descend-platform'

EXAMPLE *xiàbuliǎo tái* 'be put on the spot' ('unable to get out of something')

下乡 *xiàxiāng*	'go to the countryside'	'descend-countryside'

EXAMPLE *xià yí cì xiāng* 'be sent to (work in) the countryside one time'

Verb-plus-Object	Gloss	Literal
游泳 *yóuyǒng*	'swim'	'swim-swim'

EXAMPLE   *yóule ge yǒng* 'took a dip'

照相 *zhàoxiàng*	'take a photo'	'reflect-likeness'

EXAMPLE   *Gěi nǐ zhào ge xiàng ba.* 'Why don't I take a photo of you?'

走路 *zǒulù*	'walk'	'walk-road'

EXAMPLE   *Zǒulù qù yào jǐ fēnzhōng?* 'How long does it take to walk there?'

67. Mock Objects

In colloquial language, it is quite common to take combinations of verb-plus-adjective, whether in resultative verb compounds (*shuōqīngchu* 'say clearly'), in predicate-adjective constructions (*wánr de hěn tòngkuài* 'play happily'), or in other types of constructions with verb-plus-adjective, and recast them as if they were verbs with objects by inserting the measure word *gè* (个) between the verb and the adjective.

尽情地玩儿个痛快！
Jìnqíng de wánr ge tòngkuài! (vs. *wánr de hěn tòngkuài*)
To-one's-heart's-content DE have-fun M joyful!
'Enjoy yourself to your heart's content!'

Kuài, shuō ge míngbai. (vs. *shuō míngbai*)
Quick, say M be-plain.
'Quick, explain.'

Shuō ge qīngchu ba! (vs. *shuō qīngchu*)
Say M clear BA!
'How about a little clarification!'

一次吃个饱，吃个腻。
Yí cì chī ge bǎo, chī ge nì. (vs. *chībǎo, chīnì*)
One time eat M full, eat M fed-up.
'It's a meal that fills you up and satisfies you.'

In his grammar, Yuen Ren Chao coined the term "mock objects" for this type of *ge* phrase. Resultative verb compounds (see Section 61) are a particularly bountiful source: *shuō míngbai, chībǎo, chīnì,* and so on. Not all combinations occur. *Tòngkuài* 'joyful' is particularly common: *xǐ ge tòngkuài* 'soak to one's heart's content,' *kū ge tòngkuài* 'cry one's heart out.' Another common mock object is *méiwán<méiliǎo>* (没完<没了>)

'endless' (literally, 'not-end not-finish'): *shuō ge méiwán-méiliǎo* 'never stop talking.'

68. Ditransitive Verbs: Verbs with Two Objects

As noted in Section 48, *gěi* may take two objects, one representing the recipient and the other representing the gift—in other words, an indirect and a direct object: *gěi fúwùyuán xiǎofèi* (给服务员小费) 'give the waiter a tip.'

Unmediated Objects

Only a few verbs that take two objects follow the pattern of *gěi*, with both objects unmediated: V O O. *Jiāo* 'teach' is one: *jiāo tāmen Hànyǔ* (教他们汉语) 'teach them Chinese.' Of those verbs that allow unmediated double objects, a small number also allow, but do not require, the indirect object to be introduced by *gěi*; the pattern is V <*gěi*> O O. *Sòng* 'present, give' is one: *sòng <gěi> tā yí fèn lǐwù* (送<给>他一份礼物) 'give <to> him a present.'

Gěi with Indirect Objects

For most ditransitive verbs, *gěi* is required: V *gěi* O O. *Mài* 'sell,' for example, requires *gěi* before the indirect object: *mài gěi wǒ chē le* (卖给我车了) 'sold me a car.' The two objects are contiguous in relatively few cases; instead, direct objects will often be presented before the verb with *bǎ*: *bǎ lǐwù sòng gei tā* 'to give him the present.'

Regardless of whether the indirect object is introduced by *gěi* or not, the direct object may be omitted (see Sections 31 and 48): *Wǒ gěi nǐ.* 'It's yours.', *Qǐng gàosu tā.* 'Please tell him.', *Qǐng huán gěi tā.* 'Please return [them] to her.'

The following chart lists verbs that do not take *gěi* before indirect objects. (For two verbs, *huán* and *sòng*, *gěi* is optional.)

Chinese	Pinyin	Gloss	Example
罚	*fá*	'fine'	*fá tā yì zhōu xīnshuǐ* 'fine her a week's salary'
告诉	*gàosu*	'tell'	*gàosu tā yí jiàn shìr* 'tell him something'
给	*gěi*	'give'	*gěi tā qián* 'give him money'
还	*huán*	'return'	*huán <gěi> tā liǎng kuài qián* 'return two dollars to her'

Chinese	Pinyin	Gloss	Example
教	*jiāo*	'teach'	*jiāo tā Hànyǔ* 'teach her Chinese'
麻烦	*máfan*	'bother, trouble'	*Wǒ kěyǐ zài máfan nǐ yí jiàn shì ma?* 'Can I bother you once more for something?'
请教	*qǐngjiào*	'seek advice'	*Qǐngjiào nǐ yí jiàn shìqing.* 'I'd like to get your opinion about something.'
送	*sòng*	'present'	*sòng <gěi> tā lǐwù* 'give him a present'
问	*wèn*	'ask'	*wèn tāmen wèntí* 'ask them questions'

Far more verbs require, or at least allow, postverbal *gěi* to introduce an indirect object. The following chart lists the most common of these verbs.

Characters	Pinyin	Gloss	Example
带给	*dài gěi*	'bring to'	*dài gěi xuéxiào róngyù* 'bring honor to the school'
递给	*dì gěi*	'pass to'	*bǎ zìdiǎn dì gěi wǒ* 'pass the dictionary to me'
丢给	*diū gěi*	'toss to'	*bǎ gútou diū gěi gǒu kěn* 'toss the bones to the dog to gnaw on'
分给	*fēn gěi*	'give [a share] to'	*fēn gěi měi ge rén sān kuài* 'give each person three dollars'
还给	*huán gěi*	'return to'	*bǎ yàoshi huán gěi tā* 'give her back the keys'
寄给	*jì gěi*	'mail to'	*bǎ bāoguǒ jì gěi fùmǔ* 'send a package to one's parents'

Characters	Pinyin	Gloss	Example
交给	*jiāo gěi*	'hand to'	*jiāo gěi tā wénjiàn* 'hand the documents over to her'
卖给	*mài gěi*	'sell to'	*bǎ chē mài gěi péngyou* 'sell the car to a friend'
判给	*pàn gěi*	'award'	*bǎ yì fēn pàn gěi wǒmen duì* 'award a point to our team'
送给	*sòng gěi*	'present to'	*sòng gěi tā yí fēnr lǐwù* 'present her with a gift'

For a number of these verbs, *gěi* determines the direction of action. In the case of buying and selling, different but obviously related verbs are involved.

Chinese	Pinyin	Example
借	*jiè*	*gēn tā jiè yì běn shū* 'borrow a book from her' *jiè gěi tā yì běn shū* 'lend her a book'
买/卖	*mǎi/mài*	*gēn tā mǎi yí ge shǒubiǎo* 'buy a watch from him' *mài gěi tā ge shǒubiǎo* 'sell him a watch'
租	*zū*	*xiàng tā zū ge fángjiān* 'rent a room from him' *zū gěi tā yí ge fángjiān* 'rent him a room'

Many cases that involve multiple objects can be recast as verbs in series (in temporal order), with each object commanded by a single verb—a preferred pattern in Chinese.

sòng gěi tā yí fēnr lǐwù	~	*sòng yí fēnr lǐwù gěi tā*
'give him a present'		'present a gift to him'
mài gěi tā yì běn shū	~	*mài yì běn shū gěi tā*
'sell to him one M book'		'sell one M book to him'

Note that many ditransitive verbs in English are not so in Chinese. In English, you can say "sell him a book" or "buy him a book." In Chinese, the latter notion—"buy"—is expressed only with a prepositional or serial construction.

gěi tā mǎi yì běn shū	*mǎi yì běn shū gěi tā*
for him buy one M book	buy one M book give him
'buy a book for him'	'buy him a book'

Object plus Object-Complement

A very small set of Chinese verbs take an object plus object-complement. Unlike the direct- and indirect-object relationship, the object plus object-complement is related through identity. *Jiào* (叫) 'call' is the most common of these verbs. *Mà* (骂) 'call names, criticize, curse' is another.

我们都叫他差不多先生。
Wǒmen dōu jiào tā Chàbuduō xiānsheng.
'We all call him Mr. More-or-Less.'

他们骂他笨蛋。
Tāmen mà tā bèndàn.
'They called him a fool (literally, 'dumb-egg').'

This class of verbs can be enlarged by the addition of the copular, *shì* (是) 'be,' or one of the classificatory verbs (see Section 45), mainly *dāng* (当) 'serve as, be,' *zuò* (做) 'do,' and *wéi* (为) 'be, as,' between object and object-complement. This has the effect of distributing objects evenly across verbs (see Section 73): V-O V-O. It also makes the identity of object and object-complement explicit. These verbs require the serial construction.

有人认为他是英雄。
Yǒurén rènwéi tā shì yīngxióng.
'Some people regard him as a hero.'

请不要拿我当笨蛋。
Qǐng bú yào ná wǒ dāng bèndàn.
'Please don't take me for an idiot.'

他们选她做(~ 当)校长。
Tāmen xuǎn tā zuò (~ dāng) xiàozhǎng.
'They elected her principal of the school.'

他们任命他为主席。
Tāmen rènmìng tā wéi zhǔxí.
'They appointed him chairman.'

69. Embedded Object Clauses

Verbs of thought or perception can take whole clauses as their objects. Thus a question such as *Tā shì cóng nǎli lái de?* 'Where's she from?" can be embedded as the object of a verb like *zhīdào* (知道) 'know.'

Wǒ bù zhīdào {tā shì nǎli lái de}.
'I don't know {where she's from}.'

The expression of doubt requires the embedded clause to take the form of a question. In English, it would typically be introduced with "whether" or "if."

我应该确认{这样修改是不是可以}。
Wǒ yīnggāi quèrèn {zhè yàng xiūgǎi shì bu shì kěyǐ}.
I should check {this way correct is not is okay}.
'I should find out {whether it's okay to correct it like this (or not)}.'

看到它，我就纳闷儿{它是不是放错了地方}。
Kàndào tā, wǒ jiù nàmènr {tā shì bu shì fàngcuòle dìfang}.
See-reach it, I then puzzle {it be not be put-error-LE place}.
'When I saw it, I was wondering {if it had been put in the wrong place}.'

我在考虑{是否要买一辆新汽车}。
Wǒ zài kǎolǜ {shìfǒu yào mǎi yí liàng xīn qìchē}.
I at considering {whether-or-not want buy one M new car}.
'I'm deliberating over {whether to buy a new car (or not)}.'

Otherwise, the embedded clause is simply juxtaposed to the verb.

Wǒ pànwàng {míngtiān bú huì xiàyǔ}.
'I hope {it won't rain tomorrow}.'

我忘了{带钥匙}。
Wǒ wàngle {dài yàoshi}.
I forgot {to bring my keys}.

有人怕{去看牙医}。
Yǒu rén pà {qù kàn yáyī}.
Some people are afraid {to visit the dentist}.

70. Duration Complements

Units of duration include *tiān* 'day,' *xīngqī* 'week,' *yuè* 'month,' and *nián* 'year.' *Tiān* and *nián* are treated as measures: *yì tiān* 'one day,' *shí nián* 'ten years.' *Xīngqī* and *yuè* are nouns, counted with the measure word *gè*: *liǎng ge xīngqī* 'two weeks,' *sān ge yuè* 'three months.' (*Sān yuè* exists, but it means 'the third month,' that is, March.) *Xiǎoshí means* 'hour,' which, in colloquial language, is often counted without its measure word: *sān <ge> xiǎoshi* 'three hours.' The following chart provides a summary of the units of time.

Chinese	Pinyin	Gloss	Example
秒	*miǎo*	'second'	*yì miǎo*
分钟	*fēnzhōng*	'minute'	*yì fēnzhōng*
小时	*xiǎoshí*	'hour'	*yí ge xiǎoshí*
钟头	*zhōngtóu*	'hour' (colloquial)	*yí ge zhōngtóu*
天	*tiān*	'day'	*yì tiān*
星期	*xīngqī*	'week'	*yí ge xīngqī*
礼拜	*lǐbài*	'week' (colloquial)	*yí ge lǐbài*
周	*zhōu*	'week'	*yì zhōu*
月	*yuè*	'month'	*yí ge yuè*
年	*nián*	'year'	*yì nián*
一会儿	*yìhuǐr*[1]	'for a little while'	
半天	*bàntiān*	'quite a while' ('half-day')	
很久	*hěn jiǔ*	'a long time'	

The Chinese did not switch to 24-hour days until the late seventeenth century, and then only in administrative and official circles. Before then, several systems had coexisted. One divided the 24-hour day into 100 *kè* ('notches' on the float stick of a water clock), each 14.4 minutes in duration. Another system divided the day into 12 *chén* ('mansions of the zodiac'), each two hours long. *Xiǎoshí* 'hour' was originally a single hour within a two-hour *chén*. The more colloquial *zhōngtóu* 'hour' has *zhōng* 'clock, bell' as its root.

Traditionally, the month was divided into three 10-day periods called *xún* (旬), or into two 15-day periods called *qì* (气). The terms *xīngqī* (literally 'star period') and *lǐbài* 'worship' are recent introductions. *Lǐbài*, originally a Christian "worship week," is now rare in written language.

Duration is questioned by *duō jiǔ* (多久) 'how long' and *duōcháng shíjiān* (多长时间) 'how much time.' Questions can also be asked in terms of specific units: *jǐ ge xiǎoshí* (几个小时) 'how many hours,' *duōshao tiān* (多少天) 'how many days.'

Duration Complements

In contrast to time-when expressions, which appear before the verb, duration complements appear after the verb, as part of the predicate. There are two types of duration complements. The first type involves persistent actions or processes—working, studying, traveling; this type can be visualized as a point at the beginning of a continuous squiggly line of activity. The second type involves a persistent state, brought about by an original event—getting married, meeting someone, graduating; this type can be visualized as a point at the beginning of a straight line that represents elapsed time.

---

[1]Also pronounced *yíhuìr*.

Persistent Actions or Processes

Duration involving persistent action follows the verb directly: *děng yìhuǐr* 'wait a bit,' *shuì bā <ge> xiǎoshí* 'sleep eight hours,' *xué yì nián* 'study for a year,' *zhǎole bàntiān* 'looked for ages.' The following sentences illustrate the postverbal placement.

> *Nǐ Hànyǔ shuō de zhēn bàng. Xuéle duō jiǔ le?*
> You Chinese speak DE really great. Learn-LE how long LE?
> 'Your Chinese is terrific. How long have you been studying?'

> *Nǎli? Wǒ zhǐ xuéle yì nián, shuō de bù hǎo!*
> Where? I only learn-LE one year, speak DE not good!
> 'Nah, I've only studied a year. I don't speak very well!'

Objects. Only pronoun objects can intervene between the verb and a duration complement; this matches English word order.

> *Wǒ děngle tā bàntiān le.*
> 'I've been waiting for him for ages.'

> 昨天我陪了她差不多10个小时。
> *Zuótiān wǒ péile tā chàbuduō shí ge xiǎoshí.*
> Yesterday I accompany-LE her approximately ten M hours.
> 'Yesterday, I kept her company for about ten hours.'

If an object other than a pronoun is present, there are two options, with slightly different nuances of meaning. The first option, illustrated in the following two examples, places the verb and the object first, then the verb and the duration phrase. (See Section 57 for a similar strategy with predicate complements.)

V-O V-Duration Complement

> 他看电视看了一小时。
> *Tā kàn diànshì kànle yì xiǎoshí.*
> He watch television watch-LE one hour.
> 'He watched television for an hour.'

> 我骑马骑了一<个>上午。
> *Wǒ qímǎ qíle yí <ge> shàngwǔ.*
> I ride-horse ride-LE one late-morning.
> 'I went horseback riding the whole morning.'

The second option, illustrated in the following two examples, places the duration complement between the verb and the object. The duration complement may, optionally, be linked to the object with *de* (parallel to the use of apostrophe-"s" in the English version of the first example).

V Duration <*de*> O

他看了一小时的电视。

Tā kànle yì xiǎoshí de diànshì.

He watch-LE one hour DE television.

'He watched an hour's (worth of) television.'

讲了一个小时的话后，他的声音哑了。

Jiǎngle yíge xiǎoshí de huà hòu, tāde shēngyīn yǎ le.

Speak-LE one hour speech after, his voice hoarse LE.

'After talking for an hour, his voice got hoarse.'

Persistent States

Duration representing the length of time that an action has been taking place (the point with a squiggly line) has a different structure than duration representing the length of time that has elapsed since an event took place (the point with a straight line). In sentences such as the following, the duration phrase does not follow a verb; instead, it follows a whole clause (marked by curly braces).

{*Wǒ lái Zhōngguó*} *yí ge yuè le.*   ~   *yǒu yí ge yuè le.*
'I've been in China for a month.'

{*Wǒ rènshi tā*} *hěn jiǔ le.*   ~   *yǒu hěn jiǔ le.*
'I've known him for a long time.'

{*Tāmen jiéhūn*} *sìshí duō nián le.*   ~   *yǒu sìshí duō nián le.*
'They've been married for over 40 years.'

{*Wǒ xué Zhōngwén*} *shí duō nián le.*   ~   *yǒu shí duō nián le.*
'It's been over 10 years since I started studying Chinese.'

In such cases, the duration phrase can, optionally, be made a complement of the verb *yǒu* 'have' (as shown), which returns the duration complement to its "normal" postverbal position.

Long Time No See

Action that does not occur over a period of time is not treated as a duration complement in Chinese, but as time within which; the phrase appears before the verb. The common greeting *hěn jiǔ bú jiàn* (很久不见), which is presumably the origin of the pidgin English phrase "long time no see," is an example. The period of deprivation (*hěn jiǔ*) is stated before the verb. Two other examples follow.

我饿死了。十多个小时没吃饭了。

Wǒ èsǐ le. Shí duō ge xiǎoshí méi chīfàn le.

I hungry-death LE. Ten M hours not eat LE.

'I'm starving. I haven't eaten for over ten hours.'

我有点生疏了。一年多没说中文了。
Wǒ yǒu diǎnr shēngshū le. Yì nián duō méi shuō Zhōngwén le.
'I'm a little rusty. I haven't spoken Chinese for over a year.'

Within a Certain Time

More generally, time within which is treated like time when, appearing before the verb (either before or after the subject). Such expressions usually appear with position words <*yǐ*>*nèi* (<以 >内) 'within' or *zhōng* (中) 'in.'

三天以内在西宁有什么好玩儿的吗？
Sān tiān yǐnèi zài Xīníng yǒu shénme hǎo wánr de ma?
Three days inside at Xining have any very fun DE MA?
'With three days there, is there anything particularly fun to do in Xining?'

一个星期中绝食一天对身体有益吗？
Yí ge xīngqī zhōng juéshí yì tiān duì shēntǐ yǒuyì ma?
One M week middle fast one day to body have-benefit MA?
'Is fasting for one day a week beneficial to one's health?'

Test Yourself

Provide the Chinese versions of the following sentences.

1. He rested for half an hour. (*xiūxi* 'rest,' *bàn ge xiǎoshí* 'half an hour')
2. I've been waiting for over an hour!
3. It's two years since I graduated. (*bìyè* (vo.) 'graduate')
4. He did an hour's homework. (*zuò gōngkè* 'do homework')
5. I haven't slept for two days.
6. Last week, I was ill for two days. (*bìng* 'be ill')
7. How many hours are you in class each week? (*shàngkè* (vo.) 'be in class')
8. She drives an hour each day. (*kāichē* 'drive')
9. He's been waiting for her for ages.

Possible Answers

1. *Tā xiūxile bàn ge xiǎoshí.*
2. *Wǒ děngle yí ge duō zhōngtóu le!*
3. *Wǒ bìyè yǐjing <yǒu> liǎng nián le.*
4. *Tā zuòle yì xiǎoshí de gōngkè.*
5. *Wǒ liǎng tiān méi shuìjiào le.*
6. *Shàng xīngqī wǒ bìngle liǎng tiān.*
7. *Nǐ měi ge xīngqī shàng jǐ ge xiǎoshí de kè?*
8. *Měitiān tā kāichē kāi yí ge xiǎoshí.*
9. *Tā děngle tā hěn jiǔ le.*

71. Extent Phrases

Duration phrases are just one of several types of phrases that follow the verb to indicate the extent (or range) of verbal meaning. The reduplication of verbs (for example, *kànkan* 'take a look') and the associated forms with *yī* (*kàn yí kàn*) and *yí xiàr* (*kàn yí xiàr*) is one such pattern. One particularly common type of extent phrase involves measure words that are sometimes referred to as "verbal measures" (or "verbal classifiers"), because they are associated with an action rather than a noun. The most common verbal measures count occasions or instances: *yí cì* (一次) 'one time,' *yí biàn* (一遍) 'one time through,' *yì huí* (一回) 'one occurrence.'

他又救了我一次。
Tā yòu jiùle wǒ yí cì.
'She saved my life once again.'

我试了三次了。
Wǒ shìle sān cì le.
'I've tried three times.'

请再说一遍。
Qǐng zài shuō yí biàn.
'Please say it again.'

Associated pronouns precede verbal measures: *Wǒ yì nián jiàn tā yí cì.* 'I see her once a year.' Nouns, however, generally follow the verbal measures.

Wǒmen yì zhōu shàng sān cì Yīngyǔ kè.
'We have three English classes a week.'

Qǐng zài gàosu wǒ yí cì nín de dàmíng.
'Please tell me your name once again.'

Nǐ duō jiǔ qù yóu yí cì yǒng?
'How often do you go for a swim?'

The following chart provides a representative selection of verbal measures.

Characters	Pinyin	Literal	Verbal Measure	Example
巴掌	*bāzhang*	'palm'	'slap'	*dǎle tā liǎng bāzhang* 'slapped him a couple of times'
遍	*biàn*		'once through'	*kànguo liǎng biàn* 'read it twice'

Characters	Pinyin	Literal	Verbal Measure	Example
次	*cì*	'time'	'times, occasions'	*Zhè yào, yì tiān fú sān cì.* 'Take this medicine three times a day.'
刀	*dāo*	'knife'	'a cut'	*bèi tǒngle yì dāo* 'got stabbed'
顿	*dùn*	'pause'	'blow, beating'	*màle tā yí dùn* 'gave him a scolding'
回	*huí*	'return'	'times, occasions'	*qùguo yì huí Chángchéng* 'been to the Great Wall once'
口	*kǒu*	'mouth'	'mouthful'	*tànle yì kǒu qì* 'breathed a sigh of relief'
趟	*tàng*		'trip, journey'	*Wǒmen qùle liǎng tàng Huángshān.* 'We've been to Huangshan twice.'
眼	*yǎn*	'eye'	'a look, an eyeful'	*kànle tā liǎng yǎn* 'looked at her a couple of times'

Some verbal measures can also function as nominal measures; as such, they could be added to the chart in Section 37. *Tàng* (趟), for example, can function like *bān* (班), as a measure for regularly scheduled transport: *Shíyī diǎn, hái yǒu yí tàng huǒchē.* 'There's a train at 11 o'clock.'

72. Conjunctions

Conjunctions join words, phrases, and clauses in logical relationships that are coordinate ("and," "or," "but") or subordinate ("if," "because," "although").

Coordinate Conjunctions
Connections ("and")

The coordinate relationship is often implicit in Chinese. Nouns or noun phrases are more often juxtaposed than explicitly conjoined.

Bàbà māmā bù tóngyì.
'Mother and father don't agree.'

Gùgōng Běihǎi lí zhèr hěn jìn.
'The National Palace Museum and North Lake are quite close to here.'

If a coordinate conjunction is needed, *gēn* (跟) and *hé* (和), both of which mean 'and,' are available. Other options are used mostly in written language.

Wūzi li zhǐ yǒu yì zhāng zhuōzi gēn yì bǎ yǐzi.
'The room had only a table and a chair in it.'

Wǒ gēn péngyou yìqǐ qù de.
I and friend together go DE
'I went with a friend.'

Note that *gēn* is also a verb meaning 'follow,' but its most common function is as a preposition with verbs of speaking, teaching, and the like: *gēn tā tán* 'talk to her,' *gēn tā xué* 'study with him.' *Hé* functions only as a conjunction; it was originally a more formal or written alternative to *gēn*, although nowadays, the two seem to be interchangeable.

No coordinate conjunction, including *gēn* and *hé*, may conjoin adjectives, verbs, or clauses. Adjectives and verbs are usually conjoined by correlative adverbs rather than by specific conjunctions. The adverb *yòu* (又) 'again,' for example, may be interspersed with adjectives: *yòu kuài yòu shūfu* 'fast and comfortable' (see Section 56). The same construction may be used with verbs, provided they are governed by a single subject: *Tā yòu pǎobù yòu jǔzhòng.* 'She jogs and lifts weights.'

Other coordinate conjunctions include *bùrán* and *fǒuzé* 'otherwise.'

别走太远，不然你会迷路的。
Bié zǒu tài yuǎn, bùrán nǐ huì mílù de.
'Don't go too far, or else you'll get lost.'

Correlative adverbs often provide the effect of clausal conjunction. *Yě* (也), for example, may occur singly or, like *yòu* in the previous examples, interspersed.

Tā <yě> méi shàngkè, wǒ yě méi shàngkè.
'She didn't go to class, and neither did I.'

Yuè . . . yuè 'the more . . . the more' is always used as a pair. Where no specific first verb is available, *lái* can stand in as a default.

锅贴，越吃越想吃。
Guōtiē, yuè chī yuè xiǎng chī.
'With pot stickers, the more you eat, the more you want.'

大城市越来越危险。

Dà chéngshì yuè lái yuè wēixiǎn.

'Cities are becoming more and more dangerous.'

Another form of coordinate conjunction is provided by repeating indefinites (see Section 22).

你想吃什么就吃什么。

Nǐ xiǎng chī shénme jiù chī shénme.

You want eat whatever then eat whatever.

'Eat whatever you want.'

谁先来谁先吃。

Shéi xiān lái shéi xiān chī.

Whoever first comes whoever first eats.

'First-come, first-served.'

Alternatives ("or")

Alternatives can also be implicit in Chinese, as in the old saying cited with exceptional effect by Deng Xiaoping to promote pragmatism.

不管黑猫白猫，捉到老鼠就是好猫。

Bù guǎn hēimāo báimāo, zhuōdào lǎoshǔ jiùshì hǎo māo.

No matter black-cat white-cat, catch-success mice then-be good cat.

'Whether it's a black cat or a white cat, so long as it can catch mice, it's
   a good cat.'

Otherwise, the conjunction *huòzhě* (或者) or the alternatives *huò* (或) and *huòshì* (或是) may express "or," either singly or interspersed.

Kāfēi huòzhě chá huòzhě dòujiāng dōu xíng. Xièxie.

'Coffee, tea, or soy milk—any of them is fine, thanks.'

Duō yí ge huò shǎo yí ge, wúsuǒwèi.

'One more or one less—it makes no difference.'

Huòshì nǐ qù huòshì wǒ qù.

'Either you go or I go.'

In questions, the explicit conjunction "or" is *háishi* (see Section 21).

Adversatives ("but")

The adversative relationship ("but, however") is marked by *kěshì* (可是), *dànshì* (但是), and *búguò* (不过). *Kěshì* is more colloquial and, therefore, less written than *dànshì*, but otherwise the two are synonymous. *Búguò* has the sense 'except that, only.'

Zhōngwén, tīng shuō bǐjiào róngyi, kěshì dú xiě hěn nán.
Chinese, listening speaking rather easy, but reading writing quite hard.
'With Chinese, listening and speaking are fairly easy, but reading and
  writing are difficult.'

Wǒmen shì èrshí duō nián de línjū le, búguò hěn shǎo láiwǎng.
'We've been neighbors for over 20 years, but we rarely have any
  contact.'

Subordinate Conjunctions

Subordinate conjunction is frequently expressed with correlative adverbs.
Following is a selection of the most common ones.

CAUSAL	*yīnwei … suǒyǐ* 'because . . . [so]' *Yīnwei hěn rè suǒyǐ wǒmen dōu hěn lèi.* 'Because it's so hot, we're all quite tired.'
CONCESSION	*suīrán … kěshì ~ dànshì*, and so on 'although . . . [but]' *Tā suīrán gèzi bù gāo, kěshì zuì xǐhuan dǎ lánqiú.* 'Although he's not tall, he just loves to play basketball.'
CONDITIONAL	*yàoshi ~ rúguǒ … jiù* 'if . . . [then]' *Yàoshi qián bú gòu nǐmen jiù yòng xìnyòngkǎ.* 'If you don't have enough money, you can use a credit card.'

Conditionals are made more hypothetical by adding *de huà* (的话) at the
foot of the conditional clause. With *de huà*, *rúguǒ* or *yàoshi* can be omitted.
(*De huà*—literally, 'the saying of'—recalls the use of "say" in English to
mean 'what if': "Say you had the money, then what?")

如果有时间的话	*rúguǒ yǒu shíjiān de huà*	'if you happen to have the time'
要是你想去的话	*yàoshi nǐ xiǎng qù de huà*	'if by chance you do want to go'
如果你愿意的话	*rúguǒ nǐ yuànyi de huà*	'if you're willing'

In English, it is the subordinate conjunction that is crucial—"if," "although,"
and so on. In Chinese, however, the subordinate conjunction can often be omitted.

努力工作你就会成功。
Nǔlì gōngzuò nǐ jiù huì chénggōng.
Hard work you then will succeed.
'If you work hard, you'll succeed.'

11
Verbs and Prepositions

73. Verbs in Series

Chinese does not make use of many explicit connectors. The following proverb, for example, has the form verb-object verb-object twice over—and that is all.

看菜吃饭，量体裁衣。

Kàncài chīfàn, liángtǐ cáiyī.

View-dishes eat-food, measure-body cut-clothes.

'Judge the food before eating, measure the fit before tailoring.'

The same pared-down structure is characteristic of colloquial language, as well.

他伸手拿字典。

Tā shēn shǒu ná zìdiǎn.

He stretch-out hand take dictionary.

'He stretched out his hand to get the dictionary.'

是不是上车买票呀？

Shì bu shì shàngchē mǎi piào ya?

Be not be ascend-vehicle buy ticket SFP?

'Do you get tickets on the bus?'

她开车去火车站接他们。

Tā kāichē qù huǒchēzhàn jiē tāmen.

'She drove to the station to meet them.'

我要约时间来做身体检查。

Wǒ yào yuē shíjiān lái zuò shēntǐ jiǎnchá.

I want appoint time come do body check.

'I'd like to make an appointment for a health checkup.'

Where English requires explicit connections, such as "to" or "for," between the two verb phrases (or else recasts the sentence completely, as in the second example above), Chinese simply juxtaposes them. When the juxtaposed verb phrases indicate temporal order, they are called "verbs in series." Verbs in series, a characteristic feature of Chinese sentence organization, typically have a single overarching subject.

74. Verbs and Prepositions

Verbs in series (see Section 73) are not coordinate. The first verb is subordinate to the second, setting conditions on the realization of the latter verb. As a result, verbs that are particularly common as first verbs in a series tend to evolve prepositional functions.

用汉语交谈没问题。
Yòng Hànyǔ jiāotán méi wèntí.
Use Chinese converse not-have problem.
'[She] has no difficulty conversing in Chinese.'

他们给我们指了路。
Tāmen gěi wǒmen zhǐle lù.
They give us direct-LE route.
'They showed us the way.'

In the first example above, a literal translation of *yòng* is almost possible: "using Chinese to converse." But in the second example, only the more abstract prepositional sense of *gěi* is possible, that is, "for the benefit of" or "on behalf of."

75. Prepositions

Following is a list of the most important words that can have a prepositional function in spoken Chinese. (Written Chinese has additional prepositional forms.) Where applicable, both verbal and prepositional meanings are given.

Characters	Pinyin	Verbal ~ Prepositional Meanings	Prepositional Example(s)
按照	*ànzhào*	'according to'	*ànzhào xūyào tiáojié* 'adjusted according to need'
把	*bǎ*	'take' ~ preposed objects	*bǎ xié fàng zai wàitou* 'put your shoes outside'
被	*bèi*	'cover' ~ 'by'	*bèi <rén> tōu le* 'stolen by someone'

Characters	Pinyin	Verbal ~ Prepositional Meanings	Prepositional Example(s)
比	*bǐ*	'compare' ~ 'than'	*bǐ tā gāo* 'taller than she'
趁	*chèn*	'avail oneself of' ~ 'while, when'	*chèn rè chī ba* 'eat it while it's hot'
从	*cóng*	'follow' ~ 'from'	*cóng nǐ jiā lái* 'come from your house'
到	*dào*	'arrive' ~ 'to'	*dào xuéxiào qu* 'go to the school'
对	*duì*	'to face' ~ 'to, toward'	*duì xuésheng hěn hǎo* 'good to the students'
给	*gěi*	'give' ~ 'for (the benefit of)'	*gěi tā dǎ diànhuà* 'phone her'
跟	*gēn*	'follow' ~ 'with, to'	*gēn tā xué* 'study with her'
根据	*gēnjù*	'based on' ~ 'on the basis of'	*gēnjù zuìjìn diàochá* 'according to the latest census'
关于	*guānyú*	'concerned with' ~ 'about'	*guānyú xūnǐ de dìfang* 'about an imaginary place'
和	*hé*	'harmonize' ~ 'with'	*hé wǒ méi shénme guānxi* 'nothing to do with me'
靠	*kào*	'depend on, rely on' ~ 'on'	*kào yòu biānr kāi* 'drive on the right'
离	*lí*	'separate' ~ 'from' (distance)	*lí zhèr bù yuǎn* 'not far from here'
连	*lián*	'connect' ~ 'even'	*lián wǔfàn dōu méi chī* 'didn't even eat lunch'
拿	*ná*	'take' ~ 'with'	*ná tā dāng shūzhuō* 'use it as a desk'
上	*shàng*	'go up' ~ 'to, toward'	*Shàng nǎr qù?* 'Where are you going?'
替	*tì*	'replace' ~ 'instead of, for'	*tì nǐ zhào ge xiàng* 'take a photo for you'
同	*tóng*	'with'	*tóng tā zài yìqǐ* 'together with him'

Characters	Pinyin	Verbal ~ Prepositional Meanings	Prepositional Example(s)
往	*wǎng*	'go' ~ 'to, toward'	*wǎng qián zǒu* 'walk straight ahead'
为	*wèi*	'for (the sake of)'	*wèi rénmín fúwù* 'serve the people'
向	*xiàng*	'be facing' ~ 'toward'	*xiàng tāmen wènhǎo* 'greet them'
沿<着>	*yán <zhe>*	'follow a course' ~ 'along'	*yán hé ér xià* 'follow the river downstream'
用	*yòng*	'use' ~ 'with, in'	*yòng kuàizi chīfàn* 'eat with chopsticks,' *yòng Zhōngwén jiāotán* 'chat in Chinese'
由于	*yóuyú*	'arise from' ~ 'owing to'	*yóuyú zhèi ge yuányīn* 'for this reason'
在	*zài*	'be at' ~ 'at'	*zài chéng li gōngzuò* 'work in town'
坐	*zuò*	'sit' ~ 'by, on'	*zuò huǒchē dào Běijīng qù* 'take a train to Beijing'

Bèi is unique in not requiring an object; if it has no object, it precedes the verb directly, in effect acting as a passive marker: *bèi tōu le* 'got stolen' (see Section 77).

76. The *bǎ* (把) Construction

Giving orders or instructions often involves picking out items and then moving, changing, or otherwise manipulating them. In Chinese, the "picking out" function is typically performed by the preposition *bǎ* (把).

请把自行车放在小巷里。
Qǐng bǎ zìxíngchē fàng zài xiǎoxiàng li.
Please BA bicycle put at alley in.
'Please put your bike in the alley.'

你先把牛肉切切。
Nǐ xiān bǎ niúròu qiēqie.
You first BA beef cut-cut.
'First, slice the beef.'

他把我当做老师。

Tā bǎ wǒ dāngzuò lǎoshī.

She BA me regard-as teacher.

'She took me for a teacher.'

她没把房间钥匙给我。

Tā méi bǎ fángjiān yàoshi gěi wǒ.

She not BA room key give me.

'She didn't give me the room key.'

Bǎ derives from a verb meaning 'grasp, hold, take,' and in cases such as the one involving putting one's bike in the alley, translating *bǎ* as 'take' conveys the original sense: "Please *take the bike* and put it in the alley." However, translating *bǎ* as 'take' does not work in cases such as the last example, where its function is purely grammatical, that is, to pick out "the room key" as the object of interest. (Notice that the negative appears before *bǎ* rather than before the main verb.)

The function of *bǎ* in spotlighting the object of interest has certain consequences. First of all, such an object is of definite reference (the sort typically marked with "the" in English). This conforms to the general tendency in Chinese for nouns involving identifiable referents to appear before the verb, and those with unidentifiable referents to appear after the verb (see Section 29). Thus, *bǎ bǐ ná qǐlai* corresponds to English "pick up *the* pen"; "pick up *a* pen" would be *ná qǐ bǐ lai*. (For the position of *lái*, see Section 64.)

Another feature of *bǎ* is that, since it picks out a noun for some sort of manipulation or transformation, the associated verb cannot be plain and simple. It requires some additional articulation—not just *mài* 'sell,' but at least *màile* or *màidiào*; not just *qiē* 'slice, cut,' but at least *qiēqiē*; not just *fàng* 'put,' but *fàng zài zhuōzi shang.*

Conversely, verbs that do not perform any manipulation on their objects—no movement, transformation, or change—are not found with *bǎ*. Verbs like *chàng* (唱) 'sing,' *xǐhuan* (喜欢) 'be fond of,' and *dǒng* (懂) 'understand' are not usually found with *bǎ*. Nor are potential verb compounds like *hēbuwán* (喝不完) 'can/could not finish drinking,' which are only hypothetical.

Test Yourself

Provide the Chinese versions of the following sentences.

1. Write your name on the blackboard. (*hēibǎn* 'blackboard')
2. Please bring another pair of chopsticks. (*ná* 'bring' *yì shuāng kuàizi* 'a pair of chopsticks')
3. Who drank my beer? (*píjiǔ* 'beer')
4. Please open the window. (*chuānghu* 'window')
5. I love that movie! (*nèi bù diànyǐng* 'that movie')

6. Don't put your book bag on the table. (*shūbāo* 'book bag,' *zhuōzi* 'table')
7. I can't lift that suitcase of hers. (*xiāngzi* 'suitcase')

Possible Answers

1. *Bǎ nǐ de míngzi xiě zai hēibǎn shang.*
2. *Qǐng duō ná yì shuāng kuàizi lai.* (not definite)
3. *Shéi bǎ wǒ de píjiǔ hē le?*
4. *Qǐng bǎ chuānghu dǎkāi.*
5. *Wǒ hěn xǐhuan nèi bù diànyǐng!* (a verb of emotion)
6. *Bié bǎ shūbāo fàng zai zhuōzi shang.*
7. *Tā nèi ge xiāngzi wǒ ná bu qǐlai.* (a potential compound)

77. The Preposition *bèi* (被)

Bèi (被) 'by' is often treated in conjunction with *bǎ* (把). More or less the same types of verbs are associated with *bèi*, which—like *bǎ*— does not usually appear with a plain verb. (For an exception, see sentence 4 in "Test yourself," below.) A complement, or at least a verbal suffix, is almost always present. The difference is that while *bǎ* identifies a thing that is affected ("shoes" in the first example below), *bèi* focuses on agency.

他们把我的鞋拿走了。
Tāmen bǎ wǒ de xié názǒu le.
'They've taken my shoes.'

Wǒ de xié bèi názǒu le.
'My shoes have been taken.'

Wǒ de xié bèi háizimen názǒu le.
'My shoes have been taken by the kids.'

Here are additional examples.

等了四十五分钟，我才被救上来。
Děngle sì-shíwǔ fēnzhōng, wǒ cái bèi jiù shànglai.
Wait-LE 40 to 50 minutes, I then-and-only-then got rescued up-come.
'After waiting 40 to 50 minutes, I finally got rescued.'

他被警察抓住了。怎么办?
Tā bèi jǐngchá zhuāzhù le. Zěnme bàn?
'He was arrested by the police. What should [we] do?'

被解救的姜戈
Bèi jiějiù de Jiānggē
Get rescued DE Django
"Django Unchained" (a film)

In colloquial language, three other prepositions sometimes substitute for *bèi*: *jiào* (叫) 'call, name; cause' ~ 'by'; *ràng* (让) 'yield, allow' ~ 'by'; and *gěi* (给) 'give' ~ 'by.' *Gěi*, like *bèi*, can occur without an object (see Section 48). *Jiào* and *ràng* occur only with objects, as in the following example.

全部让他搞砸了。

Quánbù ràng tā gǎozá le.

Everything by him manage-mess le.

'Everything's been mucked up by him.'

To some degree, *bèi* sentences correspond to English passive sentences, which also serve to highlight agency. However, the similarities should not be overstated. In many cases, English passives do not correspond to *bèi* sentences, particularly when the agency is clear from the context.

Xíngli sònglai le ma?

'Have the bags been delivered?'

Bèi sentences tend to be about mishaps, but they can also be quite neutral, particularly in modern colloquial language, such as one finds in chatrooms.

他被邀请参加聚会。

Tā bèi yāoqǐng cānjiā jùhuì.

'He was invited to attend the meeting.'

Test Yourself

Provide the Chinese versions of the following sentences.

1. The food's all been eaten. (*chīdiào* 'eat')
2. Everything's been moved out. (*bānzǒu* 'move out')
3. It's probably been taken by someone by mistake. (*nácuò* 'take in error')
4. My money was taken, but not my passport. (*tōu* 'steal, take,' *hùzhào* 'passport')
5. His girlfriend sold his bike. (*mài* 'sell,' *zìxíngchē* 'bike')

Possible Answers

1. *Cài dōu bèi chīdiào le.*
2. *Dōngxi dōu bānzǒu le.* (no particular emphasis on agency)
3. *Dàgài bèi rén nácuò le.*
4. *Wǒ de qián bèi tōu le, kěshì hùzhào méi bèi tōu.*
5. *Tā nǚpéngyou bǎ tā de zìxíngchē mài le.*

78. Pivot Verbs

Not all strings of verbs or verbs with objects are verbs in series (see Section 73). Verbs in series, at least narrowly defined, involve temporally successive events. This is not the case for sentences such as the following.

我有个朋友姓张。

Wǒ yǒu ge péngyou xìng Zhāng.

I have M friend surname Zhang.

'I have a friend named Zhang.'

她不让我去。

Tā bú ràng wǒ qù.

She not let me/I go.

'She won't let me go.'

他请我帮忙。

Tā qǐng wǒ bāngmáng.

He request me/I help.

'He asked me to help.'

我还得送人上火车。

Wǒ hái děi sòng rén shàng huǒchē.

I still must take-person ride train.

'I still have to see someone off on the train.'

These examples, though they consist of unmediated verbs with objects, do not involve sequential events. The subject does not apply to both verbs. Instead, the object of the first verb is the subject of the second: *tā qǐng wǒ* 'he request me' + *wǒ bāngmáng* 'I help [him].' This is usually called a "pivotal construction": the first object, which is both object of the first verb and subject of the second, is the pivot. The closest approximation to a pivotal construction in English would be "he let me go," where "me" is the person who is "let," as well as the person who "goes." English, however, cannot have "me" as both subject and object ("me/I"), so—first-come, first-served—"me" is treated as an object of the first verb.

Pivot constructions are an example of the relative simplicity of Chinese syntax. They tend to involve causative or request-type verbs: *shǐ* (使) 'cause [someone] to,' *yǐn* (引) 'induce [someone] to,' *zhǎo* (找) 'find [someone] to.' Following is a list of pivot verbs with examples showing the pivotal construction.

Characters	Pinyin	Gloss	Example
帮	*bāng*	'help'	*bāng wǒ jiǎozhèng fāyīn* 'help me correct my pronunciation'
逼	*bī*	'force'	*Bié bī wǒ zuò!* 'Don't push me to do it!'
带	*dài*	'take, bring'	*dài háizi qù kàn mǎxì* 'take children to see the circus'
告诉	*gàosu*	'tell'	*gàosu wǒ zěnme qù* 'tell me how to get there'

Characters	Pinyin	Gloss	Example
叫	*jiào*	'make'	*jiào wǒmen bèishū* 'make us recite (from memory)'
令	*lìng*	'make, cause'	*lìng tā dàchī-yìjīng* 'surprised him greatly'
领	*lǐng*	'lead, usher'	*lǐng kèrén jìn kètīng* 'usher guests into the living room'
派	*pài*	'send [people]'	*pài rén qù qǐng yīshēng* 'send someone to get a doctor'
请	*qǐng*	'ask'	*qǐng wǒ chànggē* 'invite me to sing a song'
让	*ràng*	'let'	*bú ràng tāmen shuō Yīngwén* 'not let them speak English'
使	*shǐ*	'make'	*xūxīn shǐ rén jìnbù* 'humility helps people move forward'
送	*sòng*	'take'	*Wǒ sòng nǐ huíjiā.* 'I'll take you home.'
选	*xuǎn*	'choose'	*xuǎn tā dāng shìzhǎng* 'elected him mayor'
找	*zhǎo*	'find'	*zhǎo rén tì wǒ jiāo* 'find someone to teach for me'

Causative Sentences

The preceding list includes five members of an important subgroup of pivot verbs with the general meaning 'cause [someone to]': *bī* (逼) 'force [someone to],' *jiào* (叫) 'ask/cause [someone to],' *lìng* (令) 'make, cause,' *ràng* (让) 'allow, let,' and *shǐ* (使) 'have/make [someone do something].' Most of these verbs are not limited to the pivot function, as shown in the following examples.

Wǒmen jiào tā lǎobǎn.
'We call him boss.'

Wǒ gěi tā ràngle lù.
'I yielded the road to him.'

Lìng is particularly common in the construction *lìngrén* + disyllabic verb or adjective, which gives the equivalent of a participial phrase in English: *lìngrén tǎoyàn* 'make people annoyed,' that is, 'annoying.' Other examples follow.

令人难忘的事儿
lìngrén nánwàng de shìr
. . . hard-to-forget DE things
'unforgettable things'

令人失望的电影
lìngrén shīwàng de diànyǐng
. . . disappoint DE movies
'disappointing movies'

最令人感动的故事
zuì lìngrén gǎndòng de gùshi
most . . . move DE stories
'very moving stories'

令人吃惊的新技术
lìngrén chījīng de xīn jìshù
. . . surprise DE new technology
'spectacular new technology'

The other causative verbs are illustrated in the following examples.

她父母逼她当医生。
Tā fùmǔ bī tā dāng yīshēng.
Her parents force her to-be doctor.
'Her parents forced her into becoming a doctor.'

早一点儿叫他起床就好了。
Zǎo yìdiǎnr jiào tā qǐchuáng jiù hǎo le.
Early a-bit ask him get-up then fine LE.
'Better have him get up a little earlier.'

你的要求使我大吃一惊。
Nǐ de yāoqiú shǐ wǒ dàchī-yìjīng.
Your DE demands make me greatly-surprised.
'Your demands really surprised me.'

对不起，让你久等了。
Duìbuqǐ, ràng nǐ jiǔ děng le.
Sorry, make you long wait LE.
'Sorry, I've kept you waiting.'

12
Miscellaneous

79. Numbers

The basic numbers are as follows.

	0	1	2	3	4	5	6	7	8	9	10
	líng	yī	èr	sān	sì	wǔ	liù	qī	bā	jiǔ	shí
PLAIN	0	一	二	三	四	五	六	七	八	九	十
FORMAL	零	壹	贰	叁	肆	伍	陆	柒	捌	玖	拾

The formal written numbers (called *dàxiě* (大写)) are used on checks, bills, legal documents, and so on, where it is crucial that numbers be clear, unambiguous, and unalterable.

The ordinal numbers are formed by the addition of the prefix *dì* (第). By pinyin convention, the prefix is attached with a hyphen: *dì-yī* (第一) 'first,' *dì-èr* (第二) 'second,' *dì-bā* (第八) 'eighth,' *dì-shí* (第十) 'tenth.'

Higher numbers are formed regularly, with combinations of the unit numbers and units of ten. The units of 10 are listed as follows.

						1 million	10 million	100 million
	10	100	1,000	10,000	100,000	million	million	million
	shí	bǎi	qiān	wàn	shíwàn	bǎiwàn	qiānwàn	yì = wànwàn
PLAIN	十	百	千	万	十万	百万	千万	亿 = 万万
FORMAL	拾	佰	仟	(萬)				(亿)

The number 10,000 is a basic number in Chinese, one million is not, but 100 million is (although it can also be formed as 10,000 10,000s). A good way for a learner to understand large numbers is to remember million (*bǎiwàn*), a figure that will cover the population statistics of many of the great cities of the world: *Nánjīng rénkǒu shì 7 bǎiwàn zuǒyòu.* 'The population of Nanjing is approximately 7 million.' (*Zuǒyòu,* literally, 'left-right,' means 'approximately.')

When numbers are written in Arabic numerals in Chinese, the digits are not rationed out in threes, as in English: *10000*—not *10,000*.

Unit numbers that precede multiples of 10 are multipliers: *èrshí* (二十) '20' (2 × 10), *sānbǎi* (三百) '300' (3 × 100), *sānbǎiwàn* (三百万) '3 million' (3 × 100 × 10,000).

Numbers that follow multiples of 10 are additive: *shíyī* (十一) '11' (10 + 1); *shí'èr* (十二) '12' (10 + 2); *sìshíyī* (四十一) '41' (4 × 10 + 1).

Test Yourself

Express the following numbers in Chinese.

1. 19
2. 35
3. 165
4. 568
5. 3,426
6. 65,000
7. 6 million

Answers

1. *shíjiǔ*
2. *sānshíwǔ*
3. *yìbǎi liùshíwǔ*
4. *wǔbǎi liùshíbā*
5. *sānqiān sìbǎi èrshíliù*
6. *liùwàn wǔqiān*
7. *liùbǎiwàn*

Complications

When numbers count nouns, they are mediated by measure words (see Section 37). However, *èr* 'two' is not used before measure words; in its stead, the bound form *liǎng* (两) appears: *liǎng ge dōngxi* 'two things,' *liǎng zhāng piào* 'two tickets.' Multiples of 10 can also be considered a measure of number, so it is not surprising that "two" before multiples of 10 varies. Some Chinese say *èrbǎi* '200,' some *liǎngbǎi*; some say *èrqiān* '2000,' some *liǎngqiān*.

Counting by ten, beginning with one ten, gives *shí, èrshi, sānshí, sìshí*, and so on. However, 10 after a multiple of 10 is *yìshí*, eleven is *yìshíyī*, and so on: *liǎngbǎi yìshi* '210,' *sìqiān sìbǎi yìshísì* '4414.'

In counting, Chinese always use the highest possible multiple of ten. Thus, 1600 is always 'one thousand six hundred' (*yìqiān liùbǎi*), never 'sixteen hundred.'

Nonfinal zero is *líng*: *sānbǎi líng liù* '306,' *bābǎi líng bā* '808,' *sānqiān líng wǔshí* '3050.' Zero in the thousands place is ignored: *qīwàn yìbǎi yìshí* '70110,' *qīwàn yìbǎi líng yī* '70101.' Consecutive zeros are only *líng*: *qīwàn líng yī* '70001.'

The numeral one is often read as *yāo* instead of *yī*, presumably to give it more phonological bulk for clarity. This practice is not found in Taiwan or in many overseas communities.

Arithmetic

Mathematical

Representation	Characters	Pinyin	Literal
98.6	九十八点六	*jiǔshíbā diǎn liù*	'98 point 6'
¼	四分之一	*sì fēn zhī yī*	'4 parts ZHI 1'
2/5	五分之二	*wǔ fēn zhī èr*	'5 parts ZHI 2'
$2^2 = 4$	二的平方是四。	*Èr de píngfāng shì sì.*[1]	'2 DE squared is 4.'
$\sqrt{16} = 4$	根号下十六是四。	*Gēnhào xià shíliù shi sì.*	'square root below 16 is 4.'
$14 + 16 = 30$	十四加十六得三十。	*Shísì jiā shíliù dé sānshí.*	'14 plus 16 gets 30.'
$50 - 3 = 47$	五十减<去>三得四十七。	*Wǔshí jiǎn<qù> sān dé sìshíqī.*	'50 minus <away> 3 gets 47.'
$7 \times 6 = 42$	七乘<以>六得四十二。	*Qī chéng <yǐ> liù dé sìshí'èr.*	'7 multiply <by> 6 gets 42.'
$84 \div 6 = 14$	八十四除<以>六得十四。	*Bāshísì chú <yǐ> liù dé shísì.*	'84 divide <by> 6 gets 14.'

In a more formal reading, *děngyú* (等于) 'equals' can substitute for *dé* 'gives.'

Note how fractions are given by expressing the denominator—the total number of parts—first, then the numerator. Thus, "three quarters" is *sì fēn* 'four parts,' *zhī sān* 'three of them': *sì fēn zhī sān*.

---

[1]This colloquial usage applies only to squares. For cubes and higher powers, the more general pattern with *mì* (幂) 'power of' is used: *èrcìmì* 'to the second power,' *sāncìmì* 'to the third power'—thus, *Èr de sāncìmì shì bā.* '2 DE third-power is 8.'

Test Yourself

Express the following numbers and equations in Chinese.

1. 1.1416
2. 9 + 8 = 17
3. 17 − 11 = 6
4. 6 × 15 = 90
5. 5/6

Possible Answers

1. *yī diǎn yī-sì-yī-liù*
2. *Jiǔ jiā bā děngyú shíqī.*
3. *Shíqī jiǎn<qù> shíyī dé liù.*
4. *Liù chéng <yǐ> shíwǔ dé jiǔshí.*
5. *liù fēn zhī wǔ*

80. Money

The general word for money in Chinese, *qián* (钱), originally referred to a metal coin that, like earlier Chinese coins, had a square hole in the middle and was carried around in strings of 100 or more. These are the strings of "cash" that are often mentioned by early writers on China—"cash" being the name of the coin.

Paper money made an early appearance in China, but fell out of use after the fifteenth century. From the sixteenth century, Spanish silver dollars gained a foothold, later to be replaced by Mexican and other types of dollars. Many of these early coins can be found for sale in the antique markets of Beijing and other cities.

Currencies

Except for Macau, the names of the Chinese currencies end in *bì* (币, originally referring to gifts of silk). Foreign currencies (*wàibì*), on the other hand, are represented by their sound (*bàng* (镑) (British) 'pound,' *lúbǐ* (卢比) (Indian) 'rupee,' *lúbù* (卢布) (Russian) 'ruble', or they end in *yuán* (元, originally used for dollars).

Following is a chart of the currency units of several countries, regions, and unions.

Country/Region/Union	Characters	Pinyin	English
China	人民币	*rénmínbì*	renminbi
Taiwan	台币	*táibì*	new Taiwan dollar

Country/Region/Union	Characters	Pinyin	English
Hong Kong	港币	*gǎngbì*	Hong Kong dollar
Macau	澳门元	*àoményuán*	Macau dollar
Japan	日元	*rìyuán*	yen
Singapore	新加坡元	*xīnjiāpō yuán*	Singapore dollar
United States	美元	*měiyuán*	U.S. dollar
United Kingdom	英镑	*yīng bàng*	pound sterling
European Union	欧元	*ōuyuán*	euro

Usage

The main unit of Chinese currency is the *yuán* (written 元, a simplification of 圆 'round,' and abbreviated ¥). It is subdivided into 10 *jiǎo* (角) and 100 *fēn* (分). *Yuán* (元) and *jiǎo* (角) are the formal written terms. The spoken language makes use of *kuài* (块, originally a 'lump' of silver) for 'dollar' and *máo* (毛, also 'body hair, fur; trifles') for 'dime.' *Fēn* 'cent' is unchanged in formal and informal, as well as written and spoken, language.

Chinese paper currency comes in denominations of 100, 50, 20, 10, 5, and 1 *yuán* and 5 and 1 *jiǎo*. Coins are 1 *yuán*; 5, 2, and 1 *jiǎo*; and 5, 2, and 1 *fēn*, although change is usually rounded off nowadays to avoid having to deal with *fēn*. In citing prices, the last unit is generally omitted: *sān kuài èr* (¥3.20) rather than *sān kuài liǎng máo qián* and *sìshíjiǔ kuài bā máo bā* (¥49.88) rather than *bā fēn* or *bā fēn qián*. As with ordinary numbers, nonfinal zeros are indicated with *líng*: *yí kuài líng jiǔ* (¥1.09).

Prices can be requested by pointing to or mentioning an item, using the question words *duōshao* or *jǐ*, and—if applicable—mentioning a weight or number ("per"). Officially, China uses the metric system, but in practice, a version of the traditional market system (*shìzhì* 市制), with units of 10 instead of the earlier 16, is most current. For weights, the units are *jīn* 'catty' (= 0.5 kilogram) and *liǎng* 'ounce.' The amount ("per") can be mentioned before or after the price. The following examples show how to request and provide the price of apples.

Píngguǒ yí gè duōshao <qián>?
Apples 1 M how-much <money>?

Píngguǒ duōshao qián yí gè?
Apples how-much money 1 M?

Píngguǒ yí gè bā máo.
Apples 1 M 8 dimes.

Píngguǒ bā máo yí gè.
Apples 8 dimes 1 M.

Píngguǒ yì jīn jǐ kuài <qián>?
Apples 1 catty how-many dollars <money>?

Píngguǒ jǐ kuài <qián> yì jīn?
Apples how-many dollars <money> 1 catty?

Píngguǒ yì jīn liǎng kuài sì.
Apples 1 catty 2 dollars 4.

Píngguǒ liǎng kuài sì yì jīn
Apples 2 dollars 4 1 catty.

81. Names, Titles, and Forms of Address

Names

Han Chinese personal names are composed of a *xìng* (姓) 'surname' (almost all of one syllable, with a few that are disyllabic) followed by a one- or two-syllable *míngzi* (名字) 'given name.' Pinyin convention separates *xìng* from *míngzi* and capitalizes both. Examples from the world of sports are former basketball player *Yáo Míng* (姚明), tennis star *Lǐ Nà* (李娜), and Asian-American basketball player *Lín Shūháo* (林书豪), known as Jeremy Shu-How Lin in the United States. (The romanized spelling of Lin's name reflects his Taiwanese background.)

Disyllabic surnames (*fùxìng* 复姓) include *Sīmǎ* (司马), *Sītú* (司徒), and *Ōuyáng* (欧阳). These are more often than not combined with a one-syllable *míngzi* to conform to the dominant three-syllable pattern for names. History provides examples: *Sīmǎ Qiān* (司马迁) was a great historian who lived in the second to first century BCE, and *Sīmǎ Xiāngrú* (司马相如) was a poet and musician who lived about the same time. The latter's disyllabic *míngzi* provides a rare example of a four-syllable Han name. Most four-syllable names are non-Han, for example, *Wú'érkāixī* (吾尔开希), a Chinese student dissident whose family was Uyghur.

Although *xìng* in history number in the thousands, far fewer are used in the present day. The ten most popular surnames account for as much as 40 percent of the population. Supposedly, each of the *Zhāng* (张) and *Lǐ* (李) surnames is shared by more than 100 million people.

Foreign Names

Foreign names from outside the Sinocentric area are usually transliterated: *Yuēhàn Shǐmìsī* (约翰。史密斯) "John Smith," *Àobāmǎ* (奥巴马) "Obama," *Qiáozhì Wòkè Bùshí* (乔治。沃克。布什, also written 乔治。W。布什) "George W[alker]. Bush." For students studying Chinese, however, it is customary to create names that conform more closely to Chinese models while, ideally, also suggesting the orginal names. Thus, Anne Mauboussin becomes *Máo Xiān'ān* (茅仙安), and Robert Leonhard becomes *Léi Hànbó* (雷汉博).

Usage

Names are introduced by the classificatory verbs *xìng* (姓) or *jiào* (叫), or by *shì* (是). *Xìng* introduces surnames, while *jiào*, which requires a nonbound object of at least two syllables, can introduce disyllabic *míngzi* or full names. *Shì* identifies a person by name or by name and title.

> *Tā shì Táng Lìlì ma?*
> 'She is Tang Lili, right?'

Bù, tā xìng Tán, míngzi jiào Bìlì.
'No, she's surnamed Tan, and her given name is Bili.'

O, tā jiào Tán Bìlì, wǒ tīngcuò le.
'Oh, her name's Tan Bili. I misheard.'

Male and Female

Míngzi are not clearly divided into male and female, although certain tendencies are apparent. Names with repeated syllables, such as the misheard *Táng Lìlì* in the example above, are likely to be female, as are names that contain characters meaning beauty (美 *měi*, 丽 *lì*), elegance (秀 *xiù*), fragrance (芬 *fēn*), and other stereotypical female associations. Names that contain characters for strength (强 *qiáng*), talent (才 *cái*), mountains (山 *shān*), and the like are probably male. Surprises are common, however.

Patronymics

It is a common practice for members of the same generation to be assigned a particular syllable in their *míngzi*, often chosen from a poem. For example, *Máo Zédōng*'s siblings all had *zé* in their *míngzi*: *Máo Zémín*, *Máo Zétán*, and *Máo Zéjiàn* (also known as *Máo Zéhóng*).

Titles and Forms of Address

In Chinese society, addressing someone by his or her personal name is reserved for an intimate or a "skewed dyad" (a person of high status addressing a person of low status). Chinese are sensitive to status, which is a complex of features that includes age and professional rank. Titles are an important way of acknowledging status and establishing an appropriate tone for discourse.

In professional (including educational) settings, address usually has the form of surname plus title. Thus, students address teachers with *lǎoshī* 'teacher,' a term that can only be translated literally: *Zhào lǎoshī, nín hǎo?* 'How are you, teacher Zhao?' Where a more precise acknowledgment of rank is appropriate, the title *jiàoshòu* (教授) 'professor' can be used: *Zhào jiàoshòu*. A person working in a company can address the manager or an executive with *jīnglǐ* (经理) 'manager': *Ōuyáng jīnglǐ*. A worker in a factory can address the boss with *chǎngzhǎng* 'factory head': *Zhōu chǎngzhǎng*. Vice positions within a rank are indicated with *fù* (副) on business cards: *fùjīnglǐ* (副经理) 'vice manager.' Persons in these positions are generally addressed with the full (not the "vice") form: *Wáng jīnglǐ*. Other titles have a more generic function. *Xiānsheng* (先生), for example, is a respectful term of address for mature males: *Qián xiānsheng*. For blue-collar workers, particularly when on the job, *shīfu* (师傅) 'craftsman, master' is a polite title: *Lǐ shīfu*.

For women, address forms are more problematical. The term *xiǎojiě* (小姐), literally 'small-big sister,' in common use not very long ago, has been contaminated by various associations. It is still used with surnames, however, to refer to a youngish and presumably unmarried woman: *Nǐ rènshi Bái xiǎojiě ma?* 'Do you know Miss Bai?' For married or older women, the title *tàitai* (太太) has regained the position it once held as a term of respect. Otherwise, the title *nǚshì* (女士) 'Ms.,' formerly used only in written language, is gaining ground as a neutral term to be used to address females of working age.

Generic titles can also be used alone when names are not known (as when addressing strangers), or when they are otherwise unnecessary. For men, *xiānsheng* and *shīfu* can be used alone to get someone's attention prior to making a request, for example. Youths often address friends with *gēmenr* (哥们儿) 'brothers,' in the way that "dude" and "guys" are used in colloquial English. For addressing females, there are kinship options such as *xiǎomèi* (小妹)'young sister.' Children are often addressed as *xiǎo péngyou* (小朋友) 'young friend'; they reply with kinship terms such as *shūshu* (叔叔) 'uncle' and *áyí* (阿姨) 'auntie.'

> *Xiǎo péngyou, nǐ hǎo?*   *Shūshu hǎo. / Áyí hǎo.*
> 'How are you, kid?'   'Hello, Uncle.' / 'Hello, Auntie.'

Familiar Address

As friendships develop, there comes a point where address shifts to more informal modes, such as *xìng* plus *míngzi* or, more intimately, just *míngzi*. Familiar address includes the prefixes *lǎo* and *xiǎo*, literally, 'old' and 'young,' but here used to distinguish relative age and maturity. These prefixes may be attached to surnames, though not disyllabic ones: *lǎo Wáng, xiǎo Bì*. The Cantonese equivalent of the prefix *lǎo* is *ā*, now sometimes used in Mandarin, as well: *ā Bāo* = *lǎo Bāo*.

82. Proverbs and Sayings

Proverbs and sayings encapsulate the wisdom of the past in the form of concise, sometimes rhymed, often allusory expressions. Chinese take special pleasure in being able to cite an apt proverb for an occasion, whether it be in the course of a conversation or in a formal spoken or written presentation.

Eleven proverbs or sayings are cited here, all with some relevance to language learners. Most sayings come in several forms. For some, only the first part needs to be cited—the audience can supply the rest: *bú rù hǔxué* 'if you don't enter the tiger's lair' (you can't get any tiger cubs). Other sayings are sometimes found in the popular four-syllable format. Thus, proverb

No. 7 has a four-syllable version: *pífúhànshù* 'ant-shake-large-tree,' that is, 'a futile effort.'

1. 千里之行始于足下。
   Qiān lǐ zhī xíng shǐ yú zú xià.
   1000 mile ZHI journey begin at foot down.
   'A long journey begins with a single step.'

2. 不入虎穴，焉得虎子。
   Bú rù hǔxué, yān dé hǔzǐ.
   Not enter tiger lair, how get tiger cubs.
   'Nothing ventured, nothing gained.'

3. 世间无难事，只要有心人。
   Shì jiān wú nánshì, zhǐ yào yǒu xīn rén.
   World in not-have difficulties, only need have will person.
   'Nothing's impossible.'

4. 百闻不如一见。
   Bǎi wén bùrú yí jiàn.
   100 hear not-match 1 view.
   'A picture is worth a hundred words.'

5. 比上不足，比下有余。
   Bǐ shàng bù zú, bǐ xià yǒu yú.
   Than above not sufficient, than below have extra.
   'Could be worse,' that is, 'Adequate for one's needs.'

6. 三人行必有我师焉。
   Sān rén xíng, bì yǒu wǒ shī yān.
   Three people walking, necessarily have for-me a-teacher in-them.
   'Something to learn from almost everyone.'

7. 蚍蜉撼大树，可笑不自量。
   Pífú hàn dà shù, kěxiào bú zì liàng.
   Ant shake large tree, may-laugh not self measure.
   'A futile effort.'

8. 读书百遍，其义自见。
   Dúshū bǎi biàn, qí yì zì xiàn.
   Read 100 times, its meaning self see.
   'Read it a hundred times and you'll see the point.'

9. 玉不琢不成器。
   Yù bù zhuó, bù chéng qì.
   Jade not polish, not become utensil.
   'You won't get anywhere without refinement.' (on the need for education)

10. 吃得苦中苦，方为人上人。
    Chī dé kǔ zhōng kǔ, fāng wéi rén shàng rén.
    Eat DE bitter among bitter, then-and-only-then be person above person.
    'It takes sweat and tears to earn the respect of others.' ('No pain, no gain.')

11. 头悬梁，锥刺股。
    Tóu xuánliáng, zhuī cìgǔ.
    Head suspend-beam, awl pierce-bone.
    'Determined in one's study.'

Proverb No. 11 makes reference to two exemplary students of ancient times who became famous officials. To keep from falling asleep while studying, one tied his hair to the roof beams, while the other pricked his thigh with an awl.

Appendix

Common Verbs Organized by Semantic Area

This appendix is a list of 140 verbs, grouped by meaning, with example phrases and sentences. Although many of the verbs in the list also function as other parts of speech, particularly nouns, only the relevant verbal meanings are given.

The verbs listed here would normally be encountered in the foundation levels of spoken language study. The list is selective. Common verbs like *chī* 'eat' and *mǎi* 'buy' are excluded, because they have been well illustrated earlier in the book.

Exerting Force on Objects

推 *tuī* 'push'
tuīzhe zìxíngchē shàng shān   'push the bike up the hill'
bú yào tuī wǒ   'don't push me'

按下 *ànxia* 'push down on'
Ànxia jiǔ, ránhòu bō hàomǎ.   'Press nine, then dial the number.'

拉 *lā* 'pull'
Yòng jìnr yì lā jiù kěyǐ lākāi.   'Tug it and it'll open.'
Tā fāshāo, lā dùzi.   'He's got a temperature and has diarrhea.'

扔 *rēng* 'throw'
Wǒ rēng qiú, nǐ jiē.   'I'll throw the ball, you catch it.'
Rēng jìn lājītǒng.   'Throw it in the wastebasket.'

拍 *pāi* 'clap, pat; beat; take a photo'
pāi wénzi   'swat a mosquito'
pāi diànyǐng   'shoot a film'
pāipai shǒu   'clap one's hands'

脱 *tuō* 'take off, remove'
Tóufa dōu tuōguāng le.   'She's lost all her hair.'
Jìn mén qǐng tuō xié.   'Please remove your shoes before entering.'

摘 *zhāi* 'pluck, pick, remove'

zhāixiàle yǎnjìng	'removed one's glasses'
zài zhāi yīngtáo	'picking cherries'

抢 *qiǎng* 'snatch, grab'

bú yào qiǎng	'don't grab'
qiǎng yínháng	'rob a bank'
qiǎngdào lánbǎnqiú	'grab a rebound' ('basket-board-ball')

洗 *xǐ* 'wash'

Nǐ de chènshān zhèng zài xǐ ne.	'Your shirt's in the wash.'
Yì tiān xǐ liǎn duōshao cì bǐjiào héshì?	'How many times is it reasonable to wash your face each day?'

Breaking and Damaging

弄坏 *nònghuài* 'break'

Tāmen nònghuàile diànshì.	'They've broken the television.'
Yǒu rén bǎ yǐzi nònghuài le.	'Someone's broken the chair.'

砸坏 *záhuài* 'get crushed, get smashed'

bǎ chē záhuài le	'crushed the car'
bǎ suǒ záhuài le	'smashed the lock'

切 *qiē* 'cut'

bǎ ròu qiē chéng dīngr	'cut the meat into cubes'
Tā qiēxiàle yí piàn.	'She cut off a slice.'

撕 *sī* 'tear'

bǎ bāoguǒ shang de zhǐ sīle xiàlai	'tore off the paper around the parcel'
bǎ xìn sī de fěnsuì	'tear the letter to pieces'

断 *duàn* 'break, cut off'

Tā duànle yì tiáo tuǐ.	'She broke her leg.'
Tūrán shéngzi duàn le.	'Suddenly, the rope gave way.'

Carrying and Lifting

背 *bēi* 'carry on the back'[1]

bēile ge bāo	'carry a pack on one's back'

拿 *ná* 'hold, take, bring'

názhe huà huíqu	'returned, holding the painting'

---

[1]Compare *bèi* (背), with falling tone, 'turn one's back,' that is, 'learn by heart': *bèi xiàlai* 'learn by heart.'

挑　*tiāo* 'carry with a pole; choose, pick'

tiāozhe yì tǒng shuǐ	'carrying a pail of water'
Xǐhuan nǎ ge jiù tiāo nǎ ge.	'Pick whichever one you want.'

带　*dài* 'take, bring, carry'

Kěyǐ dài háizi ma?	'Can we bring the children?'
dài huílai yí jiàn xiǎo lǐwù	'bring back a small gift'
dàizhe shūbāo	'carry a bookbag'

扛　*káng* 'lift with two hands, lug, shoulder'

káng qiāng	'carry a gun'
kángzhe chútou	'carrying a hoe'
káng zài jiān shang	'carry on the shoulders'

提　*tí* 'lift up; raise a question'

tílai yì tǒng shuǐ	'fetch a pail of water'
xiàng shàng tí yìdiǎnr	'pry up a bit, tilt'

提供　*tígōng* 'provide, supply, offer'

tígōng miǎnfèi fúwù	'provide free service'
fúwù tígōngzhě	'service provider'

搬　*bān* 'move (house)'

Wǒmen běnyuè dǐ jiù bān jìnqu.	'We move in at the end of the month.'
Tā jiā bān dào Hūhéhàotè qu le.	'She's moved to Huhot.'

Sending and Receiving

寄　*jì* 'send'

Qǐng gěi wǒmen gōngsī jì yí fèn jiǎnlì.	'Please send a résumé to our company.'
Wǒ xiǎng jì hángkōng.	'I'd like to send it via airmail.'

送　*sòng* 'deliver; present; escort'

Mǎi yī sòng yī.	'Buy one and get one [free].'
Wǒ sòng nǐ huíjiā ba.	'I'll see you home.'

派　*pài* 'send, dispatch'

Tā bèi pài huíqu qǔ hùzhào.	'She was sent back to get her passport.'
pài rén sòng xìnjiàn	'dispatch someone to deliver the letters'

递　*dì* 'hand over, pass'

Qǐng bǎ làjiāo dì gěi wǒ.	'Please pass me the chilies.'

帮　*bāng* 'help, assist'

Wǒ bāng nǐ ná ba.	'I'll help you carry them, okay?'

帮忙 *bāngmáng* (vo.) 'give a hand, do a favor'
Xūyào bāngbang máng ma?   'May I give you a hand?'

倒 *dào* 'pour'
gěi kèrén dào chá   'pour tea for the guests'

盛 *chéng* 'dish out, ladle out, serve; contain'
chéng liǎng wǎn fàn   'serve two bowls of rice'
Tǒng li chéngzhe shuǐ.   'The tank contains water.'

交 *jiāo* 'deliver, hand in; make friends'
jiāo gōngkè   'hand in homework'
jiāo péngyou   'make friends'

交换 *jiāohuàn* 'exchange'
Zánmen jiāohuàn, hǎo ma? 'Let's exchange / do a swap.'
jiāohuàn yìjiàn   'exchange opinions'

收 *shōu* 'receive, collect'
Nǐ de diànzǐ yóujiàn shōudàole. 'I got your e-mail.'
Qǐng shōuxià zhèi ge xiǎo lǐwù. 'Please accept this small
             present.'

取 *qǔ* 'fetch, take, get'
qù qǔ xíngli   'go and get one's luggage'
qù yínháng qǔ diǎnr qián 'go to the bank to get some
             money'

Moving and Traveling

走 *zǒu* 'walk, go'
Píngcháng wǒmen zǒuzhe 'Usually, we walk to class.'
 lái shàngkè.

走路 *zǒulù* (vo.) 'walk'
Zǒulù bù fāngbiàn, háishi dǎ 'It's not convenient to
 ge dī qù ba.   walk—we'd do better
             to take a taxi.'

跑 *pǎo* 'run, run away; hurry to'
yígòng pǎole sì ge dìfang 'hurried off to four places
             altogether'

跑步 *pǎobù* 'jog'
měi gé yì tiān pǎo yí cì bù 'run every other day'

闯 *chuǎng* 'rush, dash'
chuǎng jìn jiàoshì   'burst into the classroom'
dàochù luàn chuǎng   'rush all over'

qù Shànghǎi chuǎng yi chuǎng　　'break into Shanghai (to make your fortune)'

chuǎng hóngdēng　　'run a red light'

爬 *pá* 'climb'
páshang nàme gāo de shān　　'climb such a high mountain'

爬山 *páshān* 'hike'
bēizhe bāo páshān　　'go backpacking'

趴 *pā* 'lean over, lie prone'
Bú yào pā zài zhuōzi shang.　　'Don't lean on the table.'
pā zài dìshang kànle kàn　　'got down on the ground and took a look'

飞 *fēi* 'fly'
Bèn niǎo xiān fēi.　　'Clumsy birds fly first.' (so that they can get a head start)

Yào fēi sān xiǎoshí.　　'The flight will take three hours.'

开车 *kāichē* (vo.) 'drive'
Lái, lái, wǒ kāichē sòng nǐ dào huǒchēzhàn qu.　　'Come on, I'll drive you to the station.'

游泳 *yóuyǒng* 'swim'
Jìnzhǐ yóuyǒng.　　'Swimming prohibited.'
Zuótiān wǎnshàng wǒ qù yóuyǒngchí yóule ge yǒng.　　'Last night, I took a swim in the pool.'

Falling and Rising

摔 *shuāi* 'fall, stumble'
shuāile yì jiāo　　'trip and fall'
Tā gāngcái bǎ nèi ge huāpíng shuāi de fěnsuì.　　'He just smashed the vase to pieces.'

滑 *huá* 'slip'
Tā zài bīng shang huádǎo le.　　'She slipped on the ice.'

落 *luò* 'fall, drop, come down'
Tàiyang luò xiàqu le.　　'The sun went down.'
Tā shìtúkǎnkě, sān qǐ sān luò.　　'She had a rough career, full of ups and downs.'

升 *shēng* 'rise'
Diàntī shēng dàole wǔlóu.　　'The elevator's gone up to the fifth floor.'

bèi shēngzhí le　　'got promoted'

Starting and Stopping, Opening and Closing

开始 *kāishǐ* 'start'

cóng tóu kāishǐ	'start from scratch'
Huìyì yǐjing kāishǐ le ma?	'Has the meeting begun?'

出发 *chūfā* 'set out (on a journey), depart'

Wǒmen shì bā diǎn bàn chūfā de.	'We set off at 8:30.'

启程 *qǐchéng* 'start a journey'

Wǒmen bǎ qǐchéng de shíjiān tuīchí le.	'We put off the start of our journey.'

打开 *dǎkāi* 'open; switch on'

dǎkāi chuānghu ràng kōngqì liútōng	'open the window and let the air circulate'
dǎkāi diànshìjī	'turn on the TV'

关上 *guānshang* 'close; turn off'

Líkāi de shíhou, qǐng bǎ mén guānshang.	'Close the door when you leave, please.'

Building

盖 *gài* 'cover; build [a house]'

bǎ guō gài qǐlai	'cover the pot'
gài yì suǒ fángzi	'build a house'

造 *zào* 'construct, build'

Zhè dòng fángzi shì zhuāntóu zào de.	'This house was built of brick.'
zàole yí zuò qiáo	'built a bridge'

建 *jiàn* 'build'

Zhè zuò sìmiào jiàn yú shíbā shìjì.	'This temple was contructed in the eighteenth century.'
Xuéxiào huì jiàn zài nǎr?	'Where will the school be built?'

修 *xiū* 'repair; build; study'

bǎ xié xiūhǎo le	'repaired my shoes'
Yǒu hěn duō chéngshì zài xiū dìtiě.	'There are lots of cities building subways.'

Changing

换 *huàn* 'exchange'

huàn yīfu	'change one's clothes'
bǎ gǎngbì huàn chéng měiyuán	'change Hong Kong dollars into U.S. dollars'
Dōngzhímén shì ge huànchéng chēzhàn.	'Dongzhimen is a transfer station.'

修改 *xiūgǎi* 'correct, amend'
děng xiěwánle zài xiūgǎi   'correct it after you finish writing it'

改 *gǎi* 'change'
Gǎi tiān zài shuō.   'Let's try for another day.'
Tā gǎibuliǎo shēngyīn.   'She can't alter her voice.'

变 *biàn* 'become different, change'
Tā biànle hěn duō.   'She's changed a lot.'
Shùyè biàn huáng le.   'The leaves have turned to yellow.'

改变 *gǎibiàn* 'change, alter'
Wǒ gǎibiàn zhǔyì le.   'I've changed my mind.'
gǎibiàn shēnghuó fāngshì hé yǐnshí xíguàn   'change one's lifestyle and one's eating habits'

转 *zhuǎn* 'turn, change; shift'
zhuǎn chē   'change trains/buses'
Qìhòu zhuǎn liáng.   'The weather's turning cool.'

转 *zhuàn* 'turn, revolve, rotate'
Tā zhuànle zhuàn lāshǒu bǎ mén dǎkāi.   'He turned the handle and opened the door.'
Dìqiú ràozhe tàiyang zhuàn.   'The earth revolves around the sun.'

Using the Body

出生 *chūshēng* 'be born'
Tā shì 1984 nián chūshēng de.   'She was born in 1984.'

唱 *chàng* 'sing'
chàng gēr chàng de hěn hǎo   'sing beautifully'
Tā chàng nángāoyīn.   'He sings tenor.'

住 *zhù* 'live'
Tā zài Běijīng zhùle liǎng nián le.   'He's been living in Beijing for two years.'
Tā zhù de hěn jìn.   'She lives quite close by.'

尝 *cháng* 'taste'
Cháng yi xià zhèi ge.   'Try this [food].'

运动 *yùndòng* 'move; exercise, do sports'
Bú yùndòng róngyi fāpàng.   'You'll get fat if you don't exercise.'
Tā jiānchí yùndòngle sān ge yuè.   'She stuck with her exercises for three months.'

排队 *páiduì* (vo.) 'line up'
páiduì mǎi piào　　　　　　　　　　　'line up to buy tickets'
Tā páiduì pái zài wǒ de qiánmian.　　'She lined up in front of me.'

用 *yòng* 'use'
Nǐ yòng shénme páizi de yágāo?　　　'Which brand of toothpaste do
　　　　　　　　　　　　　　　　　　 you use?'

长 *zhǎng* 'grow, develop, increase'
Tā zhǎng de hěn gāo.　　　　　　　　'She's grown up very tall.'
Tā zài Jiānádà zhǎngdà de.　　　　　 'He grew up in Canada.'

等 *děng* 'wait'
Wǒ bù néng zài děng le!　　　　　　　'I can't wait any longer!'

抽烟 *chōuyān* (vo.) 'smoke'
Nǐ bú jièyì wǒ chōuyān ba?　　　　　'Would you mind if I
　　　　　　　　　　　　　　　　　　 smoked?'

呼吸 *hūxī* 'breathe'
jīhu bù néng hūxī le　　　　　　　　　'almost not able to breathe'

休息 *xiūxi* 'rest'
Nǐ xiān xiūxi yi xiàr.　　　　　　　　'First, take a break.'

Viewing, Visiting, and Making an Appointment

瞧 *qiáo* 'look at'
Qiáo, nàr yǒu liǎng ge kòngwèir.　　'Look, there are a couple of
　　　　　　　　　　　　　　　　　　 empty seats over there.'

参观 *cānguān* 'visit, tour [a museum]'
Tā dài wǒ cānguān gōngchǎng.　　　 'She took me around the
　　　　　　　　　　　　　　　　　　 factory.'

cānguānle Zhèng Hé de mù　　　　　 'visit Zheng He's grave'
cānguān bówùguǎn　　　　　　　　　'visit a museum'

游览 *yóulǎn* 'go sightseeing, tour'
Dì-èr tiān wǒmen yóulǎnle Lìjiāng.　'The next day, we toured
　　　　　　　　　　　　　　　　　　 Lijiang.'

Yóukè cháng qù Dàlǐ de Sān Tǎ yóulǎn.　'Tourists often visit the Three
　　　　　　　　　　　　　　　　　　 Pagodas at Dali.'

约 *yuē* 'make an appointment'
Wǒmen xiǎng yuē nǐ lái cānjiā miànshì.　'We'd like to invite you to
　　　　　　　　　　　　　　　　　　 come here for an interview.'

yuē ge shíjiān jiànmiàn　　　　　　　'arrange for a time to meet'

Positioning the Body and Wearing

站 *zhàn* 'stand'

Zhànzhe gèng shūfu. 'Standing's more comfortable.'

zhàn qǐlai 'stand up'

Zhàn de yuè gāo, kàn de yuè yuǎn. 'The higher you stand, the farther you see.'

坐 *zuò* 'sit'

zuò zài yǐzi shang xiūxi 'sit on a chair and rest'

zuò yi xià 'sit down'

躺 *tǎng* 'lie down'

tǎng zài chuáng shang 'lie down on the bed'

伸 *shēn* 'extend, stretch out'

shēnkāi shǒu 'spread out one's hands'

穿 *chuān* 'wear [clothes, shoes]; pass through'

Tā cóng bù chuān báisè de yīfu. 'She never wears white.'

Dīshuǐ-chuānshí. (saying) 'Dripping water can penetrate stone.'

戴 *dài* 'wear [a hat, a watch, accessories]'

Tā xǐhuan dài ěrhuán. 'He likes to wear earrings.'

系 *jì* 'tie, fasten [a belt, a tie, shoelaces]'

Bú yòng jì lǐngdài. 'No need to wear a tie.'

Knowing and Understanding

知道 *zhīdào*[2] 'know'

bù zhīdào tā jiào shénme míngzi 'don't know his name'

认识 *rènshi* 'know, recognize'

Wǒ rènshi tā hěn jiǔ le. 'I've known her for ages.'

Wǒ bú rènshi nèi ge zì. 'I don't know that character.'

懂 *dǒng* 'understand'

Dǒng wǒ de yìsi ma? 'Do you understand what I'm getting at?'

---

[2]*Xiǎode* (晓得), originally a regional word, has much the same meaning as *zhīdào*: *Yājīn bù xiǎode néng náhuí duōshao.* 'I don't know how much of my deposit I can get back.'

了解 *liǎojiě* 'comprehend, acquaint oneself with'
liǎojiě shìshí   'get acquainted with the facts'
qù liǎojiě yi xià   'look into it'

掌握 *zhǎngwò* 'grasp, master'
zhǎngwò sìshēng   'master the four tones'

理解 *lǐjiě* 'comprehend, take in'
bù wánquán lǐjiě tā de yìsi   'not completely comprehend
                                              his meaning'

忘 *wàng* 'forget'
Tiān a! Yàoshi dōu wàng zài chē lǐ le. 'Damn! I left my keys
                                              in the car.'

记得 *jìde* 'remember'
Wǒ jìde jiànguo tā yí cì.   'I remember seeing him
                                              once.'

Experiencing Feelings

觉得 *juéde* 'feel'
Wǒ jīntiān juéde bù shūfu.   'I don't feel well today.'

以为 *yǐwéi* 'feel (mistakingly) that, believe (erroneously) that'
Wǒ yǐwéi tā shì Zhōngguórén;   'I thought she was Chinese;
  yuánlái tā shì zài Hánguó shēng de.   turns out, she was born in
                                              Korea.'

想象 *xiǎngxiàng* 'imagine'
Xiǎngxiàng bù chū nǐ shì shénme yìsi.   'I can't imagine what you
                                              mean.'

爱 *ài* 'love, like'
Tā bú ài kàn diànshì.   'She doesn't like to watch TV.'
Tā àishang tā le.   'He's in love with her.'

羡慕 *xiànmù* 'envy [but not resent], admire'
Wǒ zhēn xiànmù nǐ!   'How I envy you!'
Wǒ hǎo xiànmù nǐ a!   'I really admire you!'

同意 *tóngyì* 'agree'
Wǒ jīběn shang tóngyì nǐ de kànfǎ.   'Basically, I agree with you.'
Tā jǔshǒu biǎoshì tóngyì.   'She raised her hand to show
                                              consent.'

承认 *chéngrèn* 'recognize, admit'
Tā bù néng bù chéngrèn háishi   'He [the wind] had to admit
  tàiyang bǐ tā běnshi dà.   that the sun was more
                                              resourceful than he.'

Studying

学 *xué* 'study, learn'
gēn tā xué tàijíquán   'study tai chi with her'
Tā hěn cōngmíng, xué de hěn kuài.   'She's bright and learns fast.'

学习 *xuéxí* 'study; emulate'
Xuésheng dōu yīnggāi   'Students should all study
   xué<xí> wàiyǔ, duì ma?   foreign languages, don't you
                                                 think?'

Xiàng Léi Fēng xuéxí!   'Emulate Lei Feng!'

念书 *niàn* 'study, attend'
Tā niàn gāozhōng èrniánjí.   'She's a junior in high school.'

读书 *dúshū* (vo.) (Taiwan *niànshū*)   'study; attend school'
Nǐ mèimei hái zài dúshū a?   'Is your sister still in school?'

考 *kǎo* 'test, examine'
kǎobushàng dàxué   'couldn't get into university'
Wǒ wùlǐ kǎozá le.   'I messed up on the physics
                                               exam.'

kǎoshì kǎo de hěn lèi   'be tired of taking exams'

复习 *fùxí* 'review, revise'
fùxí bǐjì zhǔnbèi kǎoshì   'review notes for the exam'
zài fùxí yí biàn   'review once more'

练习 *liànxí* 'practice'
Duō liànxí jiù xíng le.   'It'll come with practice.'

预习 *yùxí* 'prepare lessons; rehearse'
yùxí gōngkè   'prepare ahead for class'
yùxí dì-bā kè   'prepare Lesson 8'

Speaking

说 *shuō* (Southern Mand. *jiǎng*)   'speak, talk; explain'
bú yòng shuō   'it goes without saying'
bǐfang shuō   'for example'
Míngtiān zài shuō.   'Let's talk about it tomorrow.'

讲 *jiǎng* 'discuss, explain'
Wǒ gēn nǐ jiǎng ...   'Here's the thing . . .' ('Let
                                             me explain . . .')

解释 *jiěshì* 'explain'
bù néng jiěshì de xiànxiàng   'phenomena that can't be
                                             explained'

Néng bu néng gěi wǒ jiěshì jiěshì?   'Can you explain it to me?'

介绍 *jièshào* 'introduce'
Wǒ gěi nǐ jièshao jièshao.　'Let me introduce you.'
gěi tā jièshào ge wǔbàn　'find a dance partner for her'

谈 *tán* 'speak, chat; discuss'
jiù tán dào zhèli ba　'so I'll just say this much' ('so I'll leave it at that')

Wǒ xiǎng tántan wèi rénmín fúwù de dāngdài jiàzhí.　'I'd like to talk about the value of "serving the people" in those days.'

教 *jiāo* 'teach'
jiāo tā qí zìxíngchē　'teach her to ride a bike'
Wǒ de zhíyè shì jiāo Hànyǔ.　'My job is teaching Chinese.'

劝 *quàn* 'urge, persuade'
Wǒ quànbudòng tāmen.　'I couldn't convince them.'

建议 *jiànyì* 'advise, recommend'
Wǒmen jiànyì tāmen yīnggāi jízǎo chūfā.　'We advised them to set out early.'

告诉 *gàosu* 'tell, inform, let know'
yíqiè dōu gàosu tā le　'told her everything'

问 *wèn* 'ask, inquire'
Wǒ yǒu shìqing yào wèn nǐ.　'I have something to ask you about.'

Qǐng tì wǒ xiàng tā wèn hǎo.　'Ask after her for me, please.'

请 *qǐng* 'invite'
Qǐng, qǐng, qǐng.　'After you.'
Wǒ xiǎng qǐng nǐ chīfàn.　'I'd like to invite you for a meal.'

猜 *cāi* 'guess'
Wǒ cāi bu chū nǐ shì shéi.　'I can't guess who you are.'

骂 *mà* 'call names, curse at; berate'
Màrén shì bù lǐmào de.　'It's not polite to call people names.'

Tā màle wǒ yí dùn.　'He gave me a tongue-lashing.'

Planning and Thinking

安排 *ānpái* 'arrange, plan, set up'
gěi tā ānpáile yí ge gōngzuò　'arrange a job for her'
ānpái zhuǎnjī　'arrange a connecting flight'

打算 *dǎsuàn* 'plan to, intend to'
dǎsuàn gǎn zǎobān de huǒchē   'plan to catch the early train'
dǎsuàn chūguó liúxué   'plan to study abroad'

计划 *jìhuà* 'plan, calculate, consider; amount to'
jìhuà zuò yí cì chūguó lǚxíng   'consider a trip abroad'

考虑 *kǎolǜ* 'think over, consider'
Xiān kǎolǜ yi xiàr zài juédìng.   'Think it over first, then come to a decision.'

想 *xiǎng* 'think; want'
Wǒ xiǎng bu qǐlai sǎn wàng zài nǎr le.   'I can't think where I left my umbrella.'
Méi qùguo kěshì hěn xiǎng qù.   'I haven't been yet, but I would like to go.'

算 *suàn* 'calculate; suppose; regard as'
Guòqu de shìqing jiù suàn le ba.   'Let bygones be bygones.'
Zhè bú suàn tōuqiè.   'It's not stealing.'

商量 *shāngliang* 'talk over, discuss'
Tāmen liǎ jiù shānglianghǎole shuō ...   'The two of them talked it over and said . . .'

认为 *rènwéi* 'hold that, deem it, feel it to be the case that'
Wǒ rènwéi wèi nǐ fúwù shì guāngróng de.   'I deem it an honor to serve you.'
rènwéi zìjǐ méiyǒu xīwàng   'feel there's no hope for me'

决定 *juédìng* 'decide on'
juédìng cízhí   'decide to resign'

做决定 *zuò juédìng* 'make a decision about'
Hǎohāor kǎolǜ yi xià zài zuò ge juédìng.   'Think about it, then make a decision.'

Encountering and Happening

见 *jiàn* 'catch sight of; meet; visit'
Wǒ xiǎng jiàn nǐ.   'I'd like to see you.'
Bú jiàn bú sàn.   'Don't leave without me.'

碰见 *pèngjiàn* 'run into [someone]'
Wǒ yǐqián pèngjiànguo nǐ.   'We've met before.'

发生 *fāshēng* 'happen'
Nà shì gāng qǐfēi hòu fāshēng de.   'It happened right after takeoff.'
Xīnán fāshēngle yí cì dìzhèn.   'There was an earthquake in the southwest.'

到期　*dàoqī* 'become due'

Qiānzhèng xiàyuè jiù dàoqī le.　　　'My visa expires next month.'

留　*liú* 'remain, stay; leave'

Yào bu yào liú ge yán?　　　'You want to leave a message?'

gěi rén liúxiàle bù hǎo de yìnxiàng　　　'leave people with a bad impression'

闹　*nào* 'make a noise; be troubled by, suffer'

Bié nàole, wǒ yào shuìjiào.　　　'Don't fuss; I'm trying to sleep.'

Bié nào chū xiàohuà lái.　　　'Don't make a fool of yourself.'

Tīngshuō zhè fángzi nào guǐ.　　　'I've heard this house is haunted.'

Bibliography

If you wish to continue learning Chinese—or continue learning about Chinese—here is my personal selection of books for further reading or study. I risk accusations of self-promotion for including my own textbook, *Learning Chinese*, which brings to mind another favorite saying: *Lǎo Wáng mài guā, zìmài, zìkuā.* (老王卖瓜, 自卖自夸。) 'Old Wang is selling melons; as he sells, he praises his own goods.' Perhaps true, but even so, *Learning Chinese* is one of very few textbooks that provides not only separate content for conversation and reading but also distinct methods for the two. By a similar line of reasoning, of the many fine bilingual dictionaries now available to learners of Chinese, only one is cited below: the *ABC Chinese-English comprehensive dictionary*. That is because only the *ABC* lists entries alphabetically by pinyin regardless of head character (see Section 15); this arrangement allows the learner to look up what is heard, as long as it can be rendered in pinyin.

Chao, Yuen Ren. *A grammar of spoken Chinese*. Berkeley: University of California Press, 1968.

Chen, Ping. *Modern Chinese: History and sociolinguistics*. Cambridge: Cambridge University Press, 1999.

DeFrancis, John, ed., et al. *ABC Chinese-English comprehensive dictionary*. Honolulu: University of Hawaii Press, 2003.

DeFrancis, John. *The Chinese language: fact and fantasy*. Honolulu: University of Hawaii Press, 1984.

Erbaugh, Mary S., ed. *Difficult characters: Interdisciplinary studies of Chinese and Japanese writing*. Columbus: National East Asian Languages Resource Center, Ohio State University, 2002.

McDonald, Edward. *Learning Chinese, turning Chinese: challenges to becoming sinophone in a globalised world*. Abingdon, Oxon: Routledge, 2011.

Norman, Jerry. *Chinese*. Cambridge: Cambridge University Press, 1988.

Ross, Claudia, and Jing-heng Sheng Ma. *Modern Mandarin Chinese grammar: A practical guide*, ed. 2. New York: Routledge, 2014.

Wheatley, Julian K. *Learning Chinese: A foundation course in Mandarin, elementary level*. New Haven, Connecticut: Yale University Press, 2011.

Wheatley, Julian K. *Learning Chinese: A foundation course in Mandarin, intermediate level*. New Haven, Connecticut: Yale University Press, 2014.

Yuan, Boping, and Kan Qian. *Developing writing skills in Chinese*, ed. 2. Abingdon, Oxon: Routledge, 2013.

Index

ABC Chinese-English Dictionary   31
Address, form of. *See* Titles
Adjectives   50, 107–14
  as transitive verbs   108–09
  conjoined   108
  non-gradable   107
  vivid reduplication   111–14
Adverbs   115–18
  from adjectives   116–17
  movable   115–16
  reduplicated forms   117–18
  age and weight   95
And, or, but. *See* Conjunctions,
  coordinate
Arithmetic   173
Articles ("the" and "a")   60
Attributives   50

bǎ construction   164–66
báihuà (northern vernacular)   7
bèi construction   166–67
Běijīng, names and spellings   11
Bopomofo   14

Cantonese   4, 9, 79 (note)
Causative sentences   169–70
Characters
  components of   27
  forming new ones   32
  as linguistic units   15–16, 26
  number of   31
  the simplified set   33–35
  strokes   26–27
  traditional versus
    simplified sets   33–35
Classical Chinese   6, 7, 8
Classifiers and measures   50, 74–78
Classifiers, list of   75–78
Commands   46–48
Comparison   120–23, 124

Compound nouns   53–54
Confucius   7
Conjunctions
  coordinate   157–60
  subordinate   160
Conventions and abbreviations   xii
Currencies   174–75

dǎ +objects   99–100
Dates   71–72
de
  in modification   61–62, 66
  three types   62, 124–26
Destination   39, 65–66, 139–40
Dialect writing   9
Dialects. *See* Regional languages
Dictionaries   29–31
Diglossic   8
Directional verb compounds   131–33
Ditransitive verbs   147–49
Duration   40, 151–55

Elaborate expressions   52, 118
Embedded clause. *See* Object
  clauses
Examples, format of   xi
Existence   95
Extent   156

Foreign words, representation
  in characters   26
Four-character expressions.
  See Elaborate expressions

gǎo 'deal with, etc.'   100
gěi functions   97–99, 140
gěi, with indirect objects (list)   147–49
General classifier   74
Gloss, versus definition   xi (note), xii
Guānhuà and Mandarin   6

Habitual actions   89
Hokkien (Fukienese)   4
Holidays   72–73
Hong Kong   9

Ideographic   33
Intensifiers   123–24
Interjections   51
International Phonetic Alphabet   17
IPA. *See* International Phonetic
    Alphabet

Kangxi Dictionary   30

líhécí (离合词)   80
Loanwords   54
Location   39, 65–68
Logographic   32
Low tone shift. *See* Tone shifts

Mandarin, regional variation   3–4
Measure words. *See* Classifier and
    measures
Measures, verbal (list)   156–57
Mock objects   146–47
Modal verbs, list   102–06
Modern Written Chinese
    (Written Mandarin)   7–8
Modification   61
Money   174–75
Monosyllabic   7, 51–52

Names
    personal   176–78
    for China   10, 11
    for the Chinese language   1, 2 (note 1)
Negation   46
nòng (fix, arrange)   101
Noun sentence   93
Number of speakers   3
Numbers   171–73

Object clauses   150–51
Object complements   150
Objects   137–54
    with duration   153–54
    position of   137–38
Onomatopoeia   32, 118

Particles   51
Parts of speech   49–51

Passives. *See bèi* construction
Peking versus Beijing   14–15
Phonetic sets   27–29
Phonosemantic compounds   27–28
Pinyin
    limits of   16–17
    punctuation   16
    rhymes   22–24
    the initials   18–21
    the syllable   17–18
    tones   21–22
Pivot verbs   167–70
    list   168–69
Place words   65–68
Pluricentric   2
Position words   65–68
Possession (*see* Possession and existence)
Possession and existence   95–96
Potential compounds   133–35
Predicate complements   119–20
Prepositions   50–51, 162–67
    list   162–64
Pronouns   58–60
Proverbs   178–80
Pŭtōnghuà   1–2, 6

Questions   41–42, 93
Questions and indefinites   44–45
Questions, alternative   43

r-suffix (儿)   24, 55–56
Radicals   29–30
Reading process   32–33
Regional languages (*fāngyán*)   4, 5
Regional Mandarin   3–4
Requests   46–48
Resultative verb compounds   127–31
Resultative verbs, list   128–29

Seasons   72
Separability (of compound
    verbs)   79–80, 142
Serial verbs. *See* Verbs in series
SFPs   47 (note), 51
shì in tag questions   93
shi-de construction   63–64
shì+location   93
Singapore   5, 34
Sino-Tibetan, Tibeto-Burman   10
Standard Written Chinese   7
Suffixes   54–57, 81–87

Taiwanese (*Táiyǔ*)   9–10
Test yourself   20, 39, 63, 64, 66, 83,
      85, 88, 110, 111, 120, 122, 123,
      129, 133, 134, 135, 138, 155, 165,
                              167, 172, 174
Time clauses   73–74, 155
Time words   70
Time
   calendar units   71–72
   clock time   71
   units of   69–70
   units of duration   152
Time (-when)   40, 68–74
Titles   177–78
Tone shifts   22, 112
Tones, Cantonese   21
Tones. *See also* Pinyin, tones   5
Topic-comment   37–38, 60
tou-suffix   57
Transcription
   systems   13–15
   Gwoyue Romatzyh (GR)   14
   versus orthography   16–17
   Wade-Giles system   13
   Yale system   13
Transformation (with *chéng*)   141

Verb(s)
   ambient   106
   classificatory   94, 150
   + *dào*   139–40

ditransitive. *See* Ditransitive
   verbs
   of "doing,"   101–02
   + *gěi*   140, 147–49
   of generalized meaning   99–102
   + *guo*   81–82
   + *le*   82–85
   modal   102–06
   + object compounds   142–46
      list of   143–46
   reduplication   90–91
   select list with examples   181–94
   in series   150, 161–62
   shì 'be,'   92–94
   suffixes   81–89
   + *zài*   140
   + *zhe*   86–88
Vivid reduplication. *See* Adjectives,
   vivid reduplication

Word, versus character   16, 26
Writing systems, borrowed   10

Yes and no   45–46
yǒu functions   95–96
Yuen Ren Chao   1, 15, 38, 80 (note)

zài functions   96–97, 140–42
zài+verb   88–89
Zero-pronominalization   59–60
zi-suffix   56–57